Simone de Beauvoir
and the
Politics of Ambiguity

Studies in Feminist Philosophy is designed to showcase cutting-edge monographs and collections that display the full range of feminist approaches to philosophy, that push feminist thought in important new directions, and that display the outstanding quality of feminist philosophical thought.

Published in the series:

Abortion and Social Responsibility: Depolarizing the Debate
Laurie Shrage

Gender in the Mirror: Confounding Imagery
Diana Tietjens Meyers

Autonomy, Gender, Politics
Marilyn Friedman

Setting the Moral Compass: Essays by Women Philosophers
Edited by Cheshire Calhoun

Burdened Virtues: Virtue Ethics for Liberatory Struggles
Lisa Tessman

On Female Body Experience: "Throwing Like a Girl" and Other Essays
Iris Marion Young

Visible Identities: Race, Gender, and the Self
Linda Martín Alcoff

Women and Citizenship
Edited by Marilyn Friedman

Women's Liberation and the Sublime: Feminism, Postmodernism, Environment
Bonnie Mann

Analyzing Oppression
Ann E. Cudd

Self-Transformations: Foucault, Ethics, and Normalized Bodies
Cressida J. Heyes

Family Bonds: Genealogies of Race and Gender
Ellen K. Feder

Ecological Thinking: The Politics of Epistemic Location
Lorraine Code

Moral Understandings: A Feminist Study in Ethics,
Second Edition
Margaret Urban Walker

The Moral Skeptic
Anita M. Superson

"You've Changed": Sex Reassignment and Personal Identity
Edited by Laurie J. Shrage

Dancing with Iris: The Philosophy of Iris Marion Young
Edited by Ann Ferguson and Mechthild Nagel

Philosophy of Science after Feminism
Janet A. Kourany

Shifting Ground: Knowledge and Reality, Transgression and Trustworthiness
Naomi Scheman

The Metaphysics of Gender
Charlotte Witt

Unpopular Privacy: What Must We Hide?
Anita L. Allen

Adaptive Preferences and Empowerment
Serene Khader

Out from the Shadows
Edited by Sharon L. Crasnow and Anita M. Superson

Minimizing Marriage: Marriage, Morality, and the Law
Elizabeth Brake

Simone de Beauvoir and the Politics of Ambiguity
Sonia Kruks

Simone de Beauvoir
and the
Politics of Ambiguity

SONIA KRUKS

OXFORD
UNIVERSITY PRESS

OXFORD
UNIVERSITY PRESS

Oxford University Press is a department of the University of Oxford.
It furthers the University's objective of excellence in research,
scholarship, and education by publishing worldwide.

Oxford   New York
Auckland   Cape Town   Dar es Salaam   Hong Kong   Karachi
Kuala Lumpur   Madrid   Melbourne   Mexico City   Nairobi
New Delhi   Shanghai   Taipei   Toronto

With offices in
Argentina   Austria   Brazil   Chile   Czech Republic   France   Greece
Guatemala   Hungary   Italy   Japan   Poland   Portugal   Singapore
South Korea   Switzerland   Thailand   Turkey   Ukraine   Vietnam

Oxford is a registered trade mark of Oxford University Press
in the UK and certain other countries.

Published in the United States of America by Oxford University Press
198 Madison Avenue, New York, NY 10016

Library of Congress Cataloging-in-Publication Data
Kruks, Sonia.
Simone de Beauvoir and the politics of ambiguity / Sonia Kruks.
p.   cm.—(Studies in feminist philosophy)
Includes bibliographical references (p.   ).
ISBN 978-0-19-538143-6 (pbk. : alk. paper)—ISBN 978-0-19-538144-3 (hardcover : alk. paper)
1. Beauvoir, Simone de, 1908–1986. 2. Political science—Philosophy. I. Title.
B2430.B344K78   2012
320.092—dc23   2012004968

1 3 5 7 9 8 6 4 2

Printed in the United States of America
on acid-free paper

For Leo
In memoriam

CONTENTS

ACKNOWLEDGMENTS

Nobody is an island, and this book would not have been possible without the presence of colleagues, friends, and family members who were integral parts of my world while it was being written. Over the years many, many people have contributed to the project in various ways. Some have done so by carefully reading and commenting on the text; others by acting as interlocutors at talks I have given, sharing ideas in stimulating conversations, or helping with references and translation questions. I would especially like to thank Emily Grosholz and Toril Moi for their careful readings of the entire manuscript and for their many thought-provoking suggestions. Meryl Altman, Debra Bergoffen, and Lori Jo Marso provided wonderful close readings of sections of the manuscript. Others I want to thank include Christa Acampora, Ash Amin, Ron Aronson, Robert Bernasconi, Lorraine Code, Diana Coole, Christine Daigle, Penelope Deutscher, David Drake, Mary Evans, Jill Gordon, Robert Hariman, Kimberly Hutchings, Michel Kail, Bonnie Mann, Yolanda Patterson, Anne Phillips, Margaret Simons, Roger Smith, Elaine Stavro, and Ursula Tidd. I would like especially to mention two wonderful Beauvoir scholars and friends who have recently died, both far too young: Elizabeth Fallaize and Hazel Rowley. The world is sadder for their absence. There are many other people who have contributed to this project and whom I cannot name: members of audiences before whom I have given papers; people I met and talked with perhaps only once at a conference; anonymous reviewers for earlier papers, and others. A thanks to all of you.

I have been fortunate to have held various fellowships and residencies while writing this book. These include a fellowship at the Birkbeck Institute for the Humanities; a visiting scholar appointment at the Women's Studies Program at Bucknell University; an especially wonderful term as a distinguished fellow at the Institute for Advanced Studies at Durham University; and a Visiting Scholar appointment at the Gender Institute of the London School of Economics. My profound thanks to colleagues and also to the amazingly supportive administrative staff at all of these institutions. I am also grateful to the Mellon Foundation, which provided a fellowship that relieved me of teaching for a semester.

For financial and other material support I thank Oberlin College, A sabbatical and a research status appointment allowed me some much-needed time free from teaching and other duties. Colleagues (and former colleagues) at Oberlin who have offered insightful comments include Grace An, Frances Hasso, Wendy Kozol, Maren Milligan, Ben Schiff, Harlan Wilson, and Sandra Zagarell. Thanks to Carol Tufts for helping me to stay sane. Four undergraduate research assistants have provided invaluable help: David Burnham, Gerard M. D'Emilio, Devin Gouré, and Anne Thompson.

Finally, the support of my family has been invaluable. It is not true that this book could not have been written without the assistance of my husband; however, his encouragement and suggestions have helped immensely. Thank you, Ben. Thanks also to Gabi and Sandip. Sadly, my father did not live to see this book completed. I wish he had, but it is dedicated to his memory.

ACKNOWLEDGMENTS OF PREVIOUS PUBLICATIONS

An earlier version of chapter 3 was published as "Simone de Beauvoir and the Politics of Privilege," in *Hypatia: A Journal of Feminist Philosophy*, Vol. 20, No. 1, Winter 2005, pp. 178–205. Republished by permission of Wiley-Blackwell.

A section of chapter 4 first appeared in the paper, "'Living on Rails': Freedom, Constraint, and Political Judgment in Beauvoir's 'Moral' Essays and *The Mandarins*." In *Philosophical Readings of "The Mandarins"*. Edited by Sally Scholz and Shannon Mussett, SUNY Press, Albany, NY, 2005, pp. 67–86. Reprinted by permission.

Parts of chapter 5 were first published in the work-in-progress paper, "Why Do We Humans Seek Revenge, and Should We?" in *Insights*, the online work-in-progress series of the Institute of Advanced Study, University of Durham, United Kingdom, Vol. 2, 2009. Reprinted by permission.

ABBREVIATIONS FOR THE MAIN CITED WORKS BY BEAUVOIR

Frequently cited works appear in the text using the abbreviations listed below.

Each in-text citation provides the page(s) of the English translation used, followed by the page(s) of the French edition consulted. Because many of the English translations of Beauvoir's work are of poor quality, I have frequently altered them. The abbreviation "TA" means that the translation has been altered.

The full bibliographic references for these frequently cited works are shown in the following list. Where I have not used the first French edition of a work, the original date of publication is provided at the end of the reference in square brackets.

Works by Beauvoir that are cited only occasionally are included in the general bibliography at the end of the book.

ADD   *America Day by Day*. Translated by Carol Cosman. Foreword by Douglas Brinkley. Berkeley: University of California Press, 2000.

AJJ   *L'Amérique au jour le jour: 1947*. Coll. Folio. Paris: Gallimard, 2001 [1954].

ASD   *All Said and Done*. Translated by Patrick O'Brian. Introduction by Toril Moi. New York: Paragon, 1993.

CA   *The Coming of Age*. Translated by Patrick O'Brian. New York: Putnam, 1972. [The British edition is titled *Old Age*. London: Deutsch and Weidenfeld and Nicolson, 1972].

DS I   *Le deuxième sexe*, vol. 1. Coll. Folio. Paris: Gallimard, 1989 [1949].

DS II   *Le deuxième sexe*. vol. 2. Coll. Folio. Paris: Gallimard, 1988 [1949].

EA   *The Ethics of Ambiguity*. Translated by Bernard Frechtman. New York: Citadel, 1967.

EE   "An Eye for an Eye." In *Simone de Beauvoir: Philosophical Writings*. Edited by Margaret A. Simons. Translated by Kristana Arp, 245–60. Urbana: University of Illinois Press, 2004.

FA I   *La force de l'âge*, vol. 1. Coll. Folio. Paris: Gallimard, 1981 [1960].

FA II   *La force de l'âge*, vol. 2. Coll. Folio. Paris: Gallimard, 1977 [1960].

FBS   "Faut-il brûler Sade?" In *Privilèges*, 11–89. Paris: Gallimard, 1955.

FC I   *Force of Circumstance*, vol. 1. Translated by Richard Howard. Introduction by Toril Moi. New York: Paragon, 1992.

FC II   *Force of Circumstance*, vol. 2. Translated by Richard Howard. Introduction by Toril Moi. New York: Paragon, 1992.

FC Fr I *La force des choses*, vol. 1. Coll. Folio. Paris: Gallimard, 1972 [1963].

FC Fr II *La force des choses*, vol. 2. Coll. Folio. Paris: Gallimard, 1978 [1963].

IMRP   "Idéalisme moral et réalisme politique." In *L'existentialisme et la sagesse des nations*, 55–101. Paris: Editions Nagel, 1948.

M   *The Mandarins*. Translated by Leonard M. Friedman. London: Fontana, 1972.

M Fr   *Les mandarins*. Paris: Gallimard, 1954.

MIPR   "Moral Idealism and Political Realism." In *Simone de Beauvoir: Philosophical Writings*. Edited by Margaret A. Simons. Translated by Anne Deing Cordero, 175–93. Urbana: University of Illinois Press, 2004.

MWBS   "Must We Burn Sade?" Translated by Annette Michelson. In *The Marquis de Sade: An Essay by Simone de Beauvoir with Selections from His Writings Chosen by Paul Dinnage*. London: New English Library, 1972.

OO   "Œil pour œil." In *L'existentialisme et la sagesse des nations*, 125–65. Paris: Editions Nagel, 1948.

PC   "Pyrrhus and Cinéas." In *Simone de Beauvoir: Philosophical Writings*. Edited by Margaret A. Simons. Translated by Marybeth Timmermann, 89–149. Urbana: University of Illinois Press, 2004.

PC Fr   *Pyrrhus et Cinéas*. Paris: Gallimard, 1960 [1944].

PL   *The Prime of Life*. Translated by Peter Green. Cleveland: World Publishing, 1962.

PMA   *Pour une morale de l'ambiguïté*. Paris: Gallimard, 1947.

TCF   *Tout compte fait*. Coll. Folio. Paris: Gallimard, 1978 [1972].

TSS   *The Second Sex*. Translated by Constance Borde and Sheila Malovany-Chevallier. New York: Knopf, 2010.

V   *La vieillesse*. Paris: Gallimard, 2005 [1970].

Simone de Beauvoir
and the
Politics of Ambiguity

Introduction

Simone de Beauvoir's political thinking has not received the attention it deserves. Best know as the author of *The Second Sex*, outside feminist circles she has too often been identified merely as Sartre's life companion and, in intellectual matters, as his disciple. Although the last two decades have witnessed a major "renaissance" of scholarship on Beauvoir, most of this work remains encapsulated within relatively small areas of feminist and continental philosophy and does not address her wider contributions to political theory and philosophy.[1] Indeed, very few Anglophone scholars are even aware of the extent of Beauvoir's writings on politics, and most are ignorant of her theoretical contributions. Thus my project is, in part, simply to explain what was profoundly original and significant in Beauvoir's wide-ranging thinking about politics. However, beyond that, it is also to demonstrate how her ideas continue to have a remarkable degree of currency. Her work still speaks to many questions that exercise not only academic political theorists and philosophers but also social critics and political activists.

It is particularly timely, in addition, to consider Beauvoir's thinking in the present politico-intellectual conjuncture. For some decades an impasse has existed in political theory and philosophy. Liberal rationalists, who conceive of the self as an autonomous rational agent and characterize politics as a realm of debate among such reasonable individuals, and post-structuralists, who espouse discourse-constructionist theories of the self and question both the notion of the self as an autonomous agent and

---

1. There is not, in my view, a sharp distinction to be made between political theory and political philosophy, and I use either or both terms as appropriate. I also quite often refer simply to Beauvoir's "political thinking" as a way of encompassing both her more speculative and her more immediately engaged treatments of matters political.

claims for the neutrality of reason, have for the most part persistently ignored or talked past each other. Today, the more strident versions of poststructuralism are waning. For, on the one hand, the cognitive sciences and fresh thinking about materialism are undercutting its privileging of the constitutive power of discourse, while, on the other, in the post–September 11th world, issues of human vulnerability, of the centrality of violence to politics, of the relation of ethics to violence—questions not easily encompassed by poststructuralism—have become of growing concern. Nonetheless, if the moment of high poststructuralism is now passing, this does not mean that liberal rationalism has "won," for many of the poststructuralist critiques leveled against its obfuscation of power relations and the exclusionary quality of its notions of reasonableness still hold. It is in this context that an examination of Beauvoir's highly original version of existential philosophy, in which *ambiguity* is the leitmotif, will prove especially fruitful, for she explores a set of irresolvable paradoxes and tensions in political life (and, indeed, life more broadly) of which the impasse between liberal rationalism and its poststructuralist critics is but a manifestation.

My claims for Beauvoir's continuing relevance may seem surprising since she has long been regarded, even by a great many feminists, as a quaint relic rather than as a resource for future thinking. Most feminist theory claims to have long gone "beyond" *The Second Sex* [1949]. Today, *The Second Sex* is a book that all have heard of but few actually read. Likewise, since the rise of poststructuralism, Sartre has most often been cast as a naïve "Enlightenment" thinker whose existentialist philosophy has long been surpassed by more sophisticated new theories.[2] Presumed to be but Sartre's intellectual follower, Beauvoir has been tarred with the same brush. Yet, as the recent renaissance of Beauvoir scholarship demonstrates, many of the perplexities that Beauvoir addresses in *The Second Sex*—starting with her blunt opening question, "what is a woman?"—are in no way resolved, and much of what she says remains fertile ground for further reflection. What the new scholarship also clearly demonstrates is

---

2. Sartre was never a straightforward rationalist or an idealist, although the sharp distinction he made between consciousness (being-for-itself) and the world of material things (being-in-itself) in *Being and Nothingness* [1943] implied a certain affinity with Cartesian dualism. Even so, he did not deserve the opprobrium to which he was subjected by the next generation of thinkers in France. Given his intellectual dominance in the immediate postwar period, a certain "overthrow of the father" was at play in the hostile treatment he received. It is important also to note that *Being and Nothingness* was an early work. Sartre continued to write prolifically throughout his life, and his ideas changed considerably over time.

that Beauvoir was an original philosopher in her own right. She was not merely Sartre's companion; nor was she his faithful intellectual disciple.[3]

This is not to deny that there are some strong affinities between the ideas of Beauvoir and Sartre. Both draw extensively on Hegel, as well as on Husserlian and Heideggerian phenomenology, in elaborating their respective accounts of human existence as "lived experience." Both are deeply concerned with the question of human freedom, and both insist that freedom is not a quality of a contemplative consciousness but rather requires an active engagement in the world. However, Beauvoir's version of existentialism pays far greater attention than Sartre's to the ambiguities that arise from the *embodied* qualities of freedom. She examines the body as our point of inherence in the world, thus as at once material and cultural, at once the site of both freedom and constraint. She also develops a far more nuanced appreciation than (at least the early) Sartre of the inherently social qualities of human existence, exploring how social relations both support and yet may also foreclose individual freedom.[4]

The Second Sex undoubtedly stands as the greatest work within Beauvoir's very wide-ranging œuvre. This has led to her frequent categorization exclusively as a "feminist" theorist—as if this designation excluded political theory or political philosophy "proper"! However, to theorize about sexualized social relations is already to theorize about a range of politico-philosophical questions. Feminist theory necessitates the elaboration and deployment of normative concepts such as inequality, oppression, and freedom, which are central to political theory and philosophy, and it also requires an engagement with broader philosophical issues of both an ontological and an ethical

---

3. However, it is striking that Beauvoir did frequently present herself as Sartre's disciple in matters philosophical, insisting that with regard to philosophy he had already said all there was to say. See Simons (2010) for a careful documentation of Beauvoir's persistent self-misrepresentations. But then the question arises as to why Beauvoir insisted that he, but not she, was an original philosopher. Explanations have often focused on the psychological and gendered complexities of what Michèle Le Doeuff has called the "erotico-theoretical relationship" between Beauvoir and Sartre, in which Beauvoir sometimes played a traditionally "feminine" self-abnegating role. See, for the most thoughtful discussions, Le Doeuff (1991) and Moi (1994); see also Bair (1990). However, Nancy Bauer persuasively argues that what is at issue here also concerns the nature of philosophy itself, for by "philosophy" Beauvoir meant the kind of system building that she eschewed. That Beauvoir produced no grand philosophical system is not to say that she did not ask or investigate what are profoundly philosophical questions (Bauer 2001).

4. These are issues that Sartre addressed most fully in later works, notably his *Critique of Dialectical Reason* ([1960] 1976), where he explored at length the ways in which individual actions impinge on and may alter each other.

kind. Regrettably, Beauvoir's original reflections on such matters in *The Second Sex* have too often been obscured by the assumption that (to quote from its original English translator) the book "is, after all, on woman, not on philosophy" (Parshley 1989, xxxviii). Viewed from this perspective, it would seem that Beauvoir's "existentialism" is but some minor philosophical baggage she unfortunately borrowed from Sartre and that it is irrelevant to her "real" project.[5]

However, the philosophical aspects of *The Second Sex*—and of a great many of Beauvoir's other works that I shall be discussing—are hardly minor baggage. Although Beauvoir wrote only a few, short, early essays in a conventionally philosophical style (of which *The Ethics of Ambiguity* is the best known), she articulates her philosophical positions throughout a great many other works. Not only are they are deeply woven into her account, in *The Second Sex*, of how one "becomes a woman," but they are also elaborated in many other "essays" (as she called her nonfiction works) and in her novels. Furthermore, since Beauvoir *lived* her philosophy, it was also articulated in a more intimate style throughout her letters, diaries, and autobiographical writings. Likewise, from the Second World War onward, Beauvoir experienced the political events, dilemmas, and currents of her times as deeply felt, personal concerns, and they thus became the focal point of much of her philosophical deliberation.

An orienting thread that runs throughout Beauvoir's thinking is her insistence on the *ambiguity* of human existence and the paradoxes and necessary failures of action that this implies. Within Anglophone philosophy, ambiguity is most often regarded as a fault, as indicative of the failure properly to achieve "clear and distinct ideas." However, ambiguity may also be a quality of phenomena themselves, signifying their indeterminacy.[6] In addition, it may also denote relationships in which antithetical qualities

---

5. Parshley frequently and freely rendered Beauvoir's technical philosophical concepts into what he regarded as "common sense" English, radically changing their meaning in the process. Until the publication of a new translation in 2010, Parshley's rendition of Beauvoir's book simply *was The Second Sex* for generations of Anglophone readers. His mistranslations strongly contributed to obscuring the fact that the book is a coherent work of philosophy. On the inadequacies of the Parshley translation see Simons (1999, chap. 5) and Moi (2002). The new translation by Constance Borde and Sheila Malovany-Chevallier is for the most part more accurate than the Parshley version, and unlike his, which contained many cuts, it also includes the full text. However, its style is unfortunately stilted and awkward.

6. This indeterminacy is illustrated in classic Gestalt psychology drawings (e.g., the one in which the same figure may be seen as either a duck or a rabbit, or that in which the same figure may appear either as the profiles of two faces or as a vase).

coexist in agonistic tension. For Beauvoir, this last, agonistic sense of ambiguity has the most profound significance. She argues that irresolvable antinomies are constitutive of human existence and that these extend from the ontological to the ethical and the political. At once body and consciousness but reducible to neither, we all live "the strange ambiguity of existence made body," yet we each do so in our own way (TSS 763; DS II 728). The materiality of the human condition is what both enables us to engage in free, creative action in the world and constrains us and delimits what we may do. This ambiguous admixture of freedom and constraint also suffuses human relations. We are separate, individuated existences, yet our actions may acquire their meaning only through the presence of others. "A man alone in the world would be paralyzed by the manifest vanity of all his goals," Beauvoir writes (PC 115 TA; PC Fr. 65). At the same time, because we are separate, free existences, our projects will often conflict. Desiring different ends, we will encounter others as impediments or as threats. Harms, including violent harms, as well as reciprocity, thus haunt the human world.

Herein lie the ambiguities that most fully imbue politics. Here Beauvoir's thinking also shares some interesting affinities with later poststructuralist critics of liberal rationalism. We are not autonomous or, as Beauvoir puts it, "sovereign" consciousnesses; nor are we able to resolve ambiguities or eliminate conflicts through the "correct" application of reason. Reason is not innocent of power, and to claim to act according to indubitably "right" principles or ideals does not absolve us of the harm to others that may well ensue from what we think are good actions. Accordingly, Beauvoir warns of the dangers of what she calls "moral purism." She criticizes the "intransigent moralist," who focuses only on whether her or his intentions are good and who does not acknowledge responsibility for the undesired consequences of actions. Failure in politics cannot be warded off by the incantation of mantras such as "justice," or "freedom," or "rights." For failure is a condition of life itself. Indeed, she writes, "one can never dream of eliminating [failure] without immediately dreaming of death" (EA 157; PMA 219).

Although Beauvoir anticipated compelling poststructuralist critiques of liberal rationalism and its ideal "sovereign" subject, she cannot, however, be adequately characterized as a poststructuralist *avant la lettre*. For even though she would agree that subjectivity is profoundly shaped by discursive and disciplinary practices, she still insists that it exceeds their constitutive power. Her persistent concern with freedom and with the need to create the meaning of our own lives, as well as her insistence on our responsibility for what we make of our selves and for how what we do impinges on others, would sit uncomfortably within at least high poststructuralist theory. One might thus be tempted to see Beauvoir as offering a compromise between these theoretical orientations, perhaps as developing a center ground where liberal rationalism and poststructuralism will fruitfully meld. However, such a view would be too simple. For Beauvoir does not suggest a "resolution" to the impasse by proposing either a harmonious middle way or a benign synthesis. Instead, what she propounds is an account of human existence as intrinsically riven by ambiguities and tensions that precisely are *not* amenable to a synthetic resolution. These tensions are the very stuff of life itself. Thus the impasse between liberal rationalism and poststructuralism is more than a clash of theoretical orientations. It is itself an expression of the irresolvable ambiguities that pervade human existence. Because these ambiguities cannot be eliminated, failure attends all human action, yet this cannot be a justification for inaction. How these ambiguities play out and what they come to mean in the world of politics are the central concerns of Beauvoir's political thinking. They are what this book addresses.

A Life in Writing

In the following chapters I, of course, discuss *The Second Sex*. However, I also consider a wide range of other materials drawn from across the remarkably diverse genres in which Beauvoir worked. They include explicitly philosophical essays that address ethics and politics in an existential vein; pieces written as direct interventions in political events; travel writings; volumes of autobiography; her massive book on the vicissitudes of old age; and her novel, *The Mandarins*. Since much of this material will be unfamiliar to readers who know, or know of, Beauvoir only as the author of *The Second Sex*, in what follows I introduce some of it as I also briefly review certain relevant aspects of her life. The ensuing chapters of the book are organized topically. Here, however, I proceed chronologically in order to show how knitted together are Beauvoir's works and life.

Early Days

Beauvoir's life was more or less coextensive with the short twentieth century. Born in Paris in 1908, a few years prior to the First World War, she died in the same city in 1986, only three years before the Berlin Wall was to fall. She was nine years old at the time of the Russian Revolution, and she came to adulthood during the interwar period. She lived through the rise of

Fascism; the Nazi Occupation of Paris during World War II; the development of the Cold War in the late 1940s; the eruption of anticolonial movements in the French Empire (notably the Algerian conflict in the late
1950s); the Soviet invasion of Hungary in 1956; the Vietnam War; the "May
Events" of 1968; the emergence of the women's liberation movement in the
1970s; and the Iranian Revolution of 1979. Beauvoir describes herself as
having been rather apolitical until the late 1930s, but from then on she was
avidly engaged in the currents—and cross-currents—of French and international political affairs. After the war she frequently intervened in current
events by writing about them, as well as sometimes participating in more
immediate forms of political action.

Beauvoir came from a downwardly mobile bourgeois family. She was
allowed to pursue a higher education only because her father did not have
the means to provide her with a dowry (still expected for a woman of her
class to be marriageable in the 1920s). She later described her childhood in
the first of her autobiographical volumes, *Memoirs of a Dutiful Daughter*
[1958], and there are striking affinities between her descriptions of the life
of the young girl in *The Second Sex* and her account of her own highly constrained and decorous Catholic girlhood. Beginning her university studies
in 1925, Beauvoir received the *agrégation* in philosophy (the highest teaching qualification) in 1929. The youngest member of her cohort and one of
very few women, she was ranked second in this extremely demanding
national examination—just behind Jean-Paul Sartre. They met and began
their lifelong relationship while they were preparing for the examination.[7]

Throughout most of her student days Beauvoir kept a journal, which has
only recently been published (Beauvoir 2006, 2008).[8] Reading it, one senses
the tremendous passion with which she engaged the new world of ideas she
was discovering, as well as the intensity with which she introspectively

---

7. See Moi (1994, chap. 2) for a discussion of quite how remarkable Beauvoir's
achievement was. Given the inferior quality of the girls' Catholic-school education
she had received in comparison to Sartre's at a prestigious *lycée*, the fact she began
studying philosophy only in 1926 and that, as a woman, she could not attend the
elite Ecole Normale Supérieure, her success was truly extraordinary. The examining jury is said to have discussed at some length which of the two, Beauvoir or
Sartre, it should rank first (Cohen-Solal 1987, 74).

8. The volume published in English in 2006 includes only Beauvoir's diary for
1926. The volume published in French in 2008 covers the period 1926–1930. The
remainder of the diary will soon be published in an English translation. These
translations form part of a major project to make Beauvoir's works available in
English. The project, which is being edited by Margaret A. Simons and Sylvie Le
Bon de Beauvoir, is being published by the University of Illinois Press.

scrutinized her own motives, actions, moods, and relationships. As well as her newly acquired passion for philosophy, Beauvoir also had a long-standing love of literature. She had wanted, above all, to be a great novelist, and she describes herself as now torn between literary and philosophical activity. In the 1930s, while earning her living teaching philosophy, it was the path of literature that she chose.[9]

Beauvoir wrote several early novels that she was unable to get published. However, in 1943 she finally achieved success with the publication and positive reception of *She Came to Stay [L'Invitée]*. A philosophical novel par excellence, it is preceded by an epigraph attributed to Hegel: "Each consciousness seeks the death of the other." Through the (quasi-autobiographical) story of a conflicted erotic triangle, the novel does indeed explore the experience of the "Other" as threat and antagonist—indeed, to the very point of death. The Hegelian notion of the inherent conflict of consciousnesses would later hold a prominent place in Beauvoir's political philosophy. However, she also rapidly began to complicate this notion in the series of "moral" essays that she started the following year. For here she also attends to the human potential for intersubjectivity and, indeed, solidarity. Relation, as well as separation and conflict, shapes human interactions of all kinds, she argues.

The year 1943 was also when Sartre published his magnum opus, *Being and Nothingness*, and it too portrays the fundamental human relationship as one of the conflict of consciousnesses. According to Sartre, the "look" of the Other [*le regard de L'Autre*] disrupts my world and freezes me, object-like, within his. However, I am always free also to turn the tables and to carry out an equivalent objectifying operation upon him. Thus, for many years, the standard evaluation of Beauvoir's novel was that it merely took up and presented Sartre's ideas in fictional form. More recent scholarship has effectively challenged such a reading, and Beauvoir's early diaries clearly establish that she had been meditating on the problem of "the Other" well before she had even met Sartre. With the pendulum veering in

---

9. Beauvoir's views on the relationship between literature and philosophy altered over time. In 1946, in "Literature and Metaphysics," she argued that they are closely allied, and she defended what she called the "metaphysical novel," which sought to make philosophical arguments (Beauvoir 2004, 261–77). Later, however, she criticized her early novels (which she now called "thesis-novels") for their didacticism (PL 465–66; FA II 673–74). Later still, she came to argue that the proper function of literature is, rather, the "unveiling" [*dévoilement*] of another world for the reader—a task very similar to that of phenomenological philosophy (Beauvoir 1965). For a thoughtful reading of Beauvoir's mature thinking on what literature may do, see Moi (2009).

the other direction, it has even been argued that Sartre "stole" key ideas in *Being and Nothingness* from her (Fullbrook and Fullbrook 1994). But this reading is equally problematic. For what is clear from letters and diaries is that, starting with similar preoccupations and insights, they, rather, refined each other's ideas.[10] What is also clear is that there was never a total convergence in their thinking. Instead, over the years, a crisscrossing of ideas was at play, in which at certain times their positions grew closer and at others more widely diverged.

However, in what she would later (and critically) call her "moral period" essays, written in the mid-1940s, Beauvoir was at her closest to Sartre. These philosophical essays begin with *Pyrrhus and Cinéas*, written in early 1943, and culminate in her better-known *The Ethics of Ambiguity*, published in 1947.[11] Sandwiched between are several shorter essays. Two of these are especially important resources for examining Beauvoir's political thinking: "Moral Idealism and Political Realism" [1945], which deals with problems of agency and moral responsibility in politics, and "An Eye for an Eye" [1946], in which Beauvoir reflects (in the context of the trial and execution of Robert Brasillach, an intellectual collaborator) on the nature of revenge.

From the "Moral Period" to *The Second Sex*

The German Occupation was in every way an intensely formative period for Beauvoir. The stability and normalcy of her life were shattered by the experience of living under Nazi domination and by the continual, looming presence

---

10. As Sylvie Le Bon de Beauvoir, Beauvoir's adopted daughter, has recently written about the early Beauvoir-Sartre relationship: "It is not a matter of influence but an encounter in the strong sense of the term. Beauvoir and Sartre recognized themselves in each other because each already existed independently and intensely" (2004, x).

11. Pyrrhus (319–272 BCE) was a Hellenistic king who, according to Plutarch, desired to vastly expand his empire. Beauvoir begins *Pyrrhus and Cinéas* with Plutarch's account of a conversation between Pyrrhus and his adviser, Cinéas. Cinéas asks Pyrrhus what he plans to do once all his intended conquests have been achieved. Pyrrhus replies that he plans to come home and rest afterward, whereupon Cinéas asks him why he does he not just stay at home and rest to begin with. The conversation sets the stage for Beauvoir's investigation into the meaning of human action.

Unlike her other essays of this period, *The Ethics of Ambiguity* was translated into English almost immediately, in 1948. It was only in 2004, in the volume *Simone de Beauvoir: Philosophical Writings*, that full translations of the other early essays, including *Pyrrhus and Cinéas*, became available.

of violence and death that accompanied it. Although Beauvoir herself was not directly harmed, friends and colleagues, some Jewish, some in the Resistance, disappeared, never to return. Later, Beauvoir evoked the flavor of this period in her autobiography. Even so, it is difficult for those who did not live through it (and who now know with hindsight that the Occupation was not to be a permanent condition) to grasp its overwhelming impact. All of Beauvoir's moral period works are products of the Occupation or its turbulent aftermath, and as such they are marked by a heightened, sometimes even a Manichaean, quality. They are not written with what we might call "politics as usual" in mind but rather address a world for which Picasso's *Guernica* perhaps best stands as the symbol. This is a world in which political conflict leads not to electoral defeats or to changes in government policy but to torture, destruction, and wholesale slaughter. However, reflection on extreme situations may also clarify what is at work in "politics as usual," and this is true of Beauvoir's early writings.

Pyrrhus and Cinéas, the first of the works, is a short book that Beauvoir began while *Being and Nothingness* was still in press. Invited to write an essay on "existentialism" for a series on contemporary ideologies, Beauvoir's first reaction was to refuse, saying that there was nothing she could add to Sartre's work (PL 433; FA II 627). But once having been persuaded, she wrote a work that, in fact, added a wealth of her own ideas to *Being and Nothingness*. However, she also valiantly struggled to fit her original insights within the procrustean theoretical confines of Sartre's philosophy. Consequently, *Pyrrhus and Cinéas* (and other early essays) did indeed remain too closely aligned with the idealism and voluntarism of Sartre's early ontology, in which human freedom, or "being-for-itself," was seen as indestructible. "The slave in chains is as free as his master," Sartre had proclaimed in *Being and Nothingness* ([1943] 1966, 673),[12] and his insistence on the "infinite," indeed "sovereign," quality of freedom was still echoed in *Pyrrhus and Cinéas*

---

12. His biographer, Annie Cohen-Solal, rightly locates what she calls Sartre's "declaration of the absolute supremacy of subjectivity over the world" specifically in the context of the Occupation. It expresses his defiance of Nazi oppression: "Of course, when he elaborates his theory of freedom, it is in the realm of full philosophical abstraction, but the situation out of which and under which his elaboration takes place is nonetheless concretely historical. It is in Nazi France that he shouts, loud and clear, his appeal to authenticity and responsibility and his denunciation of all forms of bad faith" (1987, 188). The same may be said of Beauvoir's early essays; it is not only Sartre's influence but her own personal experiences that give rise to her Manichaean tone. Sartre was also to criticize the idealism of his wartime notions of the absolute and indestructible nature of freedom later on (Sartre [1969] 1983).

when Beauvoir dramatically proclaimed that "one can throw a man in prison, get him out, cut off his arm, lend him wings, but his freedom remains infinite in all cases" (PC 124; PC Fr 86).

Even so, Beauvoir was already far more attuned than Sartre to the significance of what she would later call the "force of circumstance" [la force des choses]. Thus, in *Pyrrhus and Cinéas* she also introduced a distinction between this "infinite," ontological freedom [la liberté] and the practical, or effective, freedom that is required in order to act in the world [la puissance]. The latter, she argued, requires the presence and support of others; consequently, it may be curtailed by individual or societal interventions. Accordingly, in *Pyrrhus and Cinéas* Beauvoir initiated a range of arguments that Sartre had not made in *Being and Nothingness*—about human interdependencies, about the social and political prerequisites for freedom, and about the possibility of overcoming the problem of the "Other" and mitigating the conflict of consciousnesses.[13] Already, then, in this early work she was beginning to develop a conception of the self as an *ambiguous* existent: as something other than a "sovereign" freedom or consciousness. Thus, in spite of Beauvoir's own later strictures about their excessive moralism and idealism (with which I agree), *Pyrrhus and Cinéas* and her other moral period essays incipiently contain much of her mature thinking about the ambiguity of the embodied self.[14] However, as Beauvoir further developed her thinking she also began increasingly to attend to the practical material constraints on freedom and, in doing so, to incorporate elements of a non-reductionist Marxism within her analyses.

Even before the war Beauvoir considered herself a socialist, at least from an ethical standpoint. Nonetheless, she describes herself as still remaining indifferent to actual political events during the 1920s and 1930s. Seeing herself as a mere spectator, she says it never occurred to her to participate

---

13. As she later wrote about *Pyrrhus and Cinéas*, "I attempted to reconcile Sartre's ideas with the views I had upheld against him in various lengthy discussions" (PL 434; FA II 628).

14. I have written more extensively elsewhere about how Beauvoir's thinking altered over the course of the 1940s, and I do not repeat my analysis at length here (see Kruks 1991, 2001). But to summarize, although I do not believe one can point to any one moment of decisive rupture in Beauvoir's thought, and although a continuity of preoccupations persisted throughout her life, still, changes of emphasis within this continuity resulted in significant reconfigurations of her ideas about the self, freedom, responsibility, and other key concerns. I read *The Second Sex* as pivotal for many of these developments. For a more favorable reading of the moral period essays than mine (or Beauvoir's), see Arp (2001). Although I am critical of aspects of these early essays, they are far from mere juvenilia, and I draw on what is best in them in later chapters.

in a strike called at the school where she was teaching, or to join a demonstration to show her support for the Popular Front (PL 132; FA I 187). It was not until the spring of 1939 that she finally faced the fact of the inevitability of war. Then, she says, "History seized me and never let me go again" (PL 285 TA; FA II 410). Beauvoir emerged from the Occupation strongly convinced that there could be no going back to the inequitable class structure of the prewar status quo. This conviction also translated into a sympathetic but critical stance toward Communism.

After the war there was an immense wave of support for the French Communist Party (PCF) since the Communists had been the backbone of the French Resistance. Many of its members had been tortured, deported, or killed, while it was the Soviet Union that had sacrificed millions of people in order to defeat Hitler. Along with the trade unions that were allied with it, the PCF represented the largest section of the French working classes and it formed part of the Tripartite coalition government until 1947. It also attracted a large following among leftist intellectuals since, with the development of the Cold War, there appeared to be no middle ground between unqualified support for the Soviet Union and a pro-American position, which aligned one with the exploitative forces of capitalist domination and imperialism. However, the PCF took its line from Moscow. It demanded an unquestioning discipline from its members which Beauvoir would not accept, and it espoused the highly deterministic, orthodox version of Marxism (or, more precisely, Marxism-Leninism) that Stalin had formulated.

This was the political context in which, in late 1945, *Les Temps modernes*, the monthly journal of politics, ideas, and culture, began publication. A dream conceived during the Occupation, it was to become the most powerful hub of non-Communist, leftist intellectual life in postwar France. Sartre was its editor, and Beauvoir an active member of its editorial board. She would remain on the board—and actively so—until her death in 1986.[15] The journal attempted to carve out a democratic socialist "third way" between pro-Soviet and pro-American positions. It propounded a less deterministic version of Marxism than the orthodoxy of the PCF, and

---

15. Initially the political editor was Maurice Merleau-Ponty (1908–1960) but, in disagreement with Sartre's increasingly pro-Communist position, he resigned in 1952. Merleau-Ponty's major work of phenomenology, *The Phenomenology of Perception* [1945], was also an important influence on the development of Beauvoir's thinking about embodiment and about how the self is always "in situation." She wrote an extensive review of this book for an early issue of *Les Temps modernes* (Beauvoir 2004, 151–64).

it kept its distance from the Soviet-oriented Party while still offering it "critical support."[16] Accordingly, in "Moral Idealism and Political Realism," published in the second issue of *Les Temps modernes*, Beauvoir clearly distanced herself from Communist orthodoxy while embracing a less mechanistic Marxism.

In this essay she approvingly cites the saying of the young Marx that "Man represents the highest goal for man" (MIPR 181), while criticizing the determinism of those "realists" of the Left who will justify the sacrifice of the present generations to the inevitable coming of the future golden age (MIPR 2004, 186). Similarly, in *The Ethics of Ambiguity*, she criticizes the determinism of the Communist Party's "Marxism," pointing out that "the very notion of action would lose all meaning if history were a mechanical unrolling in which man appears only as a passive conductor of outside forces" (EA 20; PMA 30). At the same time, however, her discussion of oppression begins to address its material aspects in ways that are indebted to Marxism. Oppression, she says, closes down freedom for many by reducing their labor to meaninglessness, to no more than a "pure repetition of mechanical gestures," while denying them even the leisure time in which to be creative (EA 83; PMA 117). In *The Ethics of Ambiguity* we are no longer fully in the world of the conflict of consciousnesses and of Sartre's objectifying "look." Rather, this is a world where objectification also takes practical, material forms. Ambiguity is foreclosed through the treatment of persons as if they were merely physical resources, treatment that does not acknowledge that they are embodied subjectivities. Beauvoir's insights here into these dual aspects of objectification will be adapted and further extended in *The Second Sex*.

Writing *The Second Sex*

By the time *The Ethics of Ambiguity* was published, in the fall of 1947, Beauvoir had already completed considerable work on *The Second Sex*. However, she had also interrupted this work to spend four months traveling and giving

16. There was, in fact, little middle ground on which to maneuver, and various splits and feuds ensued as Sartre took the journal on a zigzag course, drawing nearer to the Communists (who were not, in the event, grateful for the journal's "critical support") in the early 1950s, veering away again after the invasion of Hungary in 1956, but still remaining hopeful until 1968 that some progressive potential remained in the Soviet Union. The story of *Les Temps modernes* and of Sartre's complicated political dance has been rehearsed elsewhere (Burnier 1968; Davies 1987; Cohen-Solal 1987; Aronson 2004; Drake 2005), and I do not repeat it here.

lectures (and beginning her passionate love affair with Nelson Algren) in America early that same year.[17] On her return she wrote an account of her travels in the United States, which was first published as a series of essays in *Les Temps modernes* and then as a book, *America Day by Day* [*L'Amérique au jour le jour*] in late 1948. *America Day by Day* reveals Beauvoir's great ambivalence about the United States. On the one hand, it is the belly of the imperialist monster, and she is disturbed by the shrill anti-Communism and the chauvinism she encounters there, even among good liberals. She also perceptively points to the disjuncture between the high-flown rhetoric of freedom and the poverty and racism she observes. Her experiences while traveling by bus in the South are especially shocking to her, and she discusses race at some length. But she is also in love with the vibrancy of America, its sheer scale, its physical and social diversity, and its lack of stuffy European formality. Although instances of race and sex oppression are in many ways different, Beauvoir's exposure to the issue of race in the United States would afterward contribute to how she theorized women's oppression in *The Second Sex*.

In the summer of 1948 Beauvoir resumed work on *The Second Sex*, which was published in two volumes, the first in June 1949 and the second in November of that year. Her explicit treatment of women's sexual initiation and her critique of compulsory maternity (the chapter on "the mother" begins with a lengthy discussion of abortion) created a considerable scandal. However, as already noted, the several hundred pages of *The Second Sex* are not only about women. They are also about the ambiguities that attend embodied human existence, about power and oppression, and about the ways in which the oppressed may become complicit in their oppression so that responsibility for it is rarely clear-cut. Oppression, she demonstrates, operates at different scales and interacting sites. It operates through the kinds of "micropractices" of power on the body that Foucault would later examine in other contexts (Foucault 1977, 1978). However, such micropractices will function to perpetuate situations of oppression only in conjunction with oppressive macro-level economic, cultural, social, and political structures. It is this symbiosis that gives rise to the situations in which women, who, like men, are free human beings capable of creative action, are required to render themselves passive and object-like. It is in this situation that they become the purported Other to "man"; to man who claims for himself the status of the "sovereign" subject. Woman, Beauvoir

---

17. Nelson Algren (1909–1981), a novelist and a leftist, lived a rather bohemian lifestyle in a run-down area of Chicago. He portrayed Chicago's lowlife in his novels and was Beauvoir's guide to that city. Much to his fury, Beauvoir later fictionalized their affair in *The Mandarins*.

writes, "is the inessential in front of the essential [*elle est l'inessentiel en face de l'essentiel*]. He is the Subject, he is the Absolute: she is the Other" (TSS 6; DS I 15).

Women's material dependence on men and their lack of control over their own fertility constitute fundamental elements of their oppression. Although Beauvoir criticizes Engels for linking the subordination of women too exclusively to the rise of private property, she concurs that an improvement in women's condition requires their "participation in production and freedom from reproductive slavery" (TSS 139; DS I 207). However, if Beauvoir's analysis in *The Second Sex* remains more informed by Marxism than is often noted, she also insists that establishing women's economic independence would not, in itself, end their oppression. Nor would improving their legal status and granting them equal rights suffice, as liberal feminism optimistically expected. Anticipating by more than two decades many of the central concerns of "second-wave" feminism, she also focused attention on the personal and "private": on sexuality as a site of power and on the "home" as a site of enforced drudgery. She pointed to the double-binds that women encounter as they begin to move from the private, domestic world into public activity. She also anticipated the focus of much recent feminist theory on the power of discourse, attending at length to the role of discursive genres as diverse as biology, Freudian psychoanalysis, myths, and works of literature, in producing Woman as man's Other. *The Second Sex* shows in fine-grained detail how the personal and the public, the economic, the political, and the cultural all converge and cohere so that, famously, "One is not born a woman: one becomes one" (TSS 283 TA; DS II 13). This is to say, one becomes an impossible, paradoxical being: an active subject who is obliged to make herself both "object and prey" (TSS 723; DS II 600) and who will thus live continuously divided against herself.

After *The Second Sex*

In the early 1950s, following the scandalous success of *The Second Sex*, Beauvoir returned to her first love, literature. After several years of intensive work she published her prize-winning novel, *The Mandarins*, in 1954. A quasi-fictionalized account of the *Temps modernes* circle during the immediate postwar period, it addresses both the personal and the political lives of its characters. It is not only a philosophical but also a deeply *political*-philosophical novel. Against the backdrop of the developing Cold War and the declining role of France in a world now dominated by the conflicting interests of the United States and the Soviet Union, its characters wrestle with a range of political dilemmas. These also lead them (as, of course, they had led Beauvoir) to speculate on thorny questions such as whether or when there is an obligation to tell the truth in politics, or what constitutes a reasonable basis for making political judgments. However, Beauvoir deliberately refrains from giving her readers replies to such questions. Her characters do not tell us what we "ought" to think about them, for, as the novel well conveys, politics is strongly pervaded by ambiguity and failure. In politics the "right" answer is rare.

While *The Mandarins* was in press, burning new political concerns were already arising for Beauvoir. The French Empire was coming under ever-growing pressure from anticolonial liberation movements, and 1954 was the year not only of the French defeat in Vietnam (at Dien Bien Phu) but also of the beginning of armed resistance in Algeria. The struggle for Algerian independence and the brutal repression with which the French responded were to affect Beauvoir's life profoundly until the early 1960s. In her autobiography, Beauvoir later described the war as invading "my thoughts, my sleep, my moods" (FC II 87 TA; FC Fr II 120). She was appalled at the massacres and the extensive use of torture and by the way the press whitewashed and the public blandly accepted what was being done in its name. She became deeply ashamed of being a French citizen and felt she was complicit in this war, which she vehemently opposed. Beauvoir reflected at length about the war, and about the nature of guilt and complicity, in *Force of Circumstance* (a volume of her autobiography that she completed in 1963, only shortly after Algeria finally received independence).

It was during the war for Algerian independence that Beauvoir became active in politics in more practical ways, notably in organizing a public campaign to pressure for the release of a young Algerian woman, Djamila Boupacha. After being subjected to many days of torture and to rape by her French captors, Boupacha had "confessed" to planting a bomb in Algiers. From then on, Beauvoir was to undertake a great many practical political interventions, and she would also continue to meditate on them in her autobiography and elsewhere. Her political activities included participation in demonstrations and other actions during the events of May 1968, lending her support to various international struggles against oppressive regimes, and long-term involvement from the early 1970s with organizations demanding women's reproductive freedom. She even served in the early 1980s as honorary chairperson of a commission on the status of women established by the Mitterand government, although by then she was elderly and quite ill.

Between 1958 and 1981 Beauvoir's writings included five large volumes of autobiography, as well as many occasional essays, several works of fiction, and a deeply touching memoir about her mother's death. These autobiographical volumes, which covered her entire life, also described a great deal of Sartre's, concluding with an account of his death in 1980.[18] As well as (rather selectively) documenting her personal life, travel experiences, books read, and so forth, the autobiographies are rich texts for examining Beauvoir's political thinking. From the rise of Fascism to the emergence of the women's liberation movement in the 1970s, Beauvoir records her intellectual and emotional responses to political events and describes her practical political involvements in them. In addition, she uses her autobiography as a site for considered reflection on politics. These volumes thus comprise an important element of her political œuvre, and I draw on them accordingly.

Beauvoir's last major "essay" (as she called it) was a book of some six hundred pages on the condition of the elderly. Published in 1970 and simply called *La viellesse* in French, it is called *The Coming of Age* in the U.S. (English) edition and, more accurately, *Old Age*, in the British edition. Written some two decades after *The Second Sex*, *The Coming of Age* has some strong affinities with the former work, but it also extends Beauvoir's earlier analyses of power and objectification in significant new ways. Although Beauvoir grants a greater weight to biology in the later work, insisting that the organic aging of bodies is a real and debilitating process, she argues that old age is above all a situation of oppression. One discovers one has "become old," she says, not from one's aches and pains but from having this identity thrust upon one by society. In *The Second Sex* Beauvoir notes that a gradual amelioration of the situation of women has accompanied the development of market society. By contrast, she argues that, a wealthy few excepted, modern capitalism has increasingly degraded the condition of the aged. Here the sometimes subterranean Marxist elements of Beauvoir's thinking again become more explicit: She argues that it is a capitalist economy that

---

18. The five volumes are *Memoirs of a Dutiful Daughter* [1958]; *The Prime of Life* [1960]; *Force of Circumstance* [1963]; *All Said and Done* [1972]; and *Adieux: Farewell to Sartre* [1981]. Because the later volumes also focus so extensively on Sartre, they have often been mined primarily as sources of information about him and "his" world. However, they have recently been examined with a more direct focus on Beauvoir herself and have been read in conjunction with her novels, essays, and (posthumously published) letters. It is now clear that on some topics (notably her erotic life), Beauvoir withheld a great deal from her readers (Rowley 2005). See Tidd (1999) for a thoughtful reading that locates Beauvoir's own autobiographical "self" within the context of her philosophical conception of a self as always embodied and situated.

gives rise to the system of values that prioritizes productivity and profit, so that the now "unproductive" aged are treated as useless, as on the scrap heap. However, as in her early moral period essays, she avoids a reductive Marxism. For responsibility for age oppression lies not only in capitalist social relations but also in the attitudes of younger adults, who, fearful of their own future old age, seek to distance themselves from it by casting the aged as the Other.

There are strong resonances between *The Coming of Age* and the last volumes of Beauvoir's autobiography, for in the latter she meditates extensively on her own advancing age and the approach of death. She was to survive Sartre by six years, but these were dogged by ill health and by conflicts with his adopted daughter and others over his literary estate. She died in April 1986 and was buried beside Sartre in Paris, in the cemetery at Montparnasse which her apartment had overlooked. Her vast funeral procession brought traffic to a standstill, and tributes poured in from around the globe—especially from women. Often vilified in life, she had also spoken inspirationally to untold thousands of women throughout the world.

Although toward the end of her life Beauvoir was harshly dismissed as a theoretical dinosaur by the "new" French feminists and their Anglophone followers, as already mentioned, in the last couple of decades there has been a remarkable development of philosophical interest in her work. Indicative of this is the striking shift in Julia Kristeva's attitude. In her influential essay "Women's Time" (1981), Kristeva had emphatically asserted that the time of Beauvoir's generation, the "time" of "suffragists and of existential feminists," was now definitively over. Yet, in 2008, she organized a major conference in Paris to celebrate the centennial of Beauvoir's birth. In her opening remarks to the conference Kristeva now claimed that Simone de Beauvoir had launched no less than an "*anthropological* revolution": a radically new way of conceiving the human. Thus, she claimed, "one hundred years after the writer's birth, the consequences of the anthropological mutation set in motion by Simone de Beauvoir are still with us" (2009, 226, 229).[19] Quite a remarkable about-face! And, one hopes, a harbinger of further serious engagement with Beauvoir's thinking to come.

---

19. The conference, the "Colloque International de Paris: Centenaire de la Naissance de Simone de Beauvoir," was held in Paris in January 2008 to coincide with the anniversary of Beauvoir's birth, on January 9, 1908. The proceedings, which include the original French version of Kristeva's opening remarks, have since been published in Kristeva et al. (2008). With a few notable exceptions (Le Doeuff in France and some northern European authors), the Beauvoir renaissance has been a predominantly Anglophone movement. However, as some of the papers presented at the conference in Paris attest, it is now also finally blossoming in France. To

An Overview: Simone de Beauvoir
and the Politics of Ambiguity

Simone de Beauvoir *lived* her philosophical orientation to the world. Thus, whether one reads *The Second Sex*, or *The Mandarins*, or her autobiographical reflections on the Algerian conflict, one discovers a striking constancy of style and preoccupations. In particular, her insistence on the *ambiguity* of human existence, first set out haltingly in her moral period essays and coming to fruition in *The Second Sex*, resonates in varying keys throughout her writings. Indeed, a musical metaphor is perhaps helpful here in capturing Beauvoir's thinking: Ambiguity is the central theme on which, over time, she develops a set of variations. This theme is set out in the first chapter, and the subsequent chapters, although each also addresses a distinct topic, present some of these variations.

Chapter 1, "Humanism after Posthumanism," sketches the main lines of Beauvoir's thinking in a fairly broad-brush fashion. It explores the major contours of her philosophy of ambiguity, while also showing how this philosophy bears on debates over the status of humanism. In recent years the political implications of the impasse between liberal rationalism and post-structuralism have come into sharp focus in clashes concerning humanism and posthumanism. Rationalism, liberalism, and humanism have long accompanied each other and have become melded together in the Western discourse of individual rights. Here "the human" has become synonymous with the "man of reason," and his claim to rights and freedoms has been based on his standing as an autonomous, rational agent. Posthumanist critics rightly point to the exclusionary nature of such a humanism since it identifies the "properly" human with elite Western men; de facto, it often functions ideologically to justify exploitation and oppression in the name of an ostensible march toward universal rights and freedoms. Even so, the values born of humanism are those still most frequently invoked to resist

---

give a sense of the extent of the Anglophone renaissance, since Beauvoir's death well over a dozen monographs that address philosophical aspects of her work have been published in (or translated into) English. These include, among others, Le Doeuff (1991); Moi (1994, 1999); Lundgren-Gothlin (1996); Vintges (1996); Bergoffen (1997); Pilardi (1999); Simons (1999); Tidd (1999); Arp (2001); Bauer (2001); Holveck (2002); Heinämaa (2003); Scarth (2004); Moser (2008); and Deutscher (2008). There have also been numerous edited volumes on Beauvoir's work. These include her belated "canonization" in the "Cambridge Companion to Philosophy" series (Card 2003) and, among others, important volumes edited by Simons (1995, 2006); Fallaize (1998); and Grosholz (2006). For my fuller discussion of the Beauvoir "renaissance," see Kruks (2005).

violence and exploitation and to demand freedoms for those who do not correspond to the Western ideal of the man of reason. Humanism thus also provides the conceptual currency with which to contest itself; it offers means with which to challenge its own exclusionary tendencies.

Accordingly, humanism should not be abandoned but needs rather to be reformulated so as to acknowledge that "the human" is not synonymous with "the man of reason" and that ambiguity and failure are intrinsic to human existence. It is here that Beauvoir becomes a vital resource. Chapter 1 draws from *The Second Sex* and from what is best in Beauvoir's moral period essays. It sets out her account of human existence as inherently ambiguous: as marked by the irresolvable antinomies of embodiment and consciousness, conflict and the interdependence of consciousnesses, separation and relation, violence and solidarity. This account, I argue, offers the resources for a self-critical, ambiguous humanism—that is, for a humanism that is aware of its own limitations and necessary failures.

If to be human is to be an ambiguous existent, then when ambiguity is foreclosed dehumanization, or what Beauvoir more frequently calls oppression, takes place. It is because we are those paradoxical existents, *embodied* subjectivities, that human beings may be oppressed. Chapter 2, "Theorizing Oppression," takes up several of Beauvoir's works as a set of lenses through which to explore the multiple and often interacting modalities through which oppression operates. Many commentators presume that the conflict of consciousnesses, as elaborated by Hegel in the "master-slave dialectic," lies at the heart of Beauvoir's theory of oppression. This is certainly an important aspect of her explanation of women's oppression in *The Second Sex*, but (as I have already pointed out) it cannot alone account for it. For oppression operates only through embodied subjects whose lives are shaped by a variety of structural phenomena. Beauvoir examined the workings of oppression in several other essays, and this chapter also considers her account of racial oppression in *America Day by Day* and of the oppression of the aged in *The Coming of Age*. Reading these works alongside *The Second Sex* reveals that Beauvoir painted a much more multifaceted picture of how oppression operates than is generally recognized: Indifference and aversion may also be central dynamics of oppression, she demonstrates. Her discussions also draw attention to the often-ambiguous interplay between submission, compliance, and contestation on the part of those who are oppressed: The lines between oppressor and oppressed are not always neat or clear-cut.

That ambiguity is inherent in contestations of oppression is also the topic of chapter 3, "Confronting Privilege," but it is approached here from a rather different angle. The oppression of one social group generally confers

privileges on another one. Those who (like Beauvoir) enjoy various privileges yet struggle to contest the oppression of others will thus encounter
the conundrum of how to address the benefits that accompany their unchosen privilege. This problem has particularly exercised white antiracists,
especially white feminist theorists. They often argue for what I call a "politics of self-transformation." Such a politics calls upon individuals to struggle to become aware of their racist ways so that they may choose to shed
them. I argue that, ironically, this project inadvertently tends to reaffirm
notions of the "sovereign" subject, since it tacitly presumes a strongly
autonomous self that is capable of radically reconstructing itself through
its own efforts.

In her autobiography Beauvoir also reflects on the question of privilege,
and she describes the dilemma of trying to shed those privileges that have
become strongly constitutive of one's very selfhood. Examining Beauvoir's
own political practices suggests, however, that there are alternative means
by which the privileged may resist their privilege. For Beauvoir developed
what I call a "politics of deployment," using the advantages that accrued
from her privileges in order to contest privilege itself. This was Beauvoir's
strategy particularly with regard to the struggle for independence in Algeria, where she effectively intervened from her position of personal privilege to contest French policies. However, I suggest, there were also some
problematic implications of her intervention, and these serve yet again to
indicate how ambiguity and failure pervade political action.

Given that ambiguity and failure pervade political action, the question
of how one arrives at the judgments on the basis of which one acts is ever
present. This becomes the direct focus of discussion in chapter 4, "Dilemmas of Political Judgment." An extensive philosophical literature addresses
the question of what characterizes a political judgment. Some authors, following Kantian notions of determinate judgment, seek formally to define
what constitutes a political judgment "proper." They claim that the task of
judgment is to determine whether or not a particular course of action may
be subsumed under a universal principle. Others, influenced by Hannah
Arendt, argue that a political judgment is, rather, an evaluation arrived at
through what Arendt calls "representative thinking." One properly arrives
at a judgment, says Arendt, by thinking through a problem from the perspectives of a multiplicity of others. Although we can never be certain that
our judgment is correct, she argues that the wider the range of perspectives
from which we think and the more we engage in an exchange of opinion
with others, the more likely are our judgments to be wise. Beauvoir would
concur with Arendt that judgment is not determinate and that it arises
through a more fluid process of deliberation. However, from Beauvoir's

perspective Arendt's account of judgment still remains too aligned with rationalism, for we do not "deliberate" with the mind alone.

Because we are embodied and situated selves, a great deal more goes into arriving at a judgment than Arendtian representative thinking. In addition to the specificities of the political situation itself, our affects, emotions and desires, our personal histories and habits, our relationships with others, and so forth (all of which "idiosyncrasies" Arendt thinks we should suspend when judging) will come to bear on how we make a particular judgment—and it could not be otherwise. Beauvoir did not set out a formal, theoretical account of what constitutes the formation of a judgment. However, the making of political judgments is a major theme in *The Mandarins*, and I draw from this novel an account of how one may arrive at judgments that are at once reasonable and yet far exceed a process of dispassionate deliberation. A recent body of work in political theory, influenced by neuroscience, has also pointed to the place of affect in the formation of political judgments, and the chapter ends by briefly discussing how Beauvoir both confirms and yet also strongly challenges some of this scholarship.

The place of affect and emotion in politics is a continuous (if sometimes implicit) theme of this book, and it moves more fully to center stage in the final chapter, " 'An Eye for an Eye': The Question of Revenge." Here I explore, with Beauvoir, the desire for revenge in the aftermath of political atrocity. In "An Eye for an Eye," Beauvoir reflects on the desire for revenge that she and many others felt during the trial and subsequent execution of Robert Brasillach (a Parisian Fascist intellectual who had collaborated with the Nazis). The desire for revenge, the passion to "get even," is usually taken to be so self-evidently "natural" that it calls for no explanation at all. However, Beauvoir's careful unpacking of this phenomenon shows that it actually involves, to the contrary, a set of complex and profoundly socially instantiated desires. Revenge, she points out, serves no useful purpose, and it cannot repair the irreparable wrongs of mass political atrocity; in this sense, it is doomed to failure. Even so, she argues that it is not to be dismissed as an irrational desire. Beauvoir explores how the desire for revenge may differ in meaning, depending on whether it is sought by the surviving victims of atrocity or by others on their behalf. She also examines, focusing on the case of Brasillach, the significance of criminal trials and legally inflicted penalties. Although she argues that these may aim at more than revenge tout court, they too present certain self-defeating qualities.

Recently, however, another set of responses has been proposed in the aftermath of mass atrocities: Since the 1990s, "truth and reconciliation" commissions have frequently been established. Deemed to be more "enlightened" and a sign of our growing "humaneness," their aim is therapeutic: to effect repair in a nonvengeful and "healing" manner. This alternative path simply was not on either the political or the intellectual radar of Beauvoir's generation after Nazism and the Holocaust. Thus I explore some of the debates that have surrounded the best known of these commissions, the one in South Africa, and I reflect on what Beauvoir might have thought about it had she still been alive. She would, I believe, have been sympathetic to the pursuit of an alternative to vengefulness. However, the many disagreements concerning the commission's effectiveness would have demonstrated for Beauvoir, yet again, the ubiquity of "failure in all success" (EA 152; PMA 213) and the impossibility of action that does not secrete ambiguity.

In writing this book I hope to provide food for thought for several, not mutually exclusive, audiences. For Beauvoir scholars, feminist and otherwise, as well as scholars of continental philosophy more generally, I hope to introduce some new facets of Beauvoir's thinking, to shed fresh light on some of her best-known texts, and to focus attention on some others that are less often examined. For scholars in political philosophy and theory who are not familiar with the range of Beauvoir's work, I hope to convince them that they should be! Beauvoir well deserves a place in their conversations alongside many more frequently invoked thinkers, and I accordingly offer some "Beauvoirian" contributions to the contemporary discussion of topics such as political judgment or revenge and reconciliation. For social critics and political activists, I suggest that Beauvoir offers a political realism that is neither cynical nor, as poststructuralist theory may sometimes become, demobilizing. My hope is that both her account of how ambiguity haunts political action and her accompanying message, that one should accept failure without being overwhelmed by frustration or despair, will offer them some sustenance in dismal times.

1

Humanism after Posthumanism

Writing between the 1940s and the early 1980s, Simone de Beauvoir was historically situated at a cusp between mid-twentieth-century humanism, with its allegedly universal yet abstract and often exclusionary claims, and its posthumanist displacements. The Universal Declaration of Human Rights was promulgated by the United Nations in 1948, while Beauvoir was at work on *The Second Sex*. Althusser, Derrida, Foucault, and others began to demarcate the terrain of posthumanism not long before her equally monumental *The Coming of Age* was published in 1970. Beauvoir was as critical of abstract humanism as many of its later poststructuralist and postcolonial critics would be, and she was as opposed to its account of a universal "human nature" that aligns "the human" above all with reason and equates freedom with the possession of an autonomous, rational will. However, she did not embrace the troubling erasures of "the human" that poststructuralism and posthumanism would often advocate or invite.

Instead, at the heart of Beauvoir's philosophy is the claim that we cannot separate consciousness from the particularities of embodiment or freedom from its situated enactments. Certainly, consciousness and freedom remain crucial aspects of "the human" for her—but not as abstract universals. For whatever there may be that is universal to human existence does not preexist particular lives and their specific projects and is brought into being only through them. "The Stoics," she observed, "rejected the ties of family, friendship, nationality in order to recognize only the universal form of man. But *man is man only through situations whose singularity is precisely a universal fact*" (EA 144 TA; PMA 201–202; my emphasis). It also follows that values do not exist as pregiven universals, for "it is not impersonal, universal man who is the source of values but the plurality of concrete, singular men projecting themselves toward their own ends" (EA 17 TA; PMA 26). This they do always as embodied subjectivities, on the basis of their particular projects, and within their particular situations.

To be human, says Beauvoir, is not to discover that one is essentially mind, or reason, or rational will. It is to discover, rather, that one is a strange and ambiguous existent: a corporeal being whose actions are "free" insofar as they are not strictly determined and yet who is always already shaped and constrained by what one is and by the world in which one finds oneself bodily situated. Furthermore, Beauvoir warns, the reduction of "the human" to the rational is not only erroneous but dangerous. Here her views anticipate, for example, Judith Butler's recent observations on the production of the category of "the human" in the West. Beauvoir would have concurred with her claim that "it is not just that some humans are treated as humans, and others are dehumanized; it is rather that dehumanization becomes the condition for the production of the human to the extent that a 'Western' civilization defines itself over and against a population understood as, by definition, illegitimate, if not dubiously human" (Butler 2004, 91). Butler notes (as had Beauvoir in her reflections on the treatment of Algerians in the 1950s) that today Islamic populations "are considered less than human or 'outside' the cultural conditions for the emergence of the human . . . [and] *they are regarded as not yet having arrived at the idea of the rational human*." She continues, "It follows from such a viewpoint that the destruction of such populations . . . constitutes the destruction of what threatens the human, but not of the human itself" (2009, 125; my emphasis).

Abstract Humanism's Recent Critics

If "the human" is constructed—at once descriptively and normatively—in an exclusionary manner, it also follows that "humanism" has rightly become suspect. I use the term *humanism* here to cover an assemblage of ethical and political doctrines that affirm the intrinsic worth and rights of "all" human beings because each possesses reason and an autonomous, rational will.[1] For such an *abstract* and allegedly universal humanism—along with the

---

1. The term *humanism* also covers the complex history of a variety of positions other than (though sharing affinities with) the ethico-political ones that are my interest here. It refers also to the intellectual site that has come to be called "the humanities" and to the advocacy of the study of literature (and originally the classical

equally abstract political liberalism of "the rights of man" in which it has been instantiated in the West—too often masks the oppression of those who are not considered to conform adequately to its conception of what essentially defines "the human."[2] As Zygmunt Bauman has nicely put it, humanism "ostensibly . . . is about 'human nature' and human beings' natural endowments. However, defining human nature also means drawing a boundary around the 'human,' to make sense of the already drawn, or intended to be drawn, political boundary separating 'human' from 'inhuman' (or more to the point, from 'inept at being human,' 'undeserving to be human,' or 'bound to be humanized')" (2003, 127).

Critiques of the exclusionary aspects of this abstract humanism are as old as its political expression in liberal theory. From Mary Astell's polite request (roughly contemporaneous with the publication of that benchmark text of rights-based liberalism, Locke's *The Second Treatise of Government*) that education be extended to women since they too have been given reason by God (Astell 1694), to the demands for recognition and rights—civil and political—made by or on behalf of the propertyless and the enslaved in the nineteenth century, and to the more recent claims of socially marginal groups such as the colonized, the formerly colonized, and the globally displaced, the abstract quality of liberal humanism has long been challenged for its exclusionary tendencies. However, until the late twentieth century these critiques were most often made in conjunction with demands simply to *widen* the scope of who is defined as within the "human." The struggles were to include the still-excluded within the boundary of the "properly" human as it was conceived by elites in the West: to extend a recognition of their humanity to women, workers, colonized peoples, those deemed racially inferior, migrants, and the socially "deviant" of various kinds and

---

languages), as well as other cultural artifacts, as a means of accessing "the human." The first explicit uses of the term were among early nineteenth-century German pedagogical reformers. In its late nineteenth-century adumbrations the term most often referred to an explicitly secular position: the affirmation of the displacement of God by man as the source of values (Davies 1997). Michel Foucault, in a late essay, takes pains to disentangle what he calls the "theme" of humanism from the "event" of the Enlightenment, writing "I am inclined to see Enlightenment and humanism in a state of tension rather than identity" (1984, 44). He may be historically correct, but over time the two have merged within liberal discourse into one strongly operative ethico-political value system, in which the assumption that it is his rational capacity that grounds the "rights of man" (or, more recently, "human rights") is pivotal.

2. While this stands as a general characterization, there was, however, an ongoing strand of counterthought. For a careful study of anti-imperialist aspects of Enlightenment thought see Muthu (2003).

also to grant them the benefits—political, economic, cultural—that should accompany this designation. The UN's Universal Declaration of Human Rights of 1948 still stands as a benchmark affirmation of humanist values in the modern world, with its assertion (at the beginning of the preamble) that "the recognition of the inherent dignity and of the equal and inalienable rights of all members of the human family is the foundation of freedom, justice and peace in the world" and its insistence (in the first article) that "all human beings are endowed with reason and conscience and should act towards one another in a spirit of brotherhood."

Recently, however, configurings of poststructuralism with feminist, queer, multicultural, and postcolonial theory have led to far more radical contestations of humanism—ones that endeavor to challenge it at its very ontological and epistemological roots. Popularly encapsulated in phrases such as "the end of man" or "the death of the subject," posthumanism has radically decentered and complicated the notion of "the human." It has called into question "the human," or "man," as the unique site of reason and autonomous rational will, as well as challenging its conventional ethico-political cognates, "humanism" and "human rights."[3] Posthumanist challenges to humanism emerge from diverse theoretical starting points, but they converge most strongly in a critique of its abstract rationalism. It is not only intellectually dubious but also politically dangerous, posthumanists argue, to assert that reason and its cognate characteristics, as conceived of in the West, are universal and inherent in all "men." For many will fall outside this conception of the human in which man-the-cogito ("man" who is both the site of indubitable "inner" self-knowledge and "man" the contemplative knower of the *res extensa*) has combined with "Enlightenment man" (the autonomous agent who asserts his rational control over nature and things) to define the "human."[4] Thus, to overcome the ideological roles that humanism has played—and continues to play—it will not be sufficient to expand the boundary and to locate previously excluded categories within the rational

---

3. For poststructuralist critiques and reconstructions of "human rights" see, for example, Cheah (2006) and Douzinas (2007). Douzinas writes: "The radical potential of right, both revealed and concealed in human rights, remains open to the idea of heterogeneous positions and traditions, when the emphasis moves from the law's promotion of pacified obedience to that of indeterminacy and openness of self and society, the boundaries of which are always contested and never coincide with the crystallizations of power and legal entitlement" (13).

4. As Lorraine Code observes, over time a further cluster of increasingly individualistic assumptions has also been added to the ideal of the autonomous Enlightenment man:

human. Rather, it is humanism's very identification of the universally human with the Western norm of "rational man" that must be cast out.

Such posthumanist critiques carry considerable weight. Yet they have still been launched from a tacit ideal of universal human flourishing that has accompanied humanism. For the objections that humanism is exclusionary and that it legitimates domination and oppression still implicitly affirm, along with abstract humanism although not on the basis of its criteria of "the human," the universal value of human lives, and the equal entitlement of all to freedom and well-being. As Kate Soper already remarked more than two decades ago, anti- (or post-) humanist argument has a tendency to "secrete a humanist rhetoric." Where, she asks, "if not from humanist sources, does the language of struggle, victimization and loss originate?" (1986, 128) Indeed, it is hard to imagine going fully "beyond" humanism of some kind except toward a nihilism in which human life is deemed to be of so little value that there is nothing objectionable to be found in its abuse or destruction. Thus, Althusser (1969), that most militant of antihumanists, rejects "Marxist humanism" in the name of a revolutionary process whose end point is still human emancipation, while Foucault, in his last works, gestures toward a humanistic (and perhaps even an "existential") notion of the free subject.[5]

It is also striking that values that have long gestated within humanist discourse continue frequently to be invoked in political struggles in order to justify the moral and political claims of the excluded or to condemn violence and oppression. Opposition to genocides and mass killings, to the forced displacement of peoples, to subjection to torture, arbitrary arrest, degrading treatment, and exploitation is still mobilized by affirming notions of human dignity and equal entitlement to respect, bodily integrity, and human rights, which are deeply rooted in humanism—and it is hard to imagine its being otherwise.[6] As Ken Plummer has remarked, while

---

Present-day autonomous man differs from the Enlightenment hero . . . A cluster of derivative assumptions now attaches to ideals of autonomy. Autonomous man is—and should be—self-sufficient, independent, and self-reliant, a self-realizing individual who directs his efforts toward maximizing his personal gains. . . . Talk of rights, rational self-interest, expediency, and efficiency permeates his moral, social, and political discourse. In short, there has been a gradual alignment of *autonomy* with *individualism*. (1991, 77–78; emphasis in the original)

5. For discussions of the late Foucault's "existential" turn, see Morris (1996) and Vintges (2001).

6. Indeed, as I write in early 2011, it is striking that it is in the name of freedom, human rights, and dignity that movements are growing to expel dictatorial regimes from power in the Middle East and North Africa.

urging what he calls a "critical" humanism, "at the simplest level . . . we need [humanism] because we have little else" (2001, 256). Similarly, after excoriating a humanism "that excludes most humans," Lila Abu-Lughod concludes that "Humanism continues to be in the West the language of human equality with the greatest force. I do not think we can abandon it" (1993, 28). The task, I suggest, is to move beyond critiques of humanism and toward its productive reconstruction. Beauvoir proves a valuable resource for this task.

Strikingly, however, since the events of September 11, 2001, a shift in politico-intellectual ethos has been emerging. Figures formerly strongly allied or identified with posthumanism are cautiously affirming notions of "the human" and even "humanism" as necessary to the repertoire of a critical politics—but no longer in an abstract, rationalist key. Thus, to return to Butler as an example, against the grain of her comments about the exclusionary nature of Western humanism, the ethos of Butler's recent, post-9/11 works has become strikingly humanistic in tenor.

In *Precarious Life*, writing in the first-person plural, Butler suggests that even though there is "not yet" a "human condition that is universally shared," still grief, loss, and bodily vulnerability do link us together. Asking "Who counts as human?" she responds that "despite our differences in location and history, my guess is that it is possible to appeal to a 'we,' for all of us have some notion of what it is to have lost somebody. Loss has made a tenuous 'we' of us all" (2004, 20).[7] In *Frames of War* her turn to "the human" is yet more explicit. Here, when considering the torture of inmates at Guantanamo (as well as widespread abuse of Arabs and Arab Americans in the United States), she urges that we reaffirm the power of "the human" as what she calls an "ideal" norm. This norm is, as she puts it, "constantly doubled" insofar as it may also operate in coercive and exclusionary ways, but it remains vitally important, and we need to assert it "precisely where it cannot be asserted" (2009, 75–77).

In the preface to one of his last works, Edward W. Said even more directly insists on the need for a modified humanism. Discussing the alleged

---

7. She also remarks that "by insisting on a 'common' corporeal vulnerability, I may seem to be positing a new basis for humanism," although she then hastily goes on to belittle this uncomfortable suggestion by commenting that it "might be true, but I am prone to consider this differently" (2004, 42–43). Her use of the phrase "prone to consider" is intriguing. "Prone" (as the OED notes) is most commonly used to suggest susceptibility, especially susceptibility to something undesirable, such as a disease. One senses here both how far Butler has moved from her earlier posthumanism and how uncomfortable she is to have to acknowledge the full extent of her shift in position.

heightening of the conflict between "the West" and "Islam," he argues that, to the contrary, conflicting cultures may actually "coexist and interact fruitfully with each other." Affirming a vision of humanistic culture as "coexistence and sharing," he argues that "it is possible to be critical of humanism in the name of humanism," for "schooled in its abuses by the experiences of Eurocentrism and empire, one could fashion a different kind of humanism" (2004, xvi, 10–11).[8]

"*To be critical of humanism in the name of humanism.*" The project is both to unmask the numerous forms of exclusion and injury justified in the name of humanism and to insist that humanism be reconstructed rather than abandoned. A humanism that is critical of itself in the name of humanism—a critical, "constantly doubled," or what, drawing on Beauvoir, I call an *ambiguous* humanism—must take seriously the posthumanist charges against abstract humanism. Yet it should not consent to erase or indefinitely to deconstruct, decenter, or defer "the human." For in doing so it becomes, at best, little more than a set of self-referential, intellectual maneuvers that have lost their purchase on the world or, at worst, a nihilism. To erase "the human" from consideration is to cut from under our feet the grounds on which we may contest certain practices and situations as oppressive. In spite of the violence that may be—and has been—done in its name, even the most flawed humanism still secretes an opposition to what *dehumanizes*.

For if to be human is not necessarily to be the individual possessor of the preconceived, essential attributes of reason and autonomous will, a critical politics does still need to be anchored in some portrayal of what it is to be human. However, this must be a sufficiently fluid depiction to accommodate the profound differences among us that abstract humanism obscures. We need a humanism that acknowledges the particularities of a multiplicity of differently embodied lives; a humanism that acknowledges that we are corporeal, sentient, affective beings; that we are beings for whom freedom is not synonymous with rational will; a humanism for which flourishing is not to be confounded with the presence of the individualistic liberal order that has accompanied abstract humanism in the West. We need, in short, the kind of humanism we may draw from Beauvoir: one that affirms the *ambiguity* of human existence.

---

8. Although Said's name has often been aligned with posthumanism, he may have always been something of a humanist. In *Orientalism*, for example, he protests that Arabs are not seen as "creatures with a potential in the process of being realized." Instead, he complains, Orientalism presumes that "the language *speaks* the Arab Oriental, not vice versa" (1978, 321).

Beauvoir's Philosophy of Ambiguity

Already in the eponymous *The Ethics of Ambiguity*, Beauvoir characterizes the key ambiguities of human existence as being at once ontological and social. "Man,"[9] as she puts it, is a material existent and, like all living organisms, his end will be decomposition: death. But while he is a part of the material world, man is also conscious of it. He is an *embodied* subject. He thus experiences himself both as "pure interiority" [*pure intériorité*] and as "a thing" [*une chose*], a thing that feels itself "crushed by the dark weight of other things" (EA 7 TA; PMA 11). This ambiguous condition, in which physical vulnerability and death are ever present, gives rise to great anxiety, and there is a powerful temptation to try to escape it in what Beauvoir calls "bad faith" [*la mauvaise foi*]. Accordingly, many attempt to deny their ambiguity by making themselves either "pure interiority or pure exteriority;" by either "escaping from the sensible world or engulfing [themselves] in it" (EA 8 TA; PMA 12–13). However, escape is not possible, and both tactics involve the self-deluding, "bad faith" attempt to flee from that which makes us human. Beauvoir demands that we instead take up our "fundamental ambiguity," accepting that it is integral to our existence. We must, she says, freely "assume" our ambiguity rather than try in vain to evade it. We must embrace the fact that each of us is this strange amalgam of consciousness and fleshly materiality, of freedom and constraint, of transcendence and immanence, of both particular qualities and generic human characteristics. For this is what it means to be an embodied subject, a human being. Beauvoir's use here of the verb "to assume" [*assumer*] has some affinities with legalistic phrases in English such as "to assume a debt" or "to assume responsibility for an injury." However, this concept, central to her thinking, has a far wider existential meaning, denoting the taking up as one's own of the "already-given" aspects of one's existence.

Although our ambiguous ontological condition must be assumed by each individually it is also a collective one, and ambiguity will also suffuse our social relations. For we are able to treat others and may be treated by them as if we were merely things (pure materiality), or else as if we were consciousness alone (pure subjectivity). Either tactic involves treating persons as abstractions and constitutes an oppression, for neither acknowledges how freedom inheres in their embodied subjectivity. Because freedom is integral

---

9. Beauvoir's continual references to "man" and "his" qualities grates on present-day sensibilities. I discuss the reasons she used such masculinist terminology later in this chapter, but I retain her usage when I am summarizing or paraphrasing her ideas.

to human existence, it is (as Sartre had said) ontological; but because it does not preexist its enactments within particular situations, it is always also social. Freedom is not an "inner" substance passively waiting there to be picked up and used. It comes into being only in action, only (to use Beauvoir's concept) as we "project" ourselves into the human world, creatively transcending what is already given. However, as Beauvoir came increasingly to emphasize (far more than the early Sartre of *Being and Nothingness*), we cannot project ourselves as disembodied freedoms; we are not free-flying consciousnesses. Contrary to neo-Cartesian views, consciousness cannot "transcend" the body which it is. For, as Beauvoir wrote in *The Second Sex*, "if the body is not a *thing*, it is a situation: it is our grasp on the world and the outline [*l'esquisse*] for our projects" (TSS 46; DS I 73).

It also follows from this, however, that since we are always corporeally instantiated in the world, our situation may come to suffuse us so strongly that it will significantly shape and delimit our projects. Between the classic antinomies of freedom and determinism, of transcendence and immanence, there lies an ambiguous in-between zone. No exterior reality *determines* our choices, in the strict sense of operating with causal necessity upon us; yet situations that we cannot but assume may so powerfully *predispose* us to act in particular ways that freedom may, in practice, be significantly curtailed.[10]

Embodiment is the site of what Beauvoir calls the *facticities* of human existence: those contingent but inerasable facts about our lives that we do not choose and yet that profoundly shape our existence and actions. They include physical "givens" such as our biological sex characteristics or our skin pigmentation, as well as where, when, and in what kind of social milieux we happen to have been born and to live. But although such facticities are contingent, this is not how we usually experience them. Instead, we encounter them as integral to who we are, and so they take on a certain kind of experiential "necessity" for us. They are aspects of our lives that we do not choose,

---

10. By the time she wrote *The Second Sex*, Beauvoir's view of freedom had moved away from Sartre's and was closer to that of Merleau-Ponty. In 1945 he had asserted, explicitly against Sartre, that "having built our life upon an inferiority complex which has been operative for twenty years, it is not probable that we shall change it" ([1945] 1962, 442). Probability, Merleau-Ponty had pointed out, is not a fiction but a real phenomenon. For if I have made my inferiority "my abode" for the last twenty years, then "this past, though not a fate, has at least a specific weight and is . . . the atmosphere of my present. . . . Our freedom does not destroy our situation but gears itself to it" (ibid.). Likewise, for Beauvoir it is not "probable" that a woman long committed to her role as her husband's inferior will choose to abandon it. Beauvoir's autobiographical comments in *All Said and Done* about having lived her own life "on rails" make a point similar to Merleau-Ponty's (ASD 12; TCF 24).

that we cannot alter, and yet which we cannot refuse to recognize and assume as "ours."[11] Thus, in *All Said and Done*, a late volume of her autobiography, Beauvoir reflects on the puzzlement of her own birth: That "that particular ovum was penetrated by that particular sperm" was an event of extremely low probability, requiring not only the birth and meeting of her parents but also of their parents and of all their forebears. It was also chance that she was born a woman, into a particular social class, and so forth. Moreover, from these initial facticities her life could also have moved toward "a thousand different futures." And yet, she remarks, "What makes me dizzy is that at the same time I am not contingent. If I had not been born, no question would have arisen: I have to take the fact that I do exist as a starting point. . . . For the person who says 'here I am' there is no other co-existing possibility [*il n'y a pas de compossible*]. Yet this necessary coincidence of the subject and its history is not enough to do away with my perplexity" (ASD 1 TA; TCF 11–12).

This is also to say that facticities such as one's sex or social class cannot *not* be assumed even though they may be taken up in many different manners, including resistant ones. However, that they must be assumed in some manner or another will shape one's possible field of action and will expand or limit one's practical possibilities for freedom. Indeed, in the most oppressive situations facticities may impinge on the ontological status of freedom itself. Then, unable even to conceive of projects that transcend the situation, subjects may become locked in immanence.

Here, in the complexities of the lived body and its always already-situated, always material, always social, existence lie perhaps the most fundamental ambiguities of human life. It is these that abstract humanism (and Western thought more generally) resolutely ignores when it identifies "the human"

---

11. Beauvoir is both following and deviating from Sartre here: In *Being and Nothingness*, Sartre writes that "the fact of not being able not to be free is the *facticity* of freedom" ([1943] 1966, 595). However, for Beauvoir, in *The Second Sex*, other facticities may impinge far more fully on freedom than Sartre concedes. Beauvoir reports in her autobiography that she had first described her more relative view of freedom to Sartre in 1940 (when he was only beginning to sketch out the ideas for *Being and Nothingness*), and she concluded, on later reflection, that she had been right: "[W]e discussed certain specific problems, above all the relation between situation and freedom. I maintained that from the point of view of freedom, as Sartre defined it—that is, not a stoical resignation but an active transcendence of the given—not all situations are equal: what transcendence is possible for the woman locked up in a harem? Even such a confined existence may be lived in different ways, Sartre told me. I stuck to my point for a long time, and I made only a token submission. Basically I was right. But to defend my position I would have had to abandon the plane of individualist, thus idealist, morality where we stood" (PL 346 TA; FA II 498).

with reason, or rational will, alone. For the lived body is the interface between self and world and so also between self and others. It *is* our situation in time and place and in the arc from birth to death that constitutes a life. Lived bodies at once particularize us and ensure our inherence in a certain generality of human existence. It follows that, because they are coextensive with human existence, the corporeal, the factic do not *in themselves* represent a loss of freedom or diminish our "humanity." To the contrary, they are integral to a meaningful existence.

Beauvoir describes the lived body as "the radiation [*le rayonnement*] of a subjectivity" (TSS 283; DS II 13). For one's body is "a way of casting oneself into the world" and not a "brute fact" (EA 41; PMA 60). This is why we may apprehend others—and they us—not only as distinct from things and other animal species but also as *particular* subjectivities. In addition to radiating subjectivity, our bodies often are also the bearers of significant social identities. Importantly, this is so irrespective of the degree to which our identities are pregiven or self-chosen. For example, to be a "man" or a "woman" is to be the bearer of certain characteristics that will self-evidently categorize one as such *in the eyes of others*, whether or not one wishes it.[12] Likewise, others' bodies may immediately communicate to us their age, race, ethnicity, social class, and other markers of differentiated social status. Thus, for example, Steven Salaita describes how his physical characteristics marked him as an "Arab" and "like Saddam" during the invasion of Iraq: "My classmates said that I resembled Saddam. We both had black hair and the same skin color, something of a high olive; these two factors— themselves not necessarily similarities—were adequate for most people to conceptualize us as identical, or close enough. It was becoming harder and harder to ignore what was symbolized by this supposed resemblance: the fact that I was an Arab" (2008, 128–29). Thus, through the perceptions of others, one's physical characteristics may come to pervade one's "being-for-oneself" regardless of whether or to what extent such categorizations are socially or culturally produced. In his situation Salaita could not *not* be "an Arab." The facticities of embodiment and their social significations adhere to us unasked for. They cannot be shed but rather must be assumed, be it willingly, resistantly, or (often) perhaps unreflectively.[13]

---

12. Moreover, as recent queer theorists have noted, those who do not fit neatly into either category are seen as profoundly disruptive of "normal" experience.

13. As Linda Alcoff also observes, "Identity designations are clearly the product of *learned* cognitive maps and *learned* modes of perception. Yet they operate through physical features and characteristics, and one cannot simply 'rise above' or ignore them" (2006, ix).

It follows that, because we must assume our identities, we do not seek from others the kind of recognition that would acknowledge us as only consciousness or subjectivity. For the body that others see us as—sexed, raced, age specific, and so forth—is *not* merely epiphenomenal to who we are. Thus, for example, reflecting on her opening question in *The Second Sex*, "What is a woman?" Beauvoir firmly rejects nominalism: It is not the case that women are "merely the human beings arbitrarily designated by the word 'woman' " (TSS 4; DS I 12). To say there are only human beings irrespective of sex is "an inauthentic flight" [*une fuite inauthentique*], for "one only has to walk with one's eyes open to observe that humanity is divided into two categories of individuals whose clothes, faces, bodies, smiles, movement, interests, and occupations are manifestly different" (TSS 4 TA; DS I 13). These differences, to which one could add many others, are profoundly constitutive of a life. If such facticities are integral to who a person is, then, far from it being dehumanizing to attend to them, a fuller recognition of others must embrace them in their factic specificities.[14] A feminism that seeks to ignore women's differences from men will be as misguided as one that seeks only to celebrate feminine difference. Long before the "equality versus difference" debates had begun to exercise Anglo-American feminism (Scott 1988), Beauvoir had already pointed to the necessary ambiguities that attend being a woman (or, indeed, a man), and she had also pointed to the dangers of oppression that attend attempts to dissolve these ambiguities through reductive "either/or" treatment.

Whether or not "oppression" must be intentional, or whether one may still say oppression takes place when a group unintentionally benefits from injustices, has been a recent topic of debate. Anne Cudd, for example, defines oppression as "a harm through which groups of persons are systematically and unfairly or unjustly constrained, burdened, or reduced by any of several forces" (2006, 23), but she also insists that such harms must be intentional if one is to call them oppressions (2006, 25; see also Frye 1983). By contrast, Iris Young argues that oppression may often be a structural phenomenon that exists independently of individual intentions. Although there will be a "privileged" group that benefits from an oppression, this does not necessarily require that its members consciously

---

14. Thus, in *Waist-High in the World*, Nancy Mairs, wheelchair bound with multiple sclerosis, writes: "Who would I be if I didn't have MS? Literally nobody. I am not 'Nancy + MS,' and no simple subtraction can render me whole. Nor do I contain MS like a tumor that might be sliced out" (1996, 8).

oppress others (1990, 40–42). Beauvoir, as we will see in the next chapter, argues both that oppression is structural and that individuals who benefit from it remain responsible insofar as they do not acknowledge and resist their advantages. For their lack of "awareness" is a way of masking their responsibility from themselves and is always a form of bad faith.[15]

In my view oppression is usefully characterized as a structural and systemic phenomenon; however, it is also more than this. For it also suffuses the experience of those who are required to occupy situations of oppression. Although an oppressed group is not necessarily visibly distinct from one that benefits from its oppression,[16] de facto oppressed groups are frequently rendered visible by bodily characteristics such as sex, or age, or physiognomic features that (as in the example of Salaita) are negatively identified as "racial" or in some other way stigmatized as "deviant." What mainly concerns Beauvoir is the kind of oppression that operates on and through such embodied, visible qualities. As I discuss further in chapter 2, sex, race, and age are the visible identities that she explores the most extensively. Viewed as no more than their perceived physical characteristics— and thus as mere abstractions—members of such groups are treated (though with varying intensities and through varying means) as if they were "things." In such oppressive relations ambiguity is suppressed. Subjectivity is arrogated to the "superior" group, who, often unthinkingly, presume themselves to be "sovereign" or "absolute" subjects, while they deem the oppressed to be, object-like, their "Other." Instantiated in structures and social relations that objectify them, the oppressed then tend to become irreversibly "Other," assuming for themselves the "alterity" [*l'altérité*] that is inflicted upon them.[17]

Here I return more directly to Beauvoir's considerations of the dangers of abstract humanism. For, in aligning the "properly" human above all with the Western "man of reason," that is, with the "sovereign" subject, and in casting his "Others" as (at best) "dubiously human," such a humanism functions ideologically; it masks and legitimizes structures of oppression.

---

15. The notion of "willful ignorance," discussed in chapter 3, similarly complicates the issues of intention and responsibility for oppression.

16. For example, there may not be visible (or other sensory) differences among social classes or among groups for whom language or religious difference is the most salient factor (Catholics in Northern Ireland come to mind).

17. Anglophone scholars use both "alterity" and "otherness" as translations of *l'altérité*, and I use either term as it better fits the context.

Beauvoir's Critique of Abstract Humanism

"The cult of Humanity," as Beauvoir dismissively calls it, affirms the existence of universal human qualities only abstractly. "Can't one find in humanity itself that absolute end that we were first looking for in heaven?" the humanist asks. "Can one speak of *a* humanity?" (PC 106; PC Fr 44–45). Beauvoir's answer is "no": "Universal, absolute man exists nowhere" (EA 112; PMA 157). Seeking, in bad faith, to find in Humanity a ready-made justification for life and action, this cult gives rise to dangerous myths of natural harmony, of the automatic "solidarity" of man with man.

The myth of universal human solidarity takes various forms. In some versions a hierarchical, yet harmonious, social order is presumed (EA 107; PMA 149–50); in others the existence of profound conflicts is acknowledged, but these are then reduced to mere moments in the great march of humankind toward its inevitable, final state of harmony. Thus, for Hegel, Beauvoir critically remarks, "one can . . . repose in a marvellous optimism where even bloody wars simply express the fertile restlessness of the Spirit" (EA 8; PMA 13). But there exists no preestablished harmony, and the alleged inevitability of "progress" simply substitutes Humanity for God as an absolute end. It fails to acknowledge that solidarities, far from being natural, must be *created*. Solidarities have to be chosen, built, and sustained in the here and now—and this means also that they cannot be universal. "Initially . . . freedoms are neither unified nor opposed but separated," Beauvoir writes, "so solidarities are created, but a man cannot enter into solidarity with all the others because they do not all choose the same goals since their choices are free" (PC 108; PC Fr 48–49).

Alterity and conflict are not only qualities of relations among individuated self-other dyads. They often characterize relations among larger social entities of various kinds. Solidarities, such as those of class or nation, often form as one social entity defines itself as conflicting with another. In politics, therefore, "one finds oneself in the presence of the paradox that no action can be undertaken for man without its being immediately undertaken against men" (EA 99 TA; PMA 139). All politics, including a humanist politics that seeks to extend human rights or justice to "all," will find that in acting for some it works against others. A more modest, self-reflective, and ambiguous humanism, such as Beauvoir proposes, will struggle for such ends while being aware of the necessary failures of political action. It will be aware that violence and other egregious harms may follow from the pursuit of commendable ideals. For "this element of failure [*cette part d'échec*] is a condition of life itself; one can never dream of eliminating it without immediately dreaming of death" (EA 157; PMA 219). Indeed, it is here that the need for ethics arises: "without failure, no ethics . . . One does not propose an ethics to a God. It is impossible to propose one to man if one defines him as nature, as given" (EA 10; PMA 16).

Abstract humanism, to the contrary, does not acknowledge this necessity of failure. So complacent in its self-certainties, its advocates often insist they bear no responsibility for ills and injuries that may "happen" to arise in the pursuit of its ideals. However,

> What is good for different men differs. Working for some often means working against others. One cannot stop at this tranquil solution: wanting *the* good of *all* men. We must define *our* own good. The error of Kantian ethics is to have claimed to make an abstraction of our own presence in the world. Therefore, it leads only to abstract formulas. *The respect of the human person in general cannot suffice to guide us because we are dealing with separate and opposed individuals.* (PC 127; PC Fr 91; my emphasis in the last sentence)

Accordingly, it is not possible unambiguously to justify injuries inflicted on others in the name of allegedly universal principles, precepts, values, or rights—not even (as we shall see later) in the name of the kind of freedom that Beauvoir herself values. To sacrifice others in pursuit of a valued end will always be what Beauvoir calls *une scandale* (a term that has been translated variously as "outrage," "abomination," and "scandal"). Although there may be plausible, even compelling, reasons why one might inflict harm on others (notably on those implicated in oppressions), such actions can never be unambiguously justifiable. Hence, Beauvoir's insistence that all political action involves a "wager" [*un pari*], as well as a moral choice (EA 148; PMA 207). No utilitarian calculus will exonerate us for violence we commit since one death is as great a *scandale* as many, while any principle in the name of which we claim to act is always contestable.

It is often argued that a distinction may be made between oppression and other kinds of harms. Oppression, it is said, is an *unjust* harm, whereas other kinds of harm are not necessarily unjust and may be acceptable (Frye 1983; Bailey 2004; Cudd 2006). However, Beauvoir puts this distinction into question. For, she argues, even a "just" harm inflicted on an oppressor remains an objectification and a closure of freedom. Severe injury or death always remains a *scandale*, irrespective of the identity or number of its victims. Discussing the moral dilemmas faced by leaders of the Resistance during the German Occupation of France, Beauvoir writes, for example:

> If I were to kill only one man in order to save millions, an absolute outrage [*scandale*] would break out in the world because of me, an outrage that could not be

compensated for by any success and that could neither be overcome nor reme-
died nor integrated into the totality of action. . . . It is for us to decide whether
one man must be killed in order to save ten or to let ten die so as not to betray
one. The decision is inscribed neither in heaven nor on earth. Whatever I may
choose to do, I will be unfaithful to my profound desire to respect human life.
(MIPR 190; IMRP 98–100)[18]

However, the abstract humanist refuses to accept this responsibility. He
(or she) is what Beauvoir calls an "intransigent moralist," or a moral "pur-
ists," claiming to be driven to action by the demands of objective principles
or indubitable values. Such people "proclaim the necessity of certain eternal
principles and insist at any cost . . . on keeping their conscience pure" irrespective of the suffering of others that might ensue (MIPR 175; IMRP 55).
Beauvoir takes Antigone to be the paradigmatic "intransigent moralist."
Antigone will rigidly follow the moral obligation to bury her brother regardless of the consequences—and the consequences are disastrous not only for
herself but also for others. Such moral intransigence constitutes an escape
into what Beauvoir (here following Sartre) calls "the spirit of the serious," in
which in bad faith one chooses "to consider values as ready-made things" (EA
35; PMA 51), as pre-given absolutes that one "must" obey.[19]

------

18. This dilemma is also treated in fictional form in *The Blood of Others* [1945],
one of Beauvoir's mostly explicitly "political" novels. The main protagonist, the
Resistance leader Jean Blomart, recognizes what he calls his own "criminality"
with regard to the murder of others that the Nazis will carry out as a reprisal for
the act of resistance he organizes: "So you would have no remorse in allowing innocent people to be shot?" he is asked by a Resistance comrade. To which Blomart
replies, "I've learned from this war that there's as much guilt in sparing blood as in
shedding it . . . in whatever way one is always criminal" (1948, 228–29 TA; 2000,
244). What Blomart comes to recognize is not only that good intentions may lead
to evil outcomes but, furthermore, that good intentions do not save us from responsibility for oppression or violence. Beauvoir has rightly been described as having a "tragic view" of violence (Frazer and Hutchings 2007).
19. "The serious" is generally a condition of childhood; it may also be imposed
on those who are most severely oppressed. However, for most adults "the serious"
involves a bad faith flight from freedom and responsibility. In *The Ethics of Ambiguity*
Beauvoir describes the origin of the serious in childhood:

Man's unhappiness, says Descartes, is due to his having first been a child. And
indeed the unfortunate choices which most men make can only be explained by
the fact that they have been taking place since childhood. What characterizes
the child's situation is that he finds himself cast into a universe which he has not
helped to constitute [*qu'il n'a pas contribué à constituer*], which has been shaped

Accordingly, Beauvoir criticizes political decisions that are made on a priori grounds. For those who make such decisions claim *already* to know the right action to choose without taking into account the particularities of the case, and such self-certainty cannot be justified. For example, the "principled" pacifist who claims always to know, before any particular situation arises, that violence is an unacceptable means, is doing so in bad faith. For pacifism may lead to more violence than a willingness to fight; there is an unjustified self-indulgence in claiming that one's hands are clean because one has made pacifism (or some other principle) one's personal choice (MIPR 185; IMRP 85). Thus, Beauvoir writes, "we challenge every condemnation as well as every a priori justification of violence practiced with a view to a valid end. They must be legitimized concretely" (EA 148; PMA 206–207). In politics, the "dream of purity" [*le rêve de pureté*] must be abandoned (MIPR 189; IMRP 97).

However, this does not mean that action should not be guided by values. That existence is ambiguous does not mean that it is absurd or meaningless but rather that "its meaning is never fixed, that it must be unceasingly won" (EA 129 TA; PMA 180). Thus, values must function as heuristics, as guidelines for arriving at judgments as to what to do in a specific situation rather than as commands to be followed blindly.[20] For Beauvoir, the guiding value, the "conducting wire" [*le fil conducteur*] for all action is freedom (EA 142; PMA 199), and the general ethical precept that should inform politics is to treat others as freedoms. However, this does not in itself tell us what action we should pursue in any particular instance, nor does it justify the injuries that a politics oriented toward expanding freedom may produce. Interestingly, here Beauvoir also anticipates recent, post-Rawlsian discussions of the gap between "ideal" and "nonideal" ethical and political theory (for example, Mills 2004; Geuss 2008; Tessman 2009, 2010). Beauvoir obviously would reject "ideal theory" of the Rawlsian variety as being too abstract, thus as masking difference and oppression. However, she would

---

without him, and which appears to him as an absolute to which he can only submit. In his eyes, human inventions, words, customs, and values are given facts, as inevitable as the sky and the trees. This means that the world in which he lives is the world of the serious, for the characteristic of the spirit of seriousness is to consider values as ready-made things. (EA 35 TA; PMA 51)

20. I take up the question of political judgment more fully in chapter 4. As should already be apparent, Beauvoir challenges the idea of determinate judgment, in which judging requires deciding whether or not a particular case may be subsumed under a preexisting general principle.

also agree with warnings, such as those Lisa Tessman gives, about the dangers of the kinds of "nonideal" theory that simply pragmatically calculate costs and benefits, and that too easily and "realistically " settle for the lesser evil.[21]

Ambiguities of Reciprocity: "Separation" and "Relation"

Beauvoir's trenchant critique of abstract humanism, with its myths of natural harmony, or of harmony-to-come, does not imply that she espouses a radically individualistic or a fundamentally conflictual conception of society. As many have noted, Beauvoir takes as an entry point for giving an account of human relations the Hegelian notion that each consciousness "seeks the death of the other." Or, as she put it rather less dramatically in *The Second Sex*, "The category of *Other* is as original as consciousness itself . . . a fundamental hostility to any other consciousness is found in consciousness itself" (TSS 6–7; DS 1 16–17). However, what few have noticed is that this hostility is not, for Beauvoir, the sole point of origin of intersubjective relations. To the contrary, she introduces her initial discussion of Hegelian alterity by locating it as supplemental to Heidegger's notion of *Mitsein* (that is, a primordial "being-with-others"). She notes that systems of opposition "could not be understood if human reality were *exclusively* [*exclusivement*] a Mitsein, based on solidarity and friendship" (TSS 7 TA; my emphasis; DS I 17), and it is only after making this observation that she offers her account of the significance of the conflict of consciousnesses. Similarly, in *The Ethics of Ambiguity* Beauvoir insists that "separation does not exclude relation, nor vice versa" (EA 122; PMA 170). An individual "is defined only by his relation to the world and other individuals . . . [and] his freedom can only be achieved through the freedom of others. He justifies his existence through a movement that, like freedom, surges up from his heart but that opens out beyond him" (EA 156 TA; PMA 218).[22] It follows

---

21. Tessman writes: "My claim is that one is not redeemed by acting in the best possible way when the best is still terrible," and she argues, probably unintentionally echoing Beauvoir, that we still need a certain kind of ideal theory since "highlighting the unattainability of ideals would serve the non-action-guiding function of signaling the irreparable moral failures that are a necessary and yet unacceptable part of the nonideal world" (2010, 811).

22. One could say that Beauvoir thus defends a certain kind of individualism, but it is a relational one. This is an individualism that insists on the interconstituency of individuated selves and social collectivities, anticipating what today is sometimes called "relational autonomy" (Mackenzie and Stoljar 2000; Nedelsky 2005; Oshana 2006).

that "to will that there be being is also to will that there be men by and for whom the world is endowed with human significations. One can reveal the world only on a basis revealed by other men. No project can be defined except by its interaction [*par son interférence*] with other projects" (EA 71; TA; PMA 100). However pervasive the conflict of consciousness might be, it is not the sole ground of human relations. And, indeed, conflictual relations themselves most often also reveal the relative quality of alterity. For what we might call "normal" alterity is rapidly tempered by the reciprocal realization that each of one of us is an object for the other, who is thus, like us, a subject. Beauvoir observes, for example, that "the native [*le natif*] traveling abroad realizes with shock [*avec scandale*] that in the neighboring country there are natives [*des natifs*] who in turn view him as the stranger" (TSS 7 TA; DS I 17).

However, it is this "normal" reciprocal alterity that is precluded, for example, in colonial situations, where the "visited" native is not allowed to return the objectifying look of the uninvited "visitor." For others to give meaning to my projects and for me to do so to theirs in a movement of mutual recognition, we must be equals—and various modes of oppression preclude this.[23] As Hegel had argued, the master cannot achieve a satisfactory recognition of his deeds from the one he has enslaved and who is thus his inferior, and Beauvoir argues in *The Second Sex* that an equivalent dilemma accompanies man's oppression of woman. "To posit Woman is to posit the absolute Other, *without reciprocity*, denying against experience that she is a subject, a fellow creature" (TSS 266 TA; DS I 396; my emphasis). Insofar as a woman assumes this status, she becomes, "as well as the incarnation of [men's] dream, also its failure" (TSS 203 TA; DS I 303). For, given her objectification, she cannot but fail to be his ideal Other. He would like to obtain recognition of his fine qualities and deeds from her, but this cannot be satisfactorily obtained from such an inferior creature.[24]

Although men certainly have the better part of the bargain, there are also ways that the oppression of women benefits neither sex. Beauvoir thus

---

23. Others do not have to be my precise equal. However, they do require sufficiently equal material conditions to be able to engage in creative activities through which they may also take up and perpetuate the meaning of mine. Accordingly, Beauvoir argues in *Pyrrhus and Cinéas* that one must want "health, knowledge, well-being, and leisure for all men so that their freedom is not consumed in fighting sickness, ignorance, and misery" (PC 137; PC Fr 115).

24. I discuss this paradoxical dynamic more fully in chapter 2, where I also argue that it is not the only kind of oppression that concerns Beauvoir. Contrary to the Hegelian model, it is not always the case that recognition is sought from those who are oppressed.

appeals for different kinds of relations among individual men and women, ones based on mutual respect and generosity, in which each recognizes that "each of them lives the strange ambiguity of existence made body in his or her own way" (TSS 763; DS II 728). She calls for relations of equality in which each recognizes the other's embodied subjectivity, where "mutually recognizing each other as subject, each will however remain for the other an *other*" (TSS 766 TA; DS II 662). Such reciprocity is epitomized in the ideal love relationship, where there is no attempt to reduce the other either to an object (to mere flesh) or to one's own mirror image or double. Beauvoir writes: "The erotic experience is one that most poignantly discloses to human beings the ambiguity of their condition; they experience themselves here as flesh and as spirit, as the other and as subject" (TSS 416 TA; DS II 190). Thus, "authentic love must be founded on the reciprocal recognition of two freedoms; each of the lovers would then experience themselves both as self and other.... For each of them, love would be a revelation of self through the gift of self and an enrichment of the world" (TSS 706 TA; DS II 579). Yet such mutual relations are in no way given, and they are always unstable. They require us to perform the ongoing and demanding task of accepting and indeed rejoicing in the other's difference.[25]

However, this ideal love relationship stands at a considerable distance from the world of politics, which involves relations among a multiplicity of social groups, and it cannot serve as a political ideal. For dyadic self-other relations do not neatly map onto the larger-scale and multivalent world of diverse social entities and identities or conflicting political agendas. Even

---

25. Beauvoir also writes, in rebutting claims that women's equality would destroy the pleasures of eroticism, that "It is absurd to claim that orgies, vice, ecstasy, passion would become impossible if man and woman were concretely equals [*concrètement des semblables*]. The contradictions that oppose flesh and spirit, the instant to time, the vertigo of immanence to the call of transcendence, the absolute of pleasure to the nothingness of oblivion will never be resolved; the tension, the anguish [*le déchirement*], the joy, the failure and the triumph of existence will always be materialized in sexuality" (TSS 765 TA; DS II 662).

A few years later, in her essay on the Marquis de Sade, Beauvoir again emphasizes how ambiguity may be present in the ideal erotic experience. She writes that the erotic relationship may enable one "to grasp existence in both oneself and the other as at once subjectivity and passivity. Through this ambiguous unity the two partners merge; each one is freed of his own presence and achieves an immediate communication with the other" (MWBS 24 TA; FBS 35). Sade, of course, epitomizes the absolute refusal of this ideal for Beauvoir. One should note in this regard how different Beauvoir's views of love relations are from those of Sartre. In *Being and Nothingness* no way out is shown beyond the objectifying-objectified dynamics of sadism and masochism (see part 3, chap. 3).

so, this ideal points toward the value of a politics that seeks to reduce inequalities and through which those differences that are irreducible may come to be mutually respected. Rather than obscuring differences in the name of an abstract universality that takes Western "rational" man as the "human" norm, Beauvoir urges a politics through which this norm will cease to be used to legitimate exclusions from the human. Respect for others who are different is perhaps the analogue in politics to love in the interpersonal domain.

The Ambiguity of Beauvoir's Ambiguous Humanism

Notwithstanding Beauvoir's demands for a politics that respects differences, some critics have claimed that she herself remains mired in some of the problems of abstract humanism. She has been accused of being male-identified and hostile to women, race-blind, class-blind, a Eurocentric "Orientalist." One certainly may point to passages, especially in *The Second Sex*, that can be read as indicative of such failings. This is hardly surprising, for Beauvoir necessarily possessed (as do we all) certain cultural blind spots of her times. We would hardly expect that a work written in France in the 1940s would be as attentive, for example, to racial differences among women as one written in the United States several decades later. The issue, however, is whether or not such blind spots significantly undermine the ambiguous humanism I am drawing from Beauvoir's work. I argue that they do not, as they are not structurally implicated in the core of her account of human ambiguity. In addition, examining certain of her alleged "failures" serves to highlight ongoing and perhaps irresolvable methodological dilemmas still faced by critical social and political theory, feminist and otherwise.

One of the most obvious contradictions in *The Second Sex*, one often taken as indicative of Beauvoir's male-identification, is that she embraces the very masculinist language she also criticizes.[26] She remarks in the introduction that "the relation of the two sexes is not like that of two electrical

---

26. Early critics also pointed to the strongly negative depiction of the female body in *The Second Sex*, especially in the chapter on "biology" (see, for example, O'Brien 1981; Evans 1985). More recently Sara Heinämaa has argued that this depiction should not be read as an expression of Beauvoir's own views but was intended as a rendition of how the biological sciences have portrayed female biology (2003, 97). I think Heinämaa is correct about Beauvoir's intentions. However, at times Beauvoir does seem to lose her critical distance from the problematic views she is presenting, so that it is not always clear how far she is merely reporting

poles: man represents both the positive and the neutral, so much so that in French one says <<*les hommes*>> to designate human beings" (TSS 5 TA; DS I 14). This observation was at the time absolutely groundbreaking, and it is arguably the point of origin for later feminist demands for gender-neutral language. However, throughout *The Second Sex* Beauvoir then repeatedly uses "man" [*l'homme*] to designate not only males but also all human beings, thus reproducing the very erasure of difference to the benefit of the privileged that she criticizes.

Beauvoir was probably not aware of the far-reaching implications of her own observation, and it seems she regarded masculinist linguistic conventions as epiphenomenal expressions of women's subordination rather than as strongly constitutive of it. However, there would have been good practical, political reasons for retaining these conventions even had she been fully aware of their implications. For Beauvoir was writing in the absence of any significant feminist movement in France of the 1940s and, had she refused to conform to existing gendered linguistic conventions, her already highly contentious work would have received even less serious attention than it did. One certainly wishes she had not, for example, ended *The Second Sex* with a call for "brotherhood" among men and women.[27] However, what her masculinist language points to is the difficulty of trying to communicate

---

"the point of view" of biology (whose claims to explain women's "destiny" she emphatically rejects) and to what extent she accepts as factually accurate some of the descriptions she presents here.

Other critics have accused Beauvoir of being an antifeminist (for example, Elshtain 1981; Lloyd 1984). Most recently Mary Hawkesworth has reiterated the antifeminist charge. Hawkesworth cites Beauvoir's remarks in the introduction to *The Second Sex*, where she states that "enough ink has been spilled in the quarreling about feminism" and that feminism is "now practically over"; on this basis she accuses Beauvoir of engaging in a "politics of extinction" with regard to feminism (2010). But by "feminism" Beauvoir was referring to the French liberal feminism of her day—and this was indeed, as she suggests, weak and ineffectual. When French women were finally granted the vote in the 1944 constitution, feminist agitation seems to have had nothing to do with it. For the (male) writers of the new constitution provided political rights to women in order to align "modern" France with the electoral practices of the liberating allies (the United States, Britain, and Canada), all of whom had granted women the vote after the First World War. Citizenship, as Michèle Le Doeuff puts it, "fell from heaven upon French women" (2006, 28). Claire Duchen suggests, in addition, that de Gaulle expected to gain electoral support by granting women the vote (1994, 34).

27. As Toril Moi points out, Beauvoir could not have substituted "sisterhood" for "fraternity" since the French *sororité* does not have the meaning that "sisterhood" later acquired in Anglophone feminism. In any event, Beauvoir's point was not

as a member of the "second" sex to an audience (of men and women alike) for whom she was already entering uncharted waters and committing outrageous transgressions of decency.[28] How and to whom one aims to speak are strategic and political questions of which Beauvoir was very well aware, noting in the introduction that she was likely to be told, " 'You think such a thing because you are a woman' "—to which, she says, the only defense would be to reply, " 'I think this because it is true' " (TSS 5 TA; DS I 14). The tension between her simultaneous critique and use of masculinist language raises enduring questions about to whom and how oppressed groups need to speak. It also complicates, without at all denying, the epistemological claims of much feminist and critical race theory that knowledge is strongly situated. For Beauvoir claims to speak both as a woman and also in the name of a truth that is not only that of women.

Other critiques of Beauvoir concern her inattention to differences among women, particularly those of race, and her alleged concentration on Europe as the site of human progress. In what has now become a widely cited critique, Elizabeth Spelman argues that by identifying "woman" primarily with women who are white, European, and middle class, like herself, Beauvoir is blind to the privileges that she and they enjoy. She argues that Beauvoir is guilty of the same erasure of women of color of which white American feminists were later accused since "she takes the story of 'woman'

---

about sisterhood but about forging a new relationship between men and women (Moi 1994, 290 n42). One should note also that it is generally much more difficult to produce gender-free language in French than in English because all nouns are gendered (for example, "a human being" and "human being" are both masculine: *un être humain* and *l'être humain*; as is "an individual": *un individu*). In the 1970s, with the emergence of *écriture feminine*, efforts were made more radically to construct a "women's language." Beauvoir was not sympathetic to this project, which she dismissively described as "cutting up and changing words around" (Wenzel 1986, 11–12).

28. As already mentioned, the initial reception of *The Second Sex* in France was virulently hostile from many quarters, and Beauvoir was subject to a torrent of personal abuse. "I received—some signed and some anonymous—epigrams, epistles, satires, admonitions, and exhortations addressed to me by, for example, 'some very active members of the First Sex.' Unsatisfied, frigid, priapic, nymphomaniac, lesbian, a hundred times aborted, I was everything, even secretly a mother" (FC I 187; FC Fr I 260). Twenty-five years later she recalled that "The fact that I had spoken about female sexuality was absolutely scandalous at the time. Men kept drawing attention to the vulgarity of the book, essentially because they were furious at what the book was suggesting—equality between the sexes" (cited in Moorehead 1974, E 16ff.). For a survey of the initial critical responses to *The Second Sex* see Galster (2004).

to be that provided by the examination of the lives of women not subject to racism, classism, anti-Semitism, imperialism, and so forth" (1988, 71). Spelman complains that Beauvoir "doesn't reflect on what her own theoretical perspective strongly suggests and what her own language mirrors: namely, that different females are constructed into different kinds of 'women'; that under some conditions certain females count as 'women' and others don't" (1988, 68). However, although Spelman, in my view rather anachronistically, chides Beauvoir for committing the same errors as later, privileged, white American women, she also agrees that, in her critique of the timeless "myth" of a feminine "essence" and in her attention to the specificities of embodiment, Beauvoir provides important *theoretical* resources with which to analyze differences among women.

Sally Markowitz (2009) offers a rather different critique, arguing that the issue is not simply one of oversight or blind spots. There are, she says, deliberate reasons for Beauvoir's Western, white, bourgeois focus, for it is expressive of her Hegelian and "Orientalist" belief in the West's great historical advancement over the East. Markowitz cites two passages from *The Second Sex* that, she claims, demonstrate Beauvoir's Orientalist proclivities, one a footnote in which Beauvoir says she will study the evolution of woman's situation in the West since "the history of woman in the East, in India, in China, has indeed been one of long and immutable slavery" (TSS 89 TA; DS I 136); the other a passage that links the alleged lack of individuality of the Oriental male to his use of "his" female only as an object of pleasure.[29]

Certainly, to the modern reader these passages sit uncomfortably in Beauvoir's text (as do many of her anthropological generalizations about other non-Western peoples, where she draws uncritically on the—now strikingly—Eurocentric scholarship then accessible to her). However, I think Markowitz badly overstates her case when she attributes Hegel's Orientalism to Beauvoir and then sweepingly asserts that it is "by contrast with an oriental other" that Beauvoir derives both "the ideal of the European male" and the ideal of the "evolved heterosexual couple" (2009, 291). For Markowitz's claims presume

---

29. "The more the male becomes individualized and lays claim to his individuality, the more he will also recognize an individual and a freedom in his companion. The Oriental, uncaring about his own fate, is satisfied with a female who is the object of his pleasure" (TSS 188 TA; DS I 281). Although Beauvoir uses the present tense here, it is important to note that the context of the passage is a discussion of the distant past; the passage is located in an overview of attitudes about women in various ancient civilizations. She does, however, distinguish early Western Christianity from other ancient value systems, suggesting it is unique in offering a certain equality to woman on the spiritual plane as long as she "renounces the flesh" (ibid.).

that Beauvoir posits a far more "evolved" European male and a much sharper divide between him and his "backward" Oriental "Other" than her account of Western masculinity warrants. Indeed, Beauvoir frequently reminds us that men (that is, European men) are also playthings of their sexual organs and hormones; they too are embodied, ambiguous. Her point is precisely that they are *not* the "sovereign" subjects they claim, in bad faith, to be: "Man claims to make Spirit triumph over Life, activity over passivity; his consciousness holds nature at a distance, his will shapes her, but in his sex organ he rediscovers in himself life, nature, and passivity" (TSS 180 TA; DS I 270).

Furthermore, as we have seen, Beauvoir's conception of history is far less "evolutionist" than Hegel's.[30] If there is a "superiority" of the West today, it is a technological but certainly not a moral one. For Beauvoir is well aware of how thoroughly it is linked to exploitative, colonial domination.[31] Interestingly, in another passage in *The Second Sex* (one that Markowitz does not choose to cite), Beauvoir actually *aligns* Oriental ("Yellow") peoples (as well as "Black" peoples) with oppressed (presumably white) European women: Opacity or "Mystery" is, she says, attributed to all of them as "insofar as they are considered absolutely as the inessential Other" (TSS 271; DS I 403).

There is, I suggest, a practical explanation for Beauvoir's predominantly Eurocentric and white "bourgeois" focus in *The Second Sex*. This has to do with the kind of materials available to her. In Paris in the 1940s, published material by and about the experiences of "third-world" or Western ethnic-minority women was still a rarity. Moreover, given the dubious content of many of the sources Beauvoir does cite on non-European peoples, one might be relieved that she did not attempt an equally full account of women's lives around the globe! Of necessity, the materials

---

30. As Markowitz points out, for Hegel the inferiority of the East lies in the alleged innate sensuousness of the Oriental spirit, and it is not (as for Marx) a historical product of oppression or exploitation. For Hegel, History passes from Asia to Greece and Rome and thence to the Christian West. Unfortunate though they are, Beauvoir's remarks about the Orient and the Oriental male hardly provide sufficient grounds to attribute such a theory of history to her.

31. *Les Temps modernes* was among the very first sites in France to argue for full decolonization of the French empire—long before the Communists and other sections of the French Left did so. Beginning in November 1946, in response to the French bombing of Haiphong, the journal took a consistently and militantly anticolonial line. Markowitz's reading is also complicated by the fact (which she does not consider) that Beauvoir refers not to the "bourgeois" West but to the Soviet Union as the place that (even though it has so far failed to live up to the promise of its early days) has offered the fullest possibilities for the liberation of women (TSS 146–48, 760; DS I 218–20; DS II 653–54).

Beauvoir used had to be in French (or other languages she could read), and for the most part these would have been written by or about educated (thus "bourgeois") European women. Claude Imbert reminds us of the difficult conditions under which Beauvoir did her research: "We must keep in mind the conditions under which Simone de Beauvoir was working: imagine post-war Paris, where the only source of research material was the Bibliothèque Nationale, rich in nineteenth-century holdings but stripped of more recent books by two successive world wars. Moreover, during that period, everyone struggled merely to find fuel and food" (2006, 12).[32]

However, there is also an important methodological issue at stake here in Beauvoir's narrow focus. Beauvoir was committed to using a phenomenological method in order to reveal women's "lived experience" to her readers as vividly as possible. Thus, her project in the second volume of *The Second Sex* was to evoke from intimate sources—women's biographies, letters, the work of women novelists, her own life and observations—the experience of "becoming" a woman and to capture this experience in both its (local) heterogeneity and its ubiquity. That *The Second Sex* has spoken so powerfully—and continues to speak—to a remarkable diversity of readers whose lives are often radically different from those she described is the confirmation of the strength of this method.[33] Absent its vivid phenomenology, *The Second Sex* would not have had the enormous impact it did. Nor would it continue to do so; it is, for example, presently an important source

---

32. Had she chosen to do so, however, Beauvoir could have found sources from which to evoke French peasant and working-class women's lived experience more fully than she did. For example, she mentions a study of women working in a Renault car plant but draws on it very little (TSS 721–22; DS II 598).

33. The range of translations, many of them surprisingly recent, is an indication of how the book speaks to remarkably diverse audiences. In addition to translations into Western European languages such as German and Swedish, the book was translated into Spanish and published in Argentina in the 1950s. This translation was, however, banned in Spain under Franco since the book was on the Roman Catholic Church's Index of Prohibited Books (Nielfa 2002, 456–57). The book was translated into Japanese very early (in 1953–1954), although more as part of a wave of interest in "existentialism" than in the situation of women, and it was better retranslated in 1997 (Inoué 2002, 463). In Russia, a translation was begun in 1989 but finally appeared only in 1998 (Aïvazova 2002, 482–83). The book has also been translated into Chinese. A partial translation of the second volume was initially published in Taiwan, and it became available in the People's Republic of China in 1986. A full translation has been available in China since 2004 (Miao 2008).

of inspiration for Iranian feminists.[34] However, her phenomenological method also carried its own constraints, for it imposed severe limits on how inclusive Beauvoir's account of "woman" could be. To elaborate such a phenomenology required her to draw in depth on the resources of her own life experience and immediate world,[35] as well as on the limited print materials that were accessible to her in Paris.

However, insofar as it may be said to be Eurocentric and not to discuss certain kinds of "difference," Beauvoir's text also points us toward a more general difficulty that besets much feminist (and other critical) political theory. For there is, I believe, an irresolvable tension between developing a nuanced and powerfully expressive phenomenology of concrete "lived experience" and the endeavor to present experience more globally. It is, of course, vital to examine some of the large-scale, structural aspects of the oppression of women and others (as I further discuss in chapter 2). But how these macro processes come to shape experience, what they mean for the daily lives of individuals, and how they come to be accepted or resisted may be grasped only by focusing on how women at local and particular sites assume them. When concrete lived experience is evoked effectively, as in good literature, its flavor may be meaningfully communicated to those whose own worlds are very different. By contrast, attempts to "bring women to voice" more globally risk sacrificing the "taste" of women's lives and erasing the nuances of their experiences in favor of a superficial inclusiveness. Yet more troubling, when Western (and white) authors narrate or interpret the experiences of "others," misrepresentation and appropriation are all too likely. Many of the virtues of Beauvoir's account of lived experience lies in its very specificity. Its "exclusions" are not only its defects but, paradoxically, also sources of its great strength.

---

34. An Iranian feminist review, published between 1998 and 2001, was actually called *The Second Sex*. The introduction to the first issue discussed the book and carried a picture of Beauvoir. Although there had been a partial translation earlier, the full text of *The Second Sex* was translated into Persian in 2001 and has since been reprinted several times. The "campaign for a million signatures," begun in 2006 to push for women's legal equality, also refers in its founding statement to women as "the second sex" (Chafiq 2008).

35. As already mentioned, there are striking parallels between Beauvoir's account of the young girl's experience in *The Second Sex* and Beauvoir's account of her own childhood in *Memoirs of a Dutiful Daughter*—as there will also be later on between her autobiography and her phenomenological study of old age. While Judith Okely's characterization of *The Second Sex* as a village ethnography, with Paris as the village, is overstated, there is a kernel of truth in it (1986, 71).

The Impossibility of the Abstract Humanist "All"

Her own exclusions notwithstanding, Beauvoir is also profoundly attuned to the existence of privilege and oppression. She is appalled at racism and anti-Semitism, at colonialism, at the treatment of women, workers, and the aged in the world around her. She demands (even though she knows it is not attainable) a world without oppression, a world in which "all" human beings may more fully assume their ambiguous freedom. This requires struggling to create conditions of sufficient social equality to enable all human beings to take up their freedom creatively. However, even as she makes this demand, Beauvoir also questions its "all." Rejecting the myths of universal reason, natural human solidarity, and unproblematic progress, hers is a humanism that acknowledges that conflicts and harm to others, that egregious failures in the pursuit of commendable goals, are inevitable.

No, we cannot treat all others as "ends," as neo-Kantians still wish. To the contrary, the claim to struggle to free all or to act for any other "universal" end, such as justice or human rights for "all," can mask a dangerous refusal of responsibility for the injuries that may ensue. Thus, even as she persists in affirming the value of freedom and in demanding a politics that facilitates its widest possibilities, Beauvoir recognizes the risks that such a politics runs: It would be in bad faith to pursue her own commitment to freedom without regard to the failures and harms that it will entail. She is well aware of the paradox that attends what Penelope Deutscher critically refers to as her "unambiguous ethics of ambiguity" (2008, 58). There is an irresolvable paradox in asserting as an absolute value the value of ambiguity in politics, and Beauvoir realizes that we can act only within the field of tensions produced by this paradox, endeavoring to be as open eyed as possible to its dangers.[36]

Beauvoir is clear that, when certain groups are labeled as (in Butler's words) "less than human" or only "dubiously human," the inhumanity inheres

---

36. Deutscher asks, "Hasn't something gone badly wrong in an unambiguous, and aspirationally 'honest,' unequivocal depiction of the equivocal?" (2008, 56–57). I do think Beauvoir may fall into this difficulty with regard to her ideal of the erotic bond, in which two lovers each unambiguously accepts the ambiguity of self and other. Nonetheless, in considering the more complex world of politics, Beauvoir is well aware that the unambiguous cannot be unambiguously pursued. In Kruks (2009) I also discuss how political action requires the suspension, or bracketing, of ambiguity: At the actual moment of action the self engages itself undividedly— and not ambiguously—in its project.

not in them but rather in their oppressors. In *The Second Sex* she writes: "Just as in America there is no black problem, but a white problem; just as 'anti-Semitism is not a Jewish problem: it is our problem;' so the woman problem has always been a men's problem" (TSS 148 TA; DS I 221).[37] She calls for a politics that focuses on resistance to oppressions and oppressors, a politics that acts against those who designate members of other groups as the "inessential," as the "absolute Other," or as mere "things." However, such a politics is most often itself objectifying. Since rational argument will rarely convert oppressors into advocates of others' freedom, Beauvoir concludes that coercion will sometimes be the most appropriate course of action. "Since, by definition, their subjectivity escapes our grasp [*échappe à notre emprise*], it will be possible to act only on their objective presence; here the other will have to be treated as a thing [*une chose*], violence must be done to him" (EA 97 TA; PMA 136).

Furthermore, acting against those who oppress necessitates a degree of *self*-objectification and thus a foreclosure of one's own ambiguity. For "since we can conquer our enemies only by acting upon their facticity, by reducing them to things, we have to turn ourselves into things; in this struggle . . . *wills are forced to confront each other through their bodies*" (EA 99 TA; PMA 138–39; my emphasis). In cases such as Nazism, which Beauvoir calls an "absolute evil," it is clear who the main enemy is. However, the lines between oppressor and oppressed are often ambiguous. There are those who are the unwitting props of oppression only by virtue of their mystification or ignorance, or else who are complicit in lesser ways. Our actions may cause harm to them and even to our allies. Contrary to Kant, we cannot treat all others, be they foe *or* friend, as ends. For, again, "no action can be undertaken for man without its being immediately undertaken against men" (EA 99 TA; PMA 139).

Beauvoir's ambiguous humanism thus affirms the impossibility of eliminating alterity and objectification from human relations, even as she insists on the obligation to struggle against practices that oppress and dehumanize. Because she acknowledges that such humanist struggles will themselves be oppressive to the extent that they are imbued with forms of objectification and violence, she anticipates Said's call for a humanism "critical of humanism in the name of humanism." Hers is a cautious and self-reflexive humanism that is aware of its always "doubled" character. It is a humanism that embraces ambiguity and accepts that "there is an element

---

37. Beauvoir takes the quoted statement about anti-Semitism from Sartre's *Anti-Semite and Jew* ([1946], 1965).

of failure in all success" (EA 152; PMA 213). While calling for political action, it acknowledges that "the dream of purity" must be abandoned. There can be no innocent pursuit of humanist ends since "man is obliged to bring forth in the world the scandal of what he does not desire" (EA 157 TA; PMA 219). However, although harms may follow from actions that strive for freedom, and although the boundaries between oppressor and oppressed may be blurred, Beauvoir still distinguishes between action whose over-arching tendency is to affirm freedom for others and that which, whether wittingly or otherwise, forecloses it. In the next chapter I take up her discussion of the latter: of various modes of dehumanization and oppression.

2

Theorizing Oppression

"There is no comparison between what others experience and what we feel. For us the strongest pain in others is absolutely nothing, but we are affected by the slightest tickle of pleasure that touches us," so says the Marquis de Sade (MWBS 56 TA; FBS 83). Sadism, the deliberate infliction of sexualized pain, even torture, on others commonly stands as the epitome of dehumanization. The sadist denies all recognition to the subjectivity of his victims, treating them as mere objects, their bodies as things to be used for the sadist's own violent pleasures—or so it seems. However, in her study of Sade, Beauvoir argues that his affective life was not as simple as he claims. For it would not satisfy him to inflict such violence on an unfeeling corpse and, contrary to the "autism" he demonstrates in this statement, the subjectivity of those he tortures is all important to him.[1] For he also wants *recognition* from his victims. His pleasure lies in their coerced recognition of his power over them, in their acknowledgment of his sovereign and unambiguous freedom. Sade engages in what I call an *asymmetrical* dialectic of recognition, and this is generally present in what we have since come to call "sadism." For a certain degree of recognition must be bestowed on the victim's subjectivity in order for her or him to serve as a source of validation—one that will never be adequate, however—for the sadist's claim that he is the Absolute Subject. "What the [sadistic] torturer demands is that, alternating between refusal and submission, whether rebelling or consenting, the victim recognizes in every case that his destiny lies in the

---

1. Likewise, Beauvoir notes, Sade's very project of writing belies this autism. "Anyone who finds it paradoxical that a 'solitary' should have engaged so passionately in an effort to communicate misunderstands Sade," she writes (MWBS 35; FBS 50–51).

freedom of the tyrant. He is then united to the tyrant by the closest of bonds. They truly form a couple" (MWBS 57–58 TA; FBS 84–85).

There is thus a paradox at the heart of sadism: It is a form of objectification that still must acknowledge, however inequitably, the distinctly human, embodied subjectivity of its victims, endeavoring through their suffering flesh to harness their subjectivity to the will of the dominator. Although, as Elaine Scarry has argued, extreme torture may sometimes go so far as to annihilate a victim's relation to the world, literally reducing the "self" to no more than a bundle of agonized sensation (Scarry 1985), this is not what one might call the "normal" sadist's project. For the latter rather demands that victims express their powerlessness and their humiliation in ways that, whether by "refusal" or "submission," appear to confirm the torturer's sovereign subjectivity.[2] Sade's relation to his victims is an intimate one. It is, as Beauvoir presents it, a relationship in which (irrespective of its coerciveness) an asymmetrical dynamic of mutual recognition is enacted within the torturer/tortured dyad.[3] But it is a dynamic that can never satisfy the torturer. Here, Beauvoir's reading of Sade is indebted to Hegel's "master-slave dialectic," in which the "master" demands recognition from his "slave" but, because he has denied the slave the status of his equal, cannot adequately obtain it. Beauvoir reads the coerced relation of sadist to victim as analogous.

Hegel was a major influence on Beauvoir's thinking, as already discussed, and many commentaries (notably on *The Second Sex*) presume her account of oppression to be but an elaboration of Hegel's master-slave dialectic. Beauvoir does draw on the Hegelian account to theorize certain

---

2. In his study of humiliation William Miller asks, with regard to modern "regimes" of torture, "what does the torturer want? To break down the victim so completely that he really will be the rat the torturer's ideology tells him the victim is? Or does he want to preserve just enough of the victim's self-respect so that the victim can feel degraded?" (1993, 166). Although contemporary "political" torture may sometimes aim at the total annihilation of subjectivity and thus to make its victim "a rat," the latter goal of degradation is probably more common. From what we know about treatment at Abu Ghraib and Guantanamo, various forms of torture were state sanctioned in order to try to obtain information from victims. However, the motives of those who directly inflicted the torture appear to have been pleasures that were detached from this "official" aim. As Miller suggests, the torturers' greatest delight lay in viewing their victims' experiences of their (often sexually inflicted) degradation.

3. The relationship is paradigmatically dyadic since it relies on the coerced recognition of individual dominators by individual victims, even though Sade often organized group sexual encounters in which it was essential that some also functioned as spectators for others. The main point here is that the site for Sade's practices was an intimate one; it was face to face and not anonymous.

objectifying, intersubjective dynamics. However, this is not her sole explanation for oppression, and critics that focus on it too exclusively occlude
the breadth and complexity of her analysis. Robin Schott, for example,
writes that Beauvoir "articulate[s] a philosophical anthropology that posits
an inter-dependency and reciprocity between individuals, following Hegel's
account of the master-slave dialectic. The master needs the slave both for
economic conquest and for the recognition of his own mastery. It is on the
basis of this need that Beauvoir portrays the attitudes of the oppressor as
defined fundamentally in relation to the oppressed" (Schott 2003, 235).[4]
Schott then goes on to criticize Beauvoir on the grounds that, in situations
of extreme evil, such as the Holocaust, not even "perverted forms of recognition" take place. Drawing on Hannah Arendt's account (Arendt 1963),
she argues that Eichmann, for example, did not seek any recognition from
the Jews whose extermination he organized; rather, his attitude was "one
of indifference and detachment." Thus, Schott argues that, "*contrary to
Beauvoir* . . . the philosophical analysis of human conflict through the dialectic of recognition is inadequate to account for how human beings create
extreme situations of evil . . . this account does not address the ability of
human beings to detach themselves from relations of interdependence
with the oppressed in a way that enables them to commit atrocities" (2003,
236; my emphasis). However, Schott's reading of Beauvoir is too uni-
dimensional, and it misses much of what Beauvoir has to tell us about the
complexities of oppression and its various modes.[5]

---

4. In addition to the extended treatments of Beauvoir and Hegel by Eva Lundgren-
Gothlin and Nancy Bauer (discussed below), other recent discussions of these Hegelian aspects of Beauvoir's thought include Hutchings (2003, esp. chap. 3); Purvis
(2003); Scarth (2004, esp. chap. 4); Mussett (2006); Altman (2007); and Green
and Roffey (2010).

5. Ann Morgan has also criticized Schott's reading of Beauvoir as being too narrow. As she points out, there are those who are able to transcend the master-slave
relationship (that is, to engage in free and equal reciprocity), and there is also "the
dehumanized person who is denied participation in this peculiarly human interac-
tivity" (Morgan 2009, 40). Morgan argues that a different variation of the master-
slave dialectic operated, in which it was Eichmann who was the slave. He was "the
slave" to dominant Nazi values, while the Jews were simply excluded from any
dialectic—they were dehumanized: "In this dialectic, the Nazi value system (and
Hitler as its exemplar) was the master, Eichmann was but a pathetic slave, and the
Jews, to the shame of everyone concerned, were simply barred from participation" (51). She suggests also that Eichmann corresponds to the "sub-man" whom
Beauvoir described in *The Ethics of Ambiguity*: the one who attempts to avoid his
ambiguity by making himself as thing-like as possible; such people easily accept
being cogs in a machine or members of a lynch mob, Beauvoir had noted.

As I argued in chapter 1, it is not only recognition but also our recognition as particular embodied subjects (thus neither as mere bodies nor as the bearers of disembodied consciousness) that human freedom and flourishing require; denial of such recognition constitutes a foreclosure of ambiguity and an oppression. However, the master-slave dialectic is not alone sufficient to account for how oppression operates in a great many situations— and Beauvoir is very well aware of this. My aim in this chapter is thus to draw on Beauvoir as a theoretical resource to think more widely about how relations of oppression may become perpetuated and be "assumed" by those whose freedom they foreclose. For, in addition to oppressions in which the Hegelian dialectic of asymmetrical recognition is indeed central, there are also those that rest primarily on "indifference and detachment" and yet others that stem primarily from profound aversion. Indeed, it is these that may lead to some of the most virulent forms of objectification, to literal dehumanization. Beauvoir considers these other modes at some length in her treatments of race and old age. However, even in *The Second Sex*, where she does indeed invoke a version of the Hegelian dialectic as intrinsic to women's oppression, she is well aware that it is not by itself sufficient to account for the situation of women. For this dialectic is sustained only through its symbiosis with large-scale social structures, institutions, norms, and practices, and Beauvoir also closely examines these.[6]

---

6. The most extended discussions of Beauvoir's appropriation of the master-slave dialectic as a model for dialectics of recognition and alterity between men and women are those of Eva Lundgren-Gothlin (1996) and Nancy Bauer (2001). Lundgren-Gothlin argues that woman in *The Second Sex* is not wholly analogous to the slave because Beauvoir truncates Hegel's dialectic: Since woman does not demand recognition from man, she is in a condition of stasis in which, unlike Hegel's slave, she continues to remain the object. This, says Lundgren-Gothlin, "makes their relationship more absolute and *non-dialectical*, and it explains why she is the *absolute Other*" (1996, 72). Bauer, by contrast, points out that Beauvoir insists on the ambiguity of *both* parties and she argues that Beauvoir thus sees their relationship as more fluid and open to change: "Beauvoir is to my knowledge wholly original in figuring reciprocal recognition as requiring the acknowledgment of one's own and the other's essential nature as *objects* as well as subjects" (2006, 186). My own reading is closer to Bauer's. For Beauvoir's point is that although men may *attempt* to deny, or drastically to curtail, women's ambiguous embodied subjectivity they cannot actually succeed in doing so (this is also the point she makes about the necessary failures of Sade's project). Beauvoir also discusses at length how some women contest their role as Absolute Other. Various passages that do suggest that woman's alterity is absolute and inescapable notwithstanding, taken over all *The Second Sex* does not portray women as in such a static condition as Lundgren-Gothlin claims.

Indifference (an accompaniment to forms of *abstraction*) is, as Schott rightly suggests, often characteristic of the most intense modes of oppression, those for which *dehumanization* is perhaps the more appropriate term. Indeed, these are modes that, as Beauvoir notes, even Sade himself rejected! Freed from the Bastille in 1790, Sade was appointed as a Grand Juror, but he would consistently dismiss charges against the accused who were brought before him. As Beauvoir observes, "What he demanded essentially of cruelty was that it reveal to him both particular individuals and his own existence as, on the one hand consciousness and freedom and, on the other, as flesh. He refused to judge, condemn, and witness anonymous deaths from afar." For, she goes on to elaborate, "when murder becomes constitutional, it is nothing more than an obnoxious expression of abstract principles: it becomes inhuman" (MWBS 19 TA; FBS 27).

Beauvoir is hardly uncritical of Sade. But her reading of him points us toward a different mode of dehumanization, one in which no degree of reciprocal recognition will be demanded from its objects. Instead, individuals are categorized and disposed of as mere abstract entities—in this instance, as members of the judicial category known as traitors.[7] Similar processes of abstraction and detachment are often at work in many other instances: in the oppressive treatment of workers as mere units of labor power, in the racial objectification of blacks in the American South, of colonized people in Algeria and elsewhere—all of which Beauvoir discusses at one time or another. Of course, absent total domination of the body, the subjectivity of the oppressed must always be minimally acknowledged since it must be harnessed (through, for example, fear or self-interest) to ensure their compliance in their own oppression. But obtaining *recognition* from them may not be an objective of the oppressor at all, while in other instances their recognition may still be sought but only as a secondary matter. In what follows I distinguish (borrowing rather loosely from Max Weber) three "ideal types" (or three distinguishable modes) of oppression and dehumanization. I call these, respectively, *asymmetrical recognition, indifference*, and *aversion*.

"Dehumanization" is a fluid term whose meanings shift according to the meanings imparted to "the human." For Beauvoir, as we have seen, "the human" is aligned not with the "sovereign" subject but with a multiply ambiguous embodied subject. Dehumanization and oppression aim to harness, to suppress, or, at the most extreme, wholly to expunge these ambiguities. However, Beauvoir herself rarely uses the term *dehumanization*, reserving

---

7. In chapter 5 we will see how she takes up the issue of abstraction in the specific case of the 1945 trial of Brasillach for treason.

it only for the most extreme instances. Instead, she refers more often to the condition in which the ambiguities of embodied subjectivity are suppressed as *oppression*. She refers to the allied processes of "objectification" (treating/being treated as a thing) and "alterity" (making/being made "Other") as the primary means through which oppression is produced. When Beauvoir does employ the term dehumanization, it is to describe the most extreme forms of objectification: those at the end point of a continuum in which lives have become so entirely disposable that the subjectivity of victims has become wholly irrelevant to the dominators. This is the situation in the Nazi extermination camps and, in her preface to J.-F. Steiner's book on Treblinka, Beauvoir refers to them as "a dehumanized world" (Beauvoir 1966, 12). Here, the objectification of the trainloads of arrivals who were to be gassed immediately was total. They were just so much material to be processed efficiently. Meanwhile, in the Sonderkommando units, the members' desperate hopes of survival were cunningly harnessed to the labor demands of the extermination process—a process to which they themselves were also doomed shortly to become victims. Even though a certain minimal subjectivity (the recognition of their desire to continue living) had tacitly to be acknowledged, the objectification of this latter group too was virtually total.

Perhaps shockingly, in *The Coming of Age* Beauvoir also describes how the aged in "normal" Western society may be subjected to a dehumanization that shares some affinities with that of the camps. For they (and, one might add, those with severe physical or cognitive disabilities) are also frequently deemed superfluous. Useless, often helpless, Beauvoir says that the aged are frequently viewed as nothing more than pure objects, and their vulnerable and inert bodies may literally be treated like things. I consider Beauvoir's treatment of old age and its wider implications later in the chapter. However, what is important to note here is that, in most other instances, the oppression of one group provides *benefits*—be they of existential recognition, social status, and/or material advantage—to members of another group and that this is its main purpose. In order for such transfers of benefits to take place, a degree of compliance on the part of the oppressed must be created. Here arises the paradox illustrated in sadism, and that Beauvoir captures at length in her discussion of women: the existence of embodied subjects who are required not only actively to objectify their own subjectivity but also to demonstrate their subjection. As Beauvoir writes in *The Second Sex*,:

> What specifically defines the situation of woman is that while being, like all human beings, an autonomous freedom, she finds and chooses herself in a world where men force her to assume herself as Other: an attempt is made to freeze

her as an object [*on prétend la figer en objet*] and to doom her to immanence . . .
Woman's drama lies in this conflict between the fundamental claim of every
subject, which always posits itself as essential, and the demands of a situation
that constitutes her as inessential. (TSS 17 TA; DS I 31)

What, adapting from Axel Honneth (2008), one might call "fictive
objectification"—the treatment of persons *as if* they were things rather
than the endeavor *literally* to render them things—is implicated in this
kind of oppression. For if women, or other categories of persons, were
literally to become things or objects, they would be of little use to their
oppressors.[8] It is true that Beauvoir sometimes makes it sound as if the
goal *were* actually to transform persons into things. For example, she
writes in *The Second Sex* that "when woman is delivered up to the male as
his property, what he demands is that, in her, flesh is present in its pure
facticity. Her body is not grasped as a radiation of subjectivity but as a
thing solidified in its immanence [*une chose empâtée dans son immanence*]"
(TSS 176 TA; DS I 264). However, she repeatedly makes it clear that what
is most often sought—and achieved—must stop short of such total objectification. Woman does not *literally* become a solidified thing; rather she
lives out, in varying intensities, a painful and impossible contradiction.
For to conform with her femininity, *as it is now designated*, she must consent to make herself "object and prey"—and yet to refuse to do so would

---

8. Beauvoir frequently refers to the making of a person into a "thing" [*une
chose*]. Her meaning is similar to Honneth's and could also be translated as "reification" instead of "objectification." However, as the verb "to reify" [*réifier*] was
already in circulation in French in the 1940s and since Beauvoir did not choose to
use it, I have retained the term *objectification* as my translation here.

Introducing the idea of "fictive reification," Honneth observes "just how im-
probable true cases of reification are for the social world as a whole," and he goes
on to make the following distinction:

Fictive reification—cases in which other persons are treated *as if* they were mere
things—is part and parcel of some of the more intensified forms of human action. In the case of both sexuality and cruelty [these cohere in sadism, of course],
we are familiar with plenty of situations in which it appears that the other is
nothing but an object to be dealt with at will, but these forms of reification have
their stimulus in the fact that beneath the surface we remain aware of the ontological difference between persons and things. (2008, 157)

The idea of "fictive reification" also has the benefit of allowing us to examine how
objectification may take place to different degrees: The "as if" may move closer to
being literal in some instances than in others.

also be to deny who she is; it would be what Beauvoir calls a "mutilation." This, then, is "the conflict that singularly characterizes the situation of the emancipated woman." For "she refuses to confine herself to her role as female, because she does not want to mutilate herself; but it would also be a mutilation to repudiate her sex. Man is a sexed human being; woman is a complete individual, and equal to the male, only if she too is a sexed human being. Renouncing her femininity means renouncing part of her humanity" (TSS 723; DS II 600–601). Woman, as flesh, as prey, is cast as the Other, as "the incidental, the inessential," vis-à-vis man's claim to represent the human.

Beauvoir argues that the production of "alterity," or "otherness," pervades human relations. However, alterity may take many different forms, and not all of them are necessarily oppressive. Thus (as discussed in chapter 1) Beauvoir makes an important distinction between what one might call "normal" alterity, in which objectifying and objectified roles, those of subject and object, are fluid and may easily be exchanged, reversed, or even (as in the ideal love relationship) reciprocally embraced by each, and the oppressive alterity in which certain groups and their individual members tend to remain *irreversibly* frozen in the role of the object or the "inessential" Other. But how does such irreversibility become stable and enduring? Even in those cases (epitomized in the master-slave dialectic) where a dynamic of coerced, asymmetrical recognition does occur, alterity cannot be sustained as a relationship of individuated subjectivities alone. It is always instantiated in—and, in turn, perpetuates—large-scale, structural forms of domination.

Thus, to return to Sade for an example, the acts of intimate violence of the Sadean boudoir must be understood as more than "private" or merely interpersonal interactions. They replicate late-feudal social hierarchies, for Sade's sexual proclivities are manifestations of how he has chosen to assume his anachronistic class position in prerevolutionary France. A member of the decadent French aristocracy but hounded for his perversions, he will not align himself with his class, and yet he still seeks to reproduce seignorial privilege over his victims. Thus, in *The Second Sex* (and later in *The Coming of Age*) Beauvoir sets out to explore the production of oppressions from two convergent and interconstituent poles: both as social structure and as individuated lived experience. It is not as autonomous individuals that men oppress women in modern Western societies since they are not the sovereign subjects beloved of abstract humanism. Rather, they do so as individuals who are themselves already socially constituted as "men"—and who may discover that they cannot but assume the privileges that accompany this status (TSS 759; DS II 650–51). It follows that the stable and usually irreversible quality of oppressive relationships is not the effect of, nor is it to be overcome by, individual action alone.[9]

Beauvoir offers her most extended explorations of oppression in three works, each of which explores the situations of a specific category of persons: women, in *The Second Sex*; racialized native and black Americans, in *America Day by Day*; and the aged in *The Coming of Age*. Each of these books also strongly typifies one of the three different modes of oppression: namely, asymmetrical recognition, indifference, and aversion. I discuss each work and the kind of oppression that it typifies in turn. However, in any particular situation of oppression, more than one mode of oppression is likely to be present. Moreover, each mode of oppression may operate with varying degrees of intensity and (except in the most extreme instances of dehumanization) may be assumed in different ways.

The Second Sex: Asymmetrical Recognition

The Second Sex is most often read as a work of phenomenology, since in it Beauvoir endeavors to capture the "lived experience" through which, as she famously put it, "one is not born but becomes a woman."[10] However, a solely phenomenological reading of *The Second Sex* fails to grasp its full significance. For Beauvoir brings to bear on women's lives not only a phenomenology of their embodied experience but also a Marxist-inflected analysis of large-scale socioeconomic and political structures of domination.[11] In

---

9. Although Beauvoir affirms the significance of subjectivity and individual agency far more than Michel Foucault, there are strong affinities between her account of the ubiquity of relations of oppression in modern societies and his conception of power as a web in which all are positioned and produced. However, Beauvoir examines the different *qualities* of such webs of power and, unlike Foucault, she asks to whose specific benefit they usually operate.

10. Indeed, Beauvoir explicitly locates herself philosophically in the phenomenological tradition, as working in the mode of Heidegger, Sartre, and Merleau-Ponty (TSS 2010 46; DS I 73).

11. However, to recall, her Marxism is not the "orthodox" communist Marxism that was prevalent in France in the 1940s but instead has strong affinities with the "early" Marx. See chapter 3 of *The Second Sex*, "The Point of View of Historical Materialism" (TSS 53–60; DS I 96–106), for her critique of Engels's reduction of women's oppression merely to a matter of private property and class relations. It should be noted (but has not often been) that Beauvoir ends *The Second Sex* with an enthusiastic endorsement of the young Marx's vision of an emancipated society as one in which women are free. Declaring that "one could not state it better," she cites from the Paris manuscripts as follows:

addition, she considers the power-effects of discourse, examining discursive forms such as myth and literature, as well as the representation of woman in the "scientific" discourses of biology, psychoanalysis, and historical materialism. Thus the two volumes of the book should be read conjointly, as dialectical and not as sequential. Volume 1, "Facts and Myths," describes the power-freighted construction of women from "without": that is, in practices, institutions, and social structures, as well as in masculinist discourses that range from biological theory to "myths."[12] Volume 2, "Lived Experience," is written phenomenologically, "from women's point of view" (TSS 17 TA; DS I 32). It is important to note Beauvoir's caveat here, however: The lived experience she presents will be that of women "in the present state of education and customs" (TSS 279; DS II 11).

Iris Young argued shortly before her death that, although a phenomenological approach is valuable for grasping the lived experience of oppression, a theory that is excessively focused on "issues of experience, identity, and subjectivity" is too constricted to support an effective politics (2005, 19; see also, for similar arguments, McNay 2008 and Fraser 2009). A critical social theory must also seek to identify and explain what Young calls the "macro" social structures that give rise to harms to oppressed groups. For women, this means that more systematic attention must be given to what she calls the gendered "structures of constraint," which operate independently of the individual intentions of either men or women (21).[13] Without

---

The immediate, natural and necessary relation of human being to human being is also *the relation of man to woman*. . . . From this relationship man's whole level of development can be assessed. It follows from the character of this relationship how far *man* has become, and has understood himself as, a *species-being*, a *human being*. The relation of man to woman is the *most natural* relation of human being to human being. It indicates, therefore, how far man's *natural* behaviour has become *human*, and how far his *human* essence has become a *natural* essence for him, how far his *human nature* has become *nature* for him. (TSS 766; DS II 662–63)

Marx's notion of what is "natural" here does not, of course, refer to some vision of a previous state of nature or to a biological condition. Rather, "nature" refers to the possibility of a non-alienated existence, in which human potentiality (for men and women alike) may be fulfilled. I cite the Marx passage as given in the English translation by Bottomore (Marx 1964, 154).

12. "We will begin by discussing the points of view taken on woman by biology, psycho-analysis, and historical materialism. We will then try to show exactly how 'feminine existence' [*la réalité feminine*] has been constituted, why woman has been defined as the Other and what, from men's point of view, have been the consequences" (TSS 17 TA; DS I 32).

13. Young notes that she borrows this useful concept from Nancy Folbre (1994).

attending to these basic structural realities—namely, the sexual division of labor, normative heterosexuality, and gendered hierarchies of power—possibilities for a politics of radical transformation are severely truncated (2005, 22). Such "gender structures" are historically given, Young says, and they "condition the action and consciousness of individual persons. They precede that action and consciousness. Each person experiences aspects of gender structures as facticity, as sociohistorical givens with which she or he must deal" (2005, 25). Young is surely correct that we must, as Beauvoir puts it, "assume" these givens in one way or another. However, if we read *The Second Sex* in its entirety, we find Beauvoir engaged—in 1949!—in exactly the kind of synthetic project that Young urges.

Indeed, right from the introduction Beauvoir introduces her claim that "exterior" social realities ineluctably suffuse and constrain individual women's lives (and those of others). "The same vicious circle can be found in all analogous circumstances," she writes. "When an individual, or a group of individuals, is kept in a situation of inferiority, the fact is that she or they *are* inferior. But the import of the verb *to be* must be understood . . . *to be* is to have become, it is to have been made as one manifests oneself [*c'est avoir été fait tel qu'on se manifeste*]. Yes, women in general *are* inferior to men today; this is to say that their situation affords fewer possibilities: the difficulty is to know whether this state of affairs must continue" (TSS 12–13 TA; DS I 25). If woman is man's Other, if she is a human being who is denied the reciprocal recognition possible only among equals, then two key questions follow: How is this situation of inferiority produced and perpetuated? And in what different ways may it be accepted or resisted?

Producing Inferiority

Women's inferiority is produced, one might say, at once wholesale and retail: that is, both through their location in "macro" social structures and through "micro," interpersonal, self-other encounters and idiosyncratic experiences. For example, the experiences of heterosexual sexual initiation that Beauvoir describes are both general and yet particular (TSS 383–416; DS II 146–91). They are general because the norms that invoke masculine agency and feminine passivity structure the "taking" of virginity on each occasion. They are also normatively linked (even today) to marriage and to all that accompanies it for women: their socioeconomic and other structural dependencies, their expected reproductive, maternal, and domestic roles, and so forth. They are also general as instances of the "normal" biophysical mechanics of heterosexual vaginal penetration. Yet, at the same time each initiation is a particular encounter of two embodied subjectivities, both of whom bring their own (already gendered) desires, fears, dispositions, and dreams to the moment.

Thus, in her discussion of psychoanalysis Beauvoir criticizes Freud for essentializing sexuality by taking it as "an irreducible given" (TSS 55; DS I 88). For it is only in light of social practices and values, as well as the individual existential choices through which these are assumed, that sexuality takes on its meanings. How we experience ourselves as sexual beings and what values we affirm through our sexuality will be at once idiosyncratic and socially structured. In a highly significant passage Beauvoir writes as follows:

> Across the separation of existents existence is one: it becomes manifest in analogous organisms; thus there will be constants in the relation between the ontological and the sexual. *At a given epoch, the technologies, the economic and social structure of a collectivity [collectivité], reveal [découvrent] an identical world to all its members.* There will also be a constant relation of sexuality to social forms; analogous individuals, located in analogous conditions, will grasp analogous significations from the given. This analogy does not ground a rigorous universality, but it does enable us to rediscover *general types within individual histories.* (TSS 56 TA; DS I 89; my emphases)

Sexuality, then, is at once general and particular. Epoch-wide technologies and economic and social structures will be assumed as particular experiences. Without asserting any essentialist claims, we may still delineate *general* descriptions of how sexuality is constitutive of objectifying and oppressive relations for women. For example, the prohibition of abortion and contraception in France in the 1940s profoundly suffused the sexual experiences of the majority of women, as well as shaping the meanings of motherhood (TSS 524 ff; DS II 330 ff). Beauvoir infamously begins the chapter of *The Second Sex* on "The Mother" with a discussion of abortion, the prohibition of which made (and, for many, still makes) a free choice of maternity virtually impossible. There are "individual histories," and women's lives and experiences are each particular, but women are also what she calls a "collectivity." That is, they are embedded within the same social structures (legal, religious, medical, familial, and so forth) as instances of a "general type," and they thus will discover themselves to belong to—and to be constrained by—an "identical world."

In using the term "collectivity" [*collectivité*] in this passage Beauvoir strikingly anticipates the notion of a "collective" [*collectif*], which Sartre will later elaborate in his *Critique of Dialectical Reason* ([1960] 1976). By a "collective" Sartre does not mean (as one might perhaps expect) an association of individuals linked by their common goals. On the contrary, a collective is an anonymous "series" of individuals who are unified passively and "externally" to their own intentions and practices (often without realizing it) through their involuntary location in one and the same set of structural constraints. Such a collective (in contradistinction to what Sartre will call a "group," which is indeed linked by a shared goal) does not produce shared internal and intentional bonds among its members. Instead, through their insertion in one and the same series each unwittingly alters the significance of the action of the others and, through them, of each individual's own action: "Each is something other than himself and behaves like someone else, who in turn is other than himself," Sartre writes ([1960] 1976, 166). Thus, women, as Beauvoir characterizes them in *The Second Sex*, may be conceptualized (although she does not use the term) as a series.[14] For each, having to accommodate to the "identical world" in which they are situated, becomes other than herself through a relation of passive, "exterior" unification with other members of the series of "women." For example, in endeavoring to conform to current beauty norms that identify the ideal feminine body with slenderness, each interchangeably imposes upon others and, through them, back onto herself the norm of slenderness.[15] How that "identical world" for women comes into being and how it passively connects

---

14. An important goal for Sartre in the *Critique* is to show the negative historical effects of seriality on the conditions of French workers. Atomized and each interchangeable, unorganized workers have competed for jobs with the effect of worsening wages and conditions for each other. However, as we see here, Sartre's mode of analysis may be extended to other collectives.

15. I explore some of the uses of Sartre's notion of seriality for gender and feminist analysis more fully in Kruks (2001, chap. 4). In Kruks (2010) I discuss the interconnections among the later works of Beauvoir and Sartre more fully than I do here, showing how Beauvoir takes up and integrates aspects of *Critique of Dialectical Reason* for her own purposes in *The Coming of Age*. See also Iris Young's argument that conceptualizing gender as "seriality" permits feminist politics to maintain the important category of "women" while avoiding the twin perils of essentialism and identity politics. Young gives additional examples of how women today experience seriality. Being a woman:

> means that I check one box rather than another on my driver's license application, that I use maxipads, wear pumps . . . I experience a serial interchangeability between myself and others. In the newspaper I read about a woman who was raped, and I empathize with her because I am rapeable, the potential object of male appropriation. But this awareness depersonalizes me, constructs me as Other to her and Other to myself in a serial interchangeability rather than defining my sense of identity. (1994, 731)

women as a series not only to men but also to each other as the Other entails the material practices that give rise to the structures of constraint. It also involves the values of masculine superiority which are most generically expressed in mythic discourse, for material structures and discourses interact. They function symbiotically, giving rise to a generalized situation of oppression that individual women must assume in one way or another.

In order for women's situation to change significantly, all of the main axes of gender oppression will have to be challenged. However, men do not, generally speaking, have an interest in such large-scale change. For the benefits—material, psychological, existential—that accrue to them from the perpetuation of women's subordination remain significant. Nevertheless, these benefits are bought at the cost of men's flight from the ambiguities of their own embodied existence. For what lies at the root of woman's oppression is man's bad faith (and in vain) affirmation of himself as Sovereign, and his desire to see his sovereignty reflected back to him by woman. Man endeavors to sunder the attributes of reason, consciousness, and autonomy from his own embodiment by fraudulently arrogating only the former to himself.

Here we must also consider masculinist values and Beauvoir's discussion of how they come to be expressed, especially in mythic forms. For myths both signify and reaffirm the asymmetrical relations between men and women. Men refuse to grant adequate recognition to women's subjectivity even as they (impossibly) demand from women recognition of their own status as the Sovereign, the Essential, the Absolute. Men "seek in the depths of two living eyes their own image haloed with admiration and gratitude, deified. If Woman has often been compared to water this is, among other reasons, because she is the mirror in which the male Narcissus contemplates himself" (TSS 202 TA; DS I 302). However, there are diverse and incompatible myths about Woman. For, as his Other, she is required by Man to affirm in him various qualities that he arrogates to himself and to acquiesce in her alleged lack of them. Thus she is Nature, carnality, flesh, and animality, and she threatens him as such. However, she is also the domesticated inversion of these, who may docilely serve him: virgin, wife, mother, muse, and so forth. She is both physis and antiphysis (TSS 178; DS I 266).[16] Yet, whatever the content of such mythic

---

16. As such, woman also mediates for man between nature and the human. As Shannon Mussett puts it, "In a peculiar doubling, woman not only acts as the embodiment of nature for man (thus making his separation from nature *and* woman easier) but because she cannot possibly *be* the totality of nature, woman can act as a mediating tool *between* man and nature" (2006, 281; Mussett's italics).

projections, the point is that "each of the myths built up around woman claims to sum her up *in toto*" (TSS 266 TA; DS I 396). Woman is thus frozen, rendered object-like. Her subjectivity and ambiguity are denied in the project to reduce her—even though she never can be fully reduced— to the object of male fantasies.[17] It also follows that Woman, in all her alleged guises, remains for man a "Mystery." She is opaque, thing-like, an "in-itself"—and she must *be so* (even though, of course, she cannot fully be so), or else she would demand from him the reciprocity between equals in which they each would mutually acknowledge their embodied and objective status, as well as their subjectivity.

Beauvoir also observes in *The Second Sex* that women are not the only category to be rendered thus "mysterious." She points out that non-Western peoples are (in Europe) similarly cast: "There is . . . a mystery of the Black, of the Yellow, insofar as they are considered absolutely as the inessential Other." However, she goes on to note that Americans (who, she says, also greatly baffle Europeans), as well as men (i.e., Western men), are not regarded as mysterious at all. Rather, one simply remarks that one does not understand them. "The point is," she says, "that rich America and the male are on the side of the Master, and Mystery is a property of the slave" (TSS 271; DS I 403). It is the identification of "the human" not only with the male but with the white Western male that is at issue here.[18]

---

17. Deutscher clarifies this important point in Beauvoir's thinking well:

> Her point is that the subjugation of women is itself a paradox. Women are equal [to men], and they are definable in terms of an irrecusable freedom. If they are nonetheless constrained, if there has been a diminishing not only of their material conditions but also of the very freedom of consciousness that, via a definition accepted by Beauvoir, is not diminishable, the paradox would belong to women's situation rather than to a deficiency in her understanding of freedom. (2008, 9)

Butler also describes this paradox in more general terms when she writes that "the norm [of the human] continues to produce the nearly impossible paradox of a human who is no human" (2009, 76).

18. This identification of "the human" with the male extends across social classes. Although it is above all within leisured elites that the myths of Woman have been elaborated, they pass into general social currency and they offer an attractive affirmation of their superiority also to lower-class men: "The taste for eternity at a bargain price, for a pocket-sized absolute, which one finds in most men, is satisfied by myths" (TSS 272 TA; DS I 405). Here, a general ideational system merges with material systems of constraint to shape the oppressive situations of individual women.

Assuming Inferiority: Submission, Complicity, and Resistance

To assure Man's place as the Absolute Subject, Woman must act not merely in accordance with his mythic projections of the "Eternal Feminine" but in a more profound way must also "become" them: "In order for any reciprocity to appear impossible, it is necessary *for the Other to be for itself an other, for its very subjectivity to be affected by otherness*" (TSS 271 TA; DS I, 403; my emphasis). Thus, even though freedom is an ontological quality of human existence, those oppressive situations that prevent meaningful action may impinge upon it so totally that its enactment will virtually cease (or in the most extreme, dehumanizing cases actually cease). Because ontological freedom is coextensive with its realization in action it is, de facto, inseparable from the conditions in which it may be practiced. Thus, in the most extreme cases oppression does not only constitute an "external" impediment to effective action but, permeating subjectivity, may also suppress the potential for ontological freedom itself. Here, the oppressed cannot be said to be complicit in their oppression or to bear any responsibility for it. What, in the introduction to *The Second Sex*, Beauvoir describes as the falling of transcendence into immanence and of freedom into facticity is, she says, a "moral fault" if it is agreed to but an oppression if it is "inflicted" (TSS 16; DS I 31).

However, Beauvoir realizes that matters are usually more ambiguous. Although the most extreme oppressions may place their victims in the quasi-infantile world of the "serious," where they cannot be held responsible for their actions,[19] this is very seldom the case. For most women considerable benefits are also attached to embracing their objectification. In these circumstances an active complicity rather then a reluctant and bare submission becomes attractive, and "men find in their women more complicity than the oppressor usually finds in the oppressed" (TSS 757 TA; DS II 649). Beauvoir argues that complicity is especially pervasive among the dependent, middle-class, European women whose lives she mainly describes in volume 2, although it is certainly not unique to them. The benefits may be material ones, being kept by a man, but they also include being able to flee from the anxiety arising from one's own ambiguous freedom. Abstract humanism, we saw, aligns itself with the masculine and evades ambiguity by affirming that "man" is a sovereign consciousness, an autonomous agent. However, an alternative evasion is possible: to embrace one's objectification.

---

19. "There are beings whose life slips by in an infantile world because, having been kept in a state of servitude and ignorance, they have no means of breaking the ceiling which is stretched over their heads" (EA 37; PMA 54).

This is the path that women are enticed to follow. Thus Beauvoir writes of woman in the introduction to *The Second Sex*:

> To refuse to be the Other, to refuse complicity with man, would be to renounce all the advantages that an alliance with the superior caste may confer on them. Man-the-sovereign will provide woman-the-liege with material protection and take care of justifying her existence: along with economic risk, she evades the metaphysical risk of a freedom that is required to invent its goals without assistance. Indeed, alongside each individual's claim to affirm oneself as subject—an ethical claim—there also lies the temptation to flee one's freedom and to make oneself into a thing: it is a pernicious path, for passive, alienated, lost, the individual is thus prey to foreign wills, cut off from transcendence, deprived of all worth. But this is an easy path: one thus avoids the anguish and stress of an authentically assumed existence. The man who constitutes woman as *Other* will thus find in her a deep-seated complicity . . . she often finds pleasure in her role as *Other*. (TSS 10; TA; DS I 21–22)

Much of volume 2 portrays the actions and experiences of women who engage in such strategies of complicity. From the woman who plays dumb and passive (who "makes herself prey") to get a man; to the housewife who automatically adopts her husband's political views or relies on him to navigate technology for her; to the narcissist who is in love with her own self-objectified image; to the mystic who tries to lose herself in mythical union with a great spiritual Other, Beauvoir describes women who willingly assume and affirm their feminine alterity. They try both to resolve the painful paradox of being a subject whom men posit as a thing and, simultaneously, to evade the ontological ambiguity of embodied subjectivity by positively identifying themselves with their objectification. "Acting" to one degree or another as if they lacked agency, they reaffirm the myths of woman as absolute Other. However, in so doing they also further reinforce all women's serial subjection to the myth of Woman, and thus they bear a degree of responsibility for its perpetuation.

A question that Beauvoir's characterization of feminine complicity raises is how far this is specific to the white middle-class women she mainly discusses, or whether it is a pervasive phenomenon among other oppressed groups of either sex. Are, for example, racially objectified groups, menial wage-workers, or the aged (of either or both sexes) similarly complicit in their own objectification? There is, of course, no one answer. However, Beauvoir suggests that there is a quality to the oppression of women that, while not unique, is particularly pervasive: This is the highly personal character of the relationship of oppressor and oppressed.

She captures this well in the analogy with feudal relations in the passage quoted earlier. For where members of the oppressed group have enduring and *particularistic* (indeed, here intimate) relations with specific members of the oppressing group (and, concomitantly, less possibility of intensive bonds with each other) they are more likely to develop the strong symbiosis that gives rise to complicity in their oppression. Women, grosso modo, do not conceive of their situation as a collective one. To the contrary, Beauvoir notes, "they do not say 'we.'" For "they live dispersed among men, bound by residence, work, economic interests, social condition, to certain men— fathers or husbands—more firmly than to other women." Indeed, anticipating the kind of divisions that were later to fracture second-wave feminism, she continues: "As bourgeois women they feel solidarity with bourgeois men, not with proletarian women; as white women their allegiance is with white men, not with black women" (TSS 8 TA; DS I 19).[20] However, for other subordinate groups oppression tends to be less embedded in particularistic relations, and the "master" often has little interest in receiving recognition from the "slave." Then the subjectivity of the oppressed will be acknowledged only to the barest extent that is necessary to harness their behavior to the interests of the dominant. In such instances a more resentful and resistant submission is the likely response. Thus, I now turn to Beauvoir's discussion of forms of objectification that are primarily grounded in depersonalization: in indifference, detachment, and abstraction.

America Day by Day: Indifference

Individuals may be treated as no more than anonymous members of a social category, as interchangeable units in a "series." This kind of objectification often facilitates economic exploitation or cultural appropriation.

---

20. Beauvoir does, however, suggest that there is something ontologically unique to oppressive man-woman relationships: They had no specific beginning (for a discussion, see Kail 2006). We can date (even though we may argue over the precise timing) the emergence of slavery or wage labor, and this means that they have a contingent quality that the oppression of women, linked to (though not explained by) dimorphic sexual reproduction, lacks. We can conceive of a world without slavery, or racism, or wage labor. However—high-tech, high-price fantasies notwithstanding—there could not be an ongoing human world without heterosexual reproduction. But what follows from reproduction by way of kinship or family forms, by way of oppressive or free gender relations, and so forth is equally contingent.

Beauvoir explores such forms of oppression most fully in her discussion of race in *America Day by Day*, her account of the four months she spent traveling coast to coast and lecturing in the United States in early 1947. Arriving from more ethnically homogenous France, she was passionately interested in learning about the lives of immigrant groups, as well as the "race" question in America. However, she did not set out systematically to investigate race as a site of oppression. Nor could she engage with race as lived experience—except insofar as it thrust upon her the startling discovery of her own whiteness. Rather, she proceeds via reportage and anecdote, describing her own encounters and offering observations (some insightful, others naïve or mistaken), relaying what others have happened to tell her on the topic of race (some of it informative, some of it inaccurate), and summarizing a certain amount of reading she did about the "Negro" question. When she was in New York, the black novelist Richard Wright (with whom she had previously become friends in Paris) provided her entrée to various events in Harlem, and he talked with her extensively about black experience. She spent about a week in New Mexico, where she was keenly interested in the situation of Native Americans, and about twelve days in the Deep South, where suddenly race confronted her as totally conditioning life. None of this amounts to anything equivalent to the amount of research and reflection that went into *The Second Sex*. Yet Beauvoir's account still captures (if at times unintentionally and against the grain) how the dynamics of race oppression are ideotypically distinct from those of sex. She describes a mode of oppression here in which the Hegelian dialectics of asymmetrical recognition are not the essential.

Beauvoir writes that America is "idealistic," but it is also the land where "abstraction" rules. High ideals are inscribed in the Constitution, such as "the essential dignity of human beings, the fundamental equality of all men, and certain inalienable rights to liberty, justice, and concrete opportunities of success" (ADD 237; AJJ 329). However, she observes, these ideals have been consigned to an "intangible heaven," while on the ground "realism escapes the bounds of morality." For, refusing to tolerate ambiguity, "the most determined idealist is also the most vulnerable as soon as someone explains to him, 'You have to take reality into account' " (ADD 295; AJJ 409). America's "sincere humanists" will all too easily consider going to war or even using nuclear weapons against the population of the Soviet Union (ADD 295; AJJ 409), while good liberals will "realistically" accommodate themselves to extreme economic inequalities and racist segregation. For the problem is not only the mouthing of grandiose abstract principles, detached from the complex realities of actual lives, but the accompanying flight from ambiguity into the ostensible certainties offered by abstraction and objectivity.[21]

When abstraction is a general societal norm, it is also conducive to the reduction of others to "objective" categories: to racist pseudoscience and to stereotyping. It thus serves to legitimize both economic exploitation and cultural appropriation. Abstraction then becomes vital to those forms of oppression that, in Schott's words, function through "indifference and detachment" (2003, 236). The instances that Beauvoir considers most fully in *America Day by Day* are white characterizations of "Indians" in the West and of "Negroes" in the South. But she observes that similar objectifying dynamics affect many groups in other places, including "natives" in the French (and other) colonies and workers from whom labor is exploitatively extracted. In none of these instances is the desire for recognition a primary impetus for oppression. Although the dominant group usually defines itself in contradistinction to the oppressed in order to justify its benefits in its *own* eyes, and although the oppressed group will discover that it cannot but assume its despised characteristics, what is different here from the case of (notably white, middle-class) women is that not even a dialectic of asymmetrical recognition is initiated.[22] In such situations, it follows, the responses of the oppressed are likely to be different, for complicity and its accompanying rewards are generally not available to them. Survival may necessitate a bare submission, but it is likely to take more resistant forms.[23]

In New Mexico, Beauvoir observes, "the exotic" is "Indian" (ADD 177; AJJ 248). Both for tourists and for the resident Anglo population, "Indians,"

---

21. Beauvoir identifies technicism, positivism, ahistoricism, "other-directedness," and money used as the criterion of what is good as symptoms of this pervasive tendency to abstraction (ADD 383–89; AJJ 527–35). None of these tendencies are, of course, as unique to the United States as Beauvoir suggests. But she clearly encountered them in heightened form there. Much of what she says anticipates the account of American life that Marcuse was to give nearly two decades later in *One Dimensional Man* (1964). I abridge Beauvoir's extended discussion of "abstraction" here, but it builds in interesting ways on her account, in *The Ethics of Ambiguity*, of the flight into self-objectification of the sub-man and the serious man. Beauvoir is careful to point out that her portrait is itself a generalization—and that it certainly does not apply to all Americans (ADD 387; AJJ 533).

22. To the contrary, among the dominant group, recognition is more likely to be sought from peers or from superiors within their own group.

23. "As for the attitude of black people, it is of course basically one of protest and refusal; but they must also adapt themselves to the conditions they have been given, so their conduct necessarily oscillates between submission and revolt" (ADD 247; AJJ 342).

stripped of other sources of livelihood, exist here above all as a category of Other for cultural appropriation. She is struck, as they enter New Mexico, by the new imagery on the roadside billboards. Now "there were Indians with feathers in their hair advertising the smoothest cigarettes or tastiest Quaker Oats," while the curio shops sell moccasins and Indian jewelry, feather head-dresses, woven blankets, and so forth (ADD 177; AJJ 248). Beauvoir is well aware of the murderous past that has left the surviving Native American population here isolated within the small confines of reservation and pue-blo, and without access to land or other economic resources. Her visits to various pueblos make it yet more obvious that the main economic activity left to them is a debasing sale of their culture; they must commoditize their historic sites, crafts, and dances for a livelihood. She is told there is no dis-crimination but notes a sign in a bar in Albuquerque that says, "Off-limits to Indians" (ADD 183; AJJ 258). She is scathing about the "aesthetes of Santa Fe," the artistic types who deck themselves in Indian clothing and jewelry while they compete "to acquire the rarest rugs, blankets, and knickknacks" (ADD 188; AJJ 264), and about the good ladies who are members of socie-ties for "Indian improvement." She sums up the views presented to her by the director of the Santa Fe museum as "they live a life rather like that of carefully kept animals in a zoo" (ADD 187; AJJ 263). At once admired and deemed inferior, "Indians" here remain (as Beauvoir later put it in *The Second Sex*) a "Mystery." Opaque, they are an Other to be appropriated, to be both romanticized and condescended to, but from whom, *unlike* the women whom she treats in *The Second Sex*, no degree of reciprocal recognition is demanded.

Accordingly, the Native Americans Beauvoir describes are not as liable to complicity.[24] They live starkly segregated on the reservations rather than scattered among the "superior" group. Given their economic constraints, they have little option but to comply with their role as exotic objects of touristic appropriation. However, their attitude, as she perceives it, is pri-marily one of antagonism. Their hostility manifests itself as the endeavor to get as much income as they can from visiting white tourists, while giving them minimum access to their inner sanctums. Visiting Taos pueblo, Beau-voir notes with irritation that there is a charge for parking and for permis-sion to take photographs, that there are limited hours when outsiders may visit, and that severe restrictions are imposed on the areas to which they have access. She describes being driven away by a group of angry women

---

24. She does not differentiate here between men and women. Almost always re-ferring to "Indians" as male, she does not consider how their situation may impact men and women in different ways. However, she does reflect on age differences, and she wonders how life may be altered for future generations (ADD 191–92; AJJ 269).

from a well that turns out to be an important sacred site. "We have violated the boundaries assigned to whites," she observes (ADD 192; AJJ 269). Likewise, the local "Indians" endeavor to keep secret the locations of their ritual dances (unsuccessfully, it seems, since Beauvoir attends one along with many of the local Anglo Indian-lovers), while they endlessly perform what Beauvoir senses are ersatz versions of the dances for tourists.

Perhaps oddly and certainly troublingly, Beauvoir does not appear to recognize the behavior of the Taos residents as a form of very justifiable resistance, and she aligns her perspective with that of her Anglo acquaintances and informants. Frustrated at being prevented from roaming freely and at being denied access to the "authentic" life of the pueblo, she writes:

> I've heard that in many villages the Indians surround themselves with prohibitions to preserve the mystery and allure that are their chief economic resources, as they largely live on money extracted from tourists. But perhaps they sincerely respect certain taboos. The most experienced Indian observers here say that no one can claim to know them. Whether they are commercial ruses or religious prejudices, all these restrictions annoy us. (ADD 192; AJJ 270)

Here, against the grain of her own arguments, Beauvoir is frustrated by the "Mystery" of the "Indians" and by the lack of reciprocity shown to her— even though this is surely an appropriate form of resistance to a white tourist. Indeed, it disturbs her to be considered a mere tourist (though this is what she is), and she seems unconscious of her position as a member of the privileged racial "caste." She is unaware of the seriality that enforces her white identity on her and that, unbidden, establishes her social designation as Other in the eyes of the Native American population, as well as theirs for her.

The same cannot be said, however, of Beauvoir's experience of antiblack racism in the Deep South. Beauvoir crossed the state line into Texas at night on a Greyhound bus. At the bus station she saw, for the first time, the signs that commanded the segregation of "whites" and "coloreds" into different waiting areas and restrooms. Unlike in New Mexico, she knew instantly that she herself was implicated: "This is the first time we're seeing with own eyes the segregation we've heard so much about," she writes, "and although we'd been well warned, something fell onto our shoulders that would not lift all through the South; it was our own skin that became heavy and stifling, its color making us burn" (ADD 202–203; AJJ 284). She discovers that she is herself a bearer of the existing structures of racism, irrespective of the fact that she is a foreigner and irrespective of her radical politics or her desire to offer solidarity to blacks. Her good intentions notwithstanding, she cannot but assume her whiteness and the superior "caste" position that attaches to it. Even enclosed in a bus, she cannot escape what Gunnar Myrdal had called "the American dilemma."[25] She cannot escape "the smell of hatred in the air—the arrogant hatred of whites, the silent hatred of blacks" that it engenders it (ADD 233; AJJ 322).

Beauvoir describes how, when she is traveling in Mississippi on a very hot day, a pregnant black woman at the back of the bus faints; the woman is jeered at by the white passengers, none of whom will help her. She would be better off in the front of the bus, where there is less jolting, but Beauvoir recounts that she did not dare to offer the woman her seat in the front: "The whole bus would oppose it, and she [the woman] would be the first victim of their indignation" (ADD 233; AJJ 323). Beauvoir was surely correct that it would have been naïve—not to mention dangerous for both of them—to think she could ignore her own "objective" classification and that of the black woman. For the dynamics of racism here locate each in the appropriate series—be it that of "white" or "colored"—from which personal intentions or volitions offer no escape. Walking across the black section of New Orleans, she realizes that here "we are the enemy despite ourselves, justifiably responsible for the color of our skin and, against our wishes, of all that it implies" (ADD 227 TA; AJJ 318).

Here no reciprocity is possible. Whites define themselves as the Subject or the Essential. However, they will seek recognition of this status from other members of their own "caste," and they regard blacks as so "dubiously human" (to use Butler's phrase) that recognition from them would be worthless. Blacks, unlike the women discussed in *The Second Sex*, are not usually invited into relationships with their oppressors that would make complicity an option. They cannot but assume their designated status, but they do so with hatred toward the dominant white Other, for whom "they" all seem the same.[26] As the bus drives through black areas, or as she and her white travel

---

25. *An American Dilemma* (1944) is the title of Gunnar Myrdal's magnum opus on race in America. Since it was, at the time, deemed the authoritative study of "the race problem," Beauvoir presents Myrdal's work at length, using it as a key resource through which to interpret her own brief experiences and impressions (ADD 236ff; AJJ 327ff). For an insightful discussion of how Beauvoir reads Myrdal, and of the tensions and resistances that arise among her readings of race and sex as sites of oppressive difference, see especially Deutscher (2008, chap. 4).

26. Some years later, in *The Colonizer and the Colonized* (a work for which Sartre wrote the preface and part of which was first published in *Les Tempes modernes*), Albert Memmi appropriately describes such use of "they" as the depersonalizing "mark of the plural." He writes: "Another sign of the colonized's depersonalization is what one might call the mark of the plural. The colonized is never characterized in an individual manner; he is entitled only to drown in an anonymous collectivity ('They are this.' 'They are all the same')" ([1957] 1991, 85).

companion walk through them, hostility is the ubiquitous response to white intrusion. She describes walking into a black area of Savannah:

> With every step, our discomfort grows. As we go by, voices drop, gestures stop, smiles die; all life is suspended in the depths of those angry eyes. This silence is so stifling, the menace so oppressive that it's almost a relief when something finally explodes. An old woman glares at us in disgust and spits twice, majestically, once for N. [Beauvoir's companion], once for me. (ADD 236; AJJ 326–27)

But Beauvoir can only observe this hatred and report on her own discomfiting experience of being its target, for she has no entry point into the lived experience expressed in the hostility she encounters.[27] Back in New York, Richard Wright is her guide to black life. His novel *Black Boy* captures for her "the black person's double face, one side of which is expressly meant for whites" (ADD 242; AJJ 335). He also takes her to Harlem to visit jazz venues and to attend a Sunday church service.[28] However, she writes about these only as an outside observer: She seems to realize that no endeavor of imagination and no goodwill attempt at recognition will overcome the separations that racism here imposes on those of different skin colors, each located in a different and antagonistic series. The facticities of embodiment and their accompanying life histories are, at least in this particular social context, overwhelming.

In *The Second Sex* Beauvoir writes both *about* women and *as* a woman,[29] and, likewise, in *The Coming of Age* (published when she was sixty-two)

---

27. Beauvoir has been accused of voyeurism and a desire to appropriate black experience, given her insistence on walking into black areas such as this. For example, Alfonso comments, "her voyeuristic, exoticizing gaze is put back in its place by the resisting stares of angry eyes" (2005, 95). There is some truth to this accusation, but then Beauvoir's whole trip may be seen as one of voyeurism and appropriation. She seeks to consume "America," hungrily gulping down each and every possible experience and, as an outsider, she has no sense (until perhaps this moment) that it is less appropriate to consume some experiences than others. As Deutscher points out, there is a naïve lack of reflection on Beauvoir's part about the nature of foreign travel and travel writing: "The questions of form that had earlier preoccupied Beauvoir vanish and she supposes that methodological problems are not hers insofar as she undertakes what she apparently understands to be the simple project of recounting her travel experiences" (2008, 66).

28. She notes that she finds less hostility toward whites in Harlem than in the South. She does, however, encounter overt and hostile racism in New York—on the part of whites as she and a white friend travel back downtown from Harlem in the company of Wright (ADD 276; AJJ 382).

29. "It would never occur to a man to write a book on the particular situation of males within humanity. If I want to define myself, I first have to state, 'I am a woman'" (TSS 5 TA; DS I 14).

autobiographical elements contribute significantly to the phenomenology of aging she elaborates. But she has no direct access to the lived experience of being subject to racial oppression.[30] Thus, in describing and analyzing her travels in the South and elsewhere she relies heavily on Gunnar Myrdal's "objective" sociological analyses to interpret (and confirm) her own observations about race, and she uses Wright as her guide to "inner" black experience. Margaret Simons has suggested that both thinkers profoundly influenced the writing of *The Second Sex*, offering Beauvoir the methodological resources for developing its double focus, on both lived experience and social construction (1999, chapter 11).[31] However, if Beauvoir may later have applied Wright's methods to grasping women's experience, she did not—and arguably could not—apply them to race. It was not possible for her to write anything analogous to the accounts of how black objectification comes to be assumed which we get from a Wright or a Du Bois or, in the Francophone context, from a Fanon. Yet what she did perceptively observe is how black compliance has very different and generally more deeply resistant qualities than that of (white) women. Apart from describing persistent black hostility she also notes, for example, that the stereotypes of black "laziness" and "dishonesty" actually describe forms of resistance: "'Laziness' means that the work doesn't have the same significance for the person who profits from it as for the person who executes it," she writes, while "lying and theft are the defense of the weak, a silent clumsy protest against unjust power" (ADD 240; AJJ 332). It is significant that the one explicit reference Beauvoir makes in *America Day by Day* to "the Hegelian dialectic of master and slave" does not refer to race (although the vestiges of historical master and slave statuses do still actually persist)

---

30. Deutscher rightly observes that "The encounters Beauvoir has with racial and cultural difference in *America Day by Day* take place 'elsewhere' and within communities described as in some ways self-enclosed" (2008, 132). However, this is not surprising since Beauvoir is profoundly trapped in her outsider status as a white tourist.

31. As mentioned earlier, Beauvoir had begun preliminary work on *The Second Sex* prior to her trip to the United States, but she wrote most of it afterward. Although Simons makes a plausible case that Myrdal's work was influential in showing Beauvoir how to move beyond the more individualistic and subjectivist perspective of her earlier existentialism, other influences were also at work. In particular, Beauvoir was also much interested in the pathbreaking structuralist anthropology of Claude Lévi-Strauss. She read the proofs of his book on kinship structures while she was writing the first volume of *The Second Sex*, and she cites it as providing evidence of the ubiquitous and fundamental presence of systems of dualistic opposition in human cultures (TSS 7; DS I 16–17). She also wrote an extensive review of the book (*The Elementary Structures of Kinship*) for *Les Temps modernes*.

but is made with regard to middle-class American women who, even as they ostensibly claim greater independence than French women, still remain in relation to man the "inessential" (ADD 330–31; AJJ 454). In racial oppression a very different logic generally predominates.

The Coming of Age: Aversion

Beauvoir can conceive of a hypothetical society (as can we) in which having a female or a male body would not make a great difference to one's life possibilities and where neither privilege nor oppression would follow from one's sex; we can also conceive of societies in which attributes such as one's physiognomy (including "race"), one's religion, or language would not oppressively delimit a life at all. However, we cannot conceive of old age without the accompanying inexorable decline of our bodies. Old age is a physiological reality, but it is not only that. Beauvoir argues in *The Coming of Age* that old age today is also a situation of oppression; indeed, sometimes it is one of profound dehumanization. What typifies oppression here is neither a master-slave relationship nor indifference but *aversion*.

Published in 1970, twenty-one years after *The Second Sex*, *The Coming of Age* is as voluminous. It is also similarly organized—except for the striking absence of an equivalent to the final section on the "Liberated Woman," for no path to liberation appears for the aged. Part 1, "The Viewpoint of Exteriority,"[32] sets forth the "data" on aging (some of it dubious, much now dated) offered by biology, anthropology, history, and postwar sociology. Part 2, "Being-in-the-World," develops a phenomenology of the lived experience of the aged. It draws extensively on memoirs, letters, surveys, and contemporary interview-based research, as well as containing strong autobiographical elements.[33] As with *The Second Sex*, the two

---

32. The English translation renders this title as "Old Age Seen from Without," a formulation that misses Beauvoir's appropriation of the idea of "exteriority" from Sartre's *Critique*. Because the English translation of *The Coming of Age* preceded that of the *Critique* by several years, English conventions for translating Sartre's neologisms were not yet in place. I have frequently altered the translation of *The Coming of Age* in order to make Beauvoir's significant use of Sartre's terminology more visible.

33. In the preface Beauvoir writes as follows:

Every human situation can be viewed from without [en *extériorité*]—as seen from the point of view of others—and from within [en *intériorité*], insofar as the subject assumes it while transcending it. For others, the aged man is an

parts of *The Coming of Age* should be read conjointly. For the lived experience of age is produced through a dialectic in which one cannot but
assume an "exterior" situation that one has not chosen and that severely
limits one's freedom.

For the most part (although not entirely), Beauvoir's focus is on men, so
that when she writes of "man" or the "aged man" [*le vieillard*], she does
indeed means male human beings.[34] Old age is above all a man's problem,
she asserts, since women, who already live mainly in the private realm, do
not suffer the abrupt descent into the category of the less-than-human
which men undergo as they are excluded from public activity. Women still
have places in the home and the family "that enable them to remain active
and to retain their identity" (CA 262 TA; V 279). This argument was already
becoming problematic in 1970 since by that time women (even in France)
had left the domestic sphere more fully than in 1949. Indeed, much of what
Beauvoir says about the crisis that old age presents for men increasingly
applies also to women, especially to professional women, who have gained
further entry into public life. In addition, women suffer acutely from other
forms of objectification as their aging bodies fall away from the norms of
feminine beauty and sexual attractiveness. As Beauvoir had argued in *The
Second Sex*, the decline in sexual attractiveness that accompanies old age
presents more of a crisis for women than men, with menopause marking a
definitive turning point in the aging process. There is thus a troubling disjuncture between Beauvoir's treatment of women's aging in *The Second Sex*
and her very scant consideration of the specificities of women's aging in

---

object of knowledge; for himself, he has a lived experience of his condition. In
the first part of the book I shall adopt the first viewpoint: I shall examine what
biology, anthropology, history and contemporary sociology have to tell us
about old age. In the second I shall endeavor to describe the way in which the
aged man interiorizes his relationship with his body, with time, and with
others. (CA 10 TA; V 16)

As with *The Second Sex*, most of the materials Beauvoir draws on for her phenomenology come from the more literate and literary European classes, but now from
the men of these classes. The account of "being-in-the-world" also has a strong autobiographical element. As Beauvoir notes in her autobiographical volume *All Said
and Done*, just as she had wanted to understand woman's situation since it was
her own, so now, on the threshold of old age, she also wanted to understand this
condition (ASD 130–31; TCF 183). For an exploration of the similarities between
Beauvoir's autobiographical account of her own aging and the account offered in
The Coming of Age see Strasser (2005–2006).

34. The feminine form, *la vieillarde*, exists in French, although it is not commonly
used.

The Coming of Age.[35] Even so, Beauvoir's central arguments about the *sui generis* nature of aging and age oppression in modern societies remain applicable. Far more than for the (younger) women whose lived experience is portrayed in *The Second Sex*, societal structures, norms, and practices that define the aged must be assumed by an embodied subject that increasingly discovers its own body *also* to be an objective impediment.

Near the beginning of the book Beauvoir points out that the topic of old age has become taboo, subject to a "conspiracy of silence" in which old age is said not to exist (CA 1–2; V 7–8).[36] It does! For although old age is a social and discursive construction it is not only this; it is also biological. Beauvoir strongly rejects the kind of nominalism implied in an adage such as "so long as you feel young, you are young" (CA 284; V 301). Thus, she would have rejected the more radical versions of poststructuralist theory that take physical conditions such as age to be discursively constituted. She would, for example, have strongly objected to Donna Haraway's appropriation of her work. Haraway writes: "One is not born a woman, Simone de Beauvoir correctly insisted. It took the political-epistemological terrain of postmodernism to be able to insist on a co-text to de Beauvoir's: one is not born an organism. Organisms are made; they are constructs of a world-changing kind. The constructions of an organism's boundaries are the job . . . of discourses" (1999, 207). In opposition to such discourse-reductionism, Beauvoir insists that organic bodies *do* have objective qualities, and these may impinge on one's ability to act. Real biological changes mark the aging process: cellular regeneration slows; hair whitens; skin wrinkles; teeth fall out; muscular strength declines; and for women, menopause ends reproductive capacity (CA 25–28; V 31–34).

With the approach of old age one makes the startling discovery that one's body, in its brute physical facticity, is *itself* "Other," and this is not only, as for (younger) women, because of its meaning for others. For one's body is increasingly encountered as the source of an immediate and unambiguous "I cannot," or as a source of pain and suffering that impinges on

---

35. However, some data on aged women is provided, and there is a discussion of sexual desire among the elderly of each sex. Beauvoir also notes that elderly women more commonly suffer from "melancholia" than men (CA 495; V 520)—surely an indication that old age is not easier for them.

36. Today, as a cohort of wealthy baby boomers become aged, the topic of aging is far less taboo than in 1970. To the contrary, the wealthy aged have become an important market for diverse commodities and services, and they are more of an organized voice in politics than Beauvoir could have anticipated. Even so, old age generally remains a profoundly despised condition, and a "conspiracy of silence" about the less visible—and far more numerous—aged poor still prevails.

one's intentions and colors one's experiences of the world: "My body" is "me," yet ever more "it" constrains me; "it" dominates me, "it" pains me. In *The Coming of Age*, Beauvoir quotes extensively from memoirs and other sources to show how pervasively the aged experience their own bodies as impediments rather than as "instruments" for their projects. Here, embodied subjectivity, integral to freedom, begins to tilt objectward; the weight of the material body becomes ever greater, ever more constraining of free action.

Thus, although its particular meanings will vary, the aged undergo what Beauvoir calls "a biological destiny" (CA 86 TA; V 95), for there develops "a 'fatigability' that spares none" (CA 28; V 34). "The coefficient of adversity in things rises: stairs are harder to climb, distances longer to cover, streets more dangerous to cross, parcels heavier to carry" (CA 304 TA; V 323), and "from being an instrument the body becomes an obstacle" (CA 317; TA; V 336). "Biological decay [*La déchéance biologique*]," she says, "brings with it the impossibility of transcendence, of becoming passionately involved; it kills projects and . . . makes death acceptable" (CA 443 TA; V 468). Such decay is also intimately linked to the temporal experience of old age: to the emergence of a horizon that is "both short and closed" (CA 373; V 395). For this militates against initiating new projects, killing the zest for life, and increasingly locking the aged into their past.[37]

This said, however, Beauvoir also insists that the body is never an unalloyed "pure nature" (CA 12; V 18). To the contrary, bodily experience is always imbued with meanings that are shaped by social structures, practices, and discourses, and Beauvoir talks of the "circularity" through which the various aspects of old age become mutually implicated in each other (CA 9; V 15–16).[38] The aged often become frozen in conditions of irreversible objectification, and these may be so profound that their dehumanization will be nearly total. Again, Beauvoir asks, why? However, her answers are significantly different from those concerning sex and race. For the advantages offered to others through the oppression of the aged are few, and what distinguishes the oppression of the aged is above all *aversion*: aversion to their deteriorating bodies and to their perceived

---

37. "'Life is a long preparation for something that never happens,' said Yeats. There comes a moment when one knows that one is no longer getting ready for anything and understands that one was deluded in believing one was advancing towards a goal" (CA 491 TA; V 516–17).

38. She writes: "An analytical description of the various aspects of old age is therefore not enough: each reacts upon the others and is affected by them, and it is in the indeterminate movement of this circularity that old age must be grasped" (CA 9 TA; V 15–16).

superfluity. This superfluity may produce a certain affinity (as mentioned earlier) between the condition of the aged and that of concentration-camp victims, and, indeed, Beauvoir remarks, "in the death-camps they were the first victims chosen; having no capacity to work they were given no chance of any kind" (CA 220 TA; V 234). But even in "normal" life the aged are subject to intense oppression: Active adults do not seek recognition from them, nor are they considered to serve any useful material ends. Now they are just "useless mouths" (CA 241; V 258), and their ineffectual bodies instill horror and disgust in still-active adults,[39] who rightly see their own future in this Other, decaying and near death. Unlike other oppressions, that of the aged is potentially ubiquitous. For, except in the case of premature death, old age awaits us all, and each of us will in turn succumb to it. However, in bad faith, still-active adults seek to flee this premonition: They refuse to acknowledge their connection with the aged.

To become old is to discover, usually against one's will, that one is already instantiated in the series of the aged. Age is an identity that cannot *not* be assumed. "In our society the elderly person is marked as such by custom, by the behaviour of others and by vocabulary itself: he must take up this reality. There is an infinite number of ways of doing so: but not one of them will allow me to coincide with the reality that I [must] assume" (CA, 291 TA; V 309). Thus, we initially realize we are becoming "old" (just as a young girl discovers she is becoming "a woman") through the words and actions of others even if we do not feel old "inside."[40] Old age comes to us as the point of view of the other (CA 286; V 304), and "it is the other within us who is old" [*en nous c'est l'autre qui est vieux*] (CA 288; V 306). There is, says Beauvoir, "an irresolvable contradiction between the personal evidence that assures our unchanging quality and the objective certainty of our transformation. We can only oscillate between them" (CA 290 TA; V 309). In the longer term, however, the oscillations normally cease; the condition of "being old" is reluctantly assumed and is most often internalized as self-disgust. "If one could die of shame and distress, I should no longer be alive," wrote the elderly Michelangelo (cited in CA 513; V 539); while, following a

---

39. "A hypocritical sense of decency forbids a capitalist society to get rid of 'useless mouths.' But it allows them only just enough to keep them on this side of death" (CA 241; V 257–58).

40. For even when our bodies begin to suffer from various disabilities of age such as rheumatism, we will not see these as symptoms of "old age" until we have, through others, interiorized and assumed that condition. Until this time, "we fail to see that [such symptoms] represent a new status. We remain what we were, with the rheumatism as something additional" (CA 285; V 303).

stroke, Churchill described himself as having become "a bundle of old rags" (CA 431; V 455). If (as an American gerontologist complained) many elderly men in nursing homes are dirty, this is in Beauvoir's view quite understandable: "They have been tossed on the rubbish-heap, so why should they obey the rules of decency and hygiene?" (CA 481 TA; V 506).

Beauvoir begins *The Coming of Age* with the story of how Buddha, as Prince Siddhartha, when he first left his father's palace encountered a feeble old man on the road. Initially astonished at the sight, he then affirmed, "I myself am the dwelling place of future old age." Born to save humankind, Buddha "wanted to assume the entire human condition," and so the young Buddha recognized both himself in the old man and the old man in himself (CA 1 TA; V 7). However, Beauvoir's point is that most of us choose to do the very opposite. Here the " 'common' corporeal vulnerability" that Butler suggests might draw human beings together (2004, 42) instead inspires dread and flight. Fearful of our own future degeneration and death, we vainly seek to evade them by casting the aged as a "foreign species," as an absolute Other—while at the same time we know only too well that they are us and we are them.

It is this fear that so often gives rise not to mere indifference to the aged but rather to a profound horror and aversion. Apart from a few exceptions, Beauvoir writes, "the old man [*le vieillard*] . . . doesn't *do* anything. He is defined by an *exis*, not a *praxis*. Time carries him toward an end—death— which is not *his* end, which is not intended as a project [*qui n'est pas posée par un projet*]. And this is why he appears to active individuals as a 'foreign species' in which they don't recognize themselves." She continues: "Old age inspires a biological repugnance; in a kind of self-defense one pushes it far away from oneself" (CA 217 TA; V 231).[41] Here vulnerability arouses not compassion but rather a visceral aversion. Mockery, frequently sadistic in tone, is used as a distancing device. The aged are objects of manipulation,

---

41. Beauvoir is drawing here on Sartre's notion of *exis* in the *Critique*. Exis is a condition of inertia so severe that it precludes the ability to engage in further meaningful action (*praxis*). In a condition of exis the *very being* of a person comes to be constituted by his or her membership in an unchosen, passively formed "collective." In exis, the self is so fully constituted from without that the possibility of future praxis is foreclosed. Selfhood now comes to be defined, in its fixity, above all by a person's "being" and no longer by his or her actions (Sartre [1960] 1976, 255). McBride notes that Sartre is adapting for his own use the Aristotelian notion of exis (or, more properly transliterated, hexis). For Aristotle, *hexis*, meaning habit, is conceived as a desirable component of education, but for Sartre it carries only the negative connotation of the blockage of the possibility of praxis (McBride 1991, 121–22).

condescension, infantilization, and dishonesty even when they are still relatively sound in mind and body (CA 218–19; V 232–233).[42]

If fear and disgust and the aversion they inspire provide the major impetus for the objectification of the aged, this arises, however, not only from their bodily decrepitude but also from its accompanying social superfluity and dependence. From a practical perspective the aged are superfluous in a way that younger women, workers, the colonized and/or racially denigrated are not; the dependent housewife, for example, still offers valuable services to her husband, as does the menial black worker in the American South to a white employer, while the dependent child has a productive future ahead. The aged person thus has no *value* in our productivity-oriented society and is not acknowledged as a subject. Instead, "he is condemned to stagnate in boredom and loneliness, just a throw-out . . . a piece of scrap" (CA 6; V 13). No longer considered a subject, others treat him as a "nullity" [*en quantité négligeable*] (CA 219 TA; V 233)—and this is how he will come to feel and regard himself.

In all societies, Beauvoir argues, younger adults seek to distance themselves from the aged because they so profoundly fear their own old age. In some traditional societies the aversion this provokes is mitigated by respect for the aged as transmitters of knowledge or as interceders with ancestors or gods. But in modern Western society, where rapid change renders experience irrelevant and where productivity, profit, and the cult of novelty are the most prevalent values (CA 380–82; V 402–404), no positive value is associated with age. Moreover, since one's occupation and income are also vital to an individual's identity, retirement constitutes its sudden destruction (CA 266; V 283–84). Because retirement rarely provides opportunities to acquire meaningful new identities, it means "losing one's place in society, losing one's dignity and almost one's existence [*presque sa réalité*] " (CA 266 TA; V 284). Once retired (or "redundant"), the elderly (with the exception of the wealthy few, who may purchase a degree of recognition) are often reduced "to the condition of sub-man" [*à l'état de sous-homme*] (CA 505 TA; V 531).[43] Now, "fictive" objectification may indeed yield to literal

---

42. Beauvoir quotes Doctor Johnson's nice example: "There is a wicked inclination in most people to suppose an old man decayed in his intellects. If a young or middle-aged man, when leaving a company, does not recollect where he has laid his hat, it is nothing and people laugh. But if the same inattention is discovered in an old man, people will shrug up their shoulders and say, 'His memory is going' " (CA 479 TA; V 504).

43. In *The Ethics of Ambiguity*, Beauvoir uses the term *les sous-hommes* [sub-men] to describe those who, rather than run the risks and assume the responsibilities associated with free action, try in bad faith try to make themselves as passive and thing-like as possible. The sub-man's acts "are never positive choices, only flights.

objectification in the treatment of those who become physically helpless or demented. Whether attended to by family members or paid domestic "carers," or warehoused in homes for the elderly or hospitals to await death, they may be subjected to callousness, neglect, and sometimes direct physical and psychological abuse.

Far more than for women or even black Americans, Beauvoir frames the oppressive situation of the aged as structured by contemporary capitalism. In a for-profit economy not only are those who are no longer economically productive objects of contempt and disgust but, for many, a prior life of alienated labor also means that they have no existential resources to enjoy the enforced "leisure" of retirement. Indeed, with strong echoes of Marx's notion of the proletariat as a universal class, Beauvoir ends *The Coming of Age* by suggesting that the treatment of the aged "exposes the failure of our entire civilization." More generous pensions and so forth—although vital—would not be sufficient to make old age more meaningful. For in modern society old age is usually but the terminus of a lifetime of objectification and exploitation in the labor force: "It is the whole system that is at issue and our demand cannot be other than radical—change life itself" (CA 543 TA; V 569–70).

But who will change it? Not the aged. For their very condition precludes effective resistance. Each isolated and each "the same," passively unified through structures and practices that locate each in the series of "the aged," powerlessness is their common hallmark. Dispersed and excluded from public activities and spaces, apart from a small elite, the aged have virtually no capacity for resistance.[44] The individual would-be liberated woman has some ability to resist her objectification in spite of the limits she encounters and, as Beauvoir described in *America Day by Day*, resistant responses are open to those subjected to racial objectification. In addition, both groups have also developed organized movements of collective resistance that have met with some success. Likewise, workers and colonized peoples have at various times developed effective collective resistance. However, the aged, especially as they become increasingly debilitated, inactive, and isolated, cannot do so.

He cannot prevent himself from being a presence in the world, but he maintains this presence on the plane of bare facticity" (EA 42–45; PMA 61–65). Here, however, Beauvoir is suggesting that this becomes a *condition* for the aged; that is, it is imposed on them without their consent.

44. As Beauvoir said a few years later, "The split in class is very important. There is an immense difference between an old tramp and an old oil millionaire. One can just imagine, though it doesn't exist yet, a movement of solidarity among women; but one can't possibly imagine solidarity among the old" (cited in Moorehead 1974).

Of course, and as Beauvoir herself occasionally notes, her overwhelmingly negative depiction of old age does not apply to all elderly people, and some continue to enjoy warm relationships with family and friends and to have meaningful projects.[45] One also needs to distinguish more carefully than Beauvoir does between those we might call the "active" aged, who still have a range of different ways in which they may assume their status, and the "debilitated" aged, whose lives are constricted through and through by bodily decline and whose vulnerability to oppression—and indeed dehumanization—are far greater. Reading Beauvoir today, one is struck by how greatly extended active old age has become for many in Western societies since 1970. This is especially so for members of the upper and professional classes (for whom life expectancy itself has also increased). Still, her diagnosis of the role poverty plays in reducing many others to a life of exclusion and incapacity remains disturbingly accurate, as does her portrayal of the aversion—the disgust, derision, hostility—with which younger adults generally respond to the aged. This is an aversion that the aged most often internalize in the form of self-disgust, for "becoming aged" offers no equivalent to the rewards of complicity that may attend "becoming a woman."

The Multiple Ambiguities of Oppression

My aim in this chapter has been to move beyond readings of Beauvoir that focus too exclusively on her appropriation of Hegel's master-slave dialectic as offering *the* key characterization of oppression. This project is important both in terms of how we should read Beauvoir and because she offers us the resources for thinking about the complexities of oppression and the different modes through which it is perpetuated. Drawing from Beauvoir's discussions of sex, race, and age, I have elicited three "ideal types," or modes, of oppression each of which has a different core dynamic: asymmetrical recognition, indifference, and aversion. Up to now I have tended, like Beauvoir, to write as if individuals pertain only to one particular series of the oppressed but, of course, they are often instantiated in more than one. Thus, women's experiences are more inflected by race or ethnicity, class, age, and so forth than Beauvoir often considers in *The Second Sex*. Similarly, as I have noted, Beauvoir's treatment of race tends to occlude gender (and

---

45. She gives a couple of extended examples of more positive experiences of old age: Victor Hugo (CA 505–11; V 531–37) and Lou Andreas-Salomé (CA 518–19; V 544–45), both of whom were writers.

other) differences, while in *The Coming of Age* she misguidedly claims that "Old age is a problem of men" even though she draws on examples concerning women when it suits her purposes. Although, for example, Beauvoir describes the condition of Woman as one that, paradigmatically, is constituted by asymmetrical recognition, this will not be the case for every individual woman. For some men will not seek recognition from aged women of any description, or from women whom they perceive as their inferiors in class or race status. Conversely, a higher economic or race status may diminish the degree of objectification that accompanies aging, and so forth. This also means, of course, that particular individuals may occupy ambiguous positions, in which they are at once members of an oppressive and an oppressing series.[46]

Additionally, even within a fairly homogenous series, more than one mode of oppression is often operative. The aged of all descriptions, including those who are male, wealthy, and white, may be subject to indifference as well as to aversion or to an oscillating between them, while even elite women may also be subject to profound aversion on the part of men. Indeed, men's disgust for women's bodily processes may sometimes be as intense as the repugnance the young feel toward the aged, and it may displace or alternate with men's desire for recognition from women.[47] Likewise, antiblack racism on the part of whites does not always proceed through indifference and objectifying abstraction alone. Although Fanon, Ellison, and others confirm the centrality of the dynamic of indifference by pointing to "absence" or "invisibility" as fundamental to black experience (Fanon [1952] 1967; Ellison 1990), racism may also be propelled by a fear of (and perhaps an envious desire for) the sexual prowess that is often projected by whites onto black men. It may also be driven by the desire that blacks should recognize white superiority, since such recognition may help to assuage white guilt and to justify economic exploitation.[48]

---

46. This phenomenon is often explored now through the lens of "intersectionality." However, the concept is used so variously that I do not find it very helpful. For an excellent survey of the diversity of conceptions and uses of "intersectionality" in both North American and European research see Bilge (2010).

47. "In all civilizations and still today, she inspires horror in man: the horror of his own carnal contingence, that he projects on her" (TSS 167; DS I 249). There are some intriguing anticipations of Kristeva's notion of "abjection" in Beauvoir's treatment of the disgust that female and aged bodies may incite (Kristeva 1982).

48. Alfonso, for example, writes, drawing on Zizek: "It is what we feel as lacking in ourselves, and our own tortured relationship to our own desires, that makes us susceptible to racist fear, guilt and hatred" (2005, 98). On the vicious circle of guilt and racism see also Memmi [1957] 1991, especially 45–76.

Irrespective of which particular modes and dynamics are at play, what always makes a situation one of oppression is that it curtails the ambiguities of an embodied subject and forecloses freedom. To return to Honneth's notion of fictive reification, such a situation always involves the treatment of persons (through whatever modes or admixture of modes) *as if* they are merely "things." In both *The Second Sex* and *The Coming of Age* (though much less in *America Day by Day*), Beauvoir focuses extensively on the experiential, "lived," aspects of this objectification. She captures, in vignette after vignette, how oppression is variously assumed by those who are subjected to it, and she vividly portrays its "taste" in a myriad of instances. However, in addition, she theorizes how these particular experiences are situated within the general societal "structures of constraint" that make them stably possible, and she shows how individual actions and social structures iteratively reinforce each other.

Oppression creates for the oppressed constrained situations in which change is nearly impossible since whatever they may individually choose to do will only tend further to consolidate oppression. This is what Marilyn Frye has described as the "double bind" of oppression, in which whatever one does confirms one's oppressed status.[49] As we have seen, women are serially caught up in the perpetuation of their subordination, so that even the would-be liberated woman, whom Beauvoir applauds for resisting complicity, finds she must still attend to the demands of "femininity": "The individual is not free to shape [the idea of femininity] as she pleases. The woman who does not conform to it devaluates herself sexually and, consequently, socially . . . It is a bad move to choose defiance unless it represents a positively efficacious action: one consumes more time and energy than one saves" (TSS 724 TA; DS II 601–602). For example, a woman will need to dress "properly," perhaps flatter a male boss (or more) to retain the job that will provide her "independence." The black American who, exploited and working for a pittance, puts little effort into his (or her) work reinscribes the stereotype of black laziness. But whether it is through the resentful compliance that bare survival required of blacks in the American South (and that poverty and economic insecurity still demand of so many today), or the resignation and self-aversion of the aged, or the active choice of complicity of many women, the oppressed become implicated in their own oppression.

---

49. "One of the most characteristic and ubiquitous features of the world as experienced by the oppressed is the double-bind situations in which options are reduced to very few and all of them expose one to penalty, censure or deprivation" (Frye 1983, 2). For example, today, the young woman who flouts norms of sexual restraint may be labeled "promiscuous," while the one who does not is "frigid."

However, if structures of constraint are perpetuated not only by those who benefit from them but also by those who are oppressed, then the obverse may also be the case. For those who benefit from oppression may also find ways to contest it. This is the ambiguous situation of those privileged would-be "progressives" who discover that they are not free to refuse the social rewards conferred on them because of the chance of their beneficial location in large-scale structures of constraint and oppression. Beauvoir herself was such an individual. As she turned increasingly to political activism in the 1950s she also began to confront her own complicity in structures of oppression. "I am a woman," she had written in *The Second Sex* (TSS 5; DS I 14). But she was not simply a woman. Beauvoir was a particular woman in a particular time and place: French, educated, wealthy, famous. It was the struggle for independence in Algeria and the brutal war that ensued that concretely thrust her own complicity in oppression upon her. She began to reflect on questions about whether or how one may contest oppressions of which one is also a beneficiary. This is the topic to which I turn in the next chapter.

3

Confronting Privilege

In 1955 Simone de Beauvoir published a collection of essays that she titled *Privilèges* [*Privileges*]. In the foreword she says that one key question
links together the essays: How are the privileged able to think about their
situation? She argues that they cannot think about it honestly and without
self-delusion since "to justify the possession of particular advantages in the
mode of the universal is not an easy undertaking." The privileged thus
engage in bad faith: in modes of thought marked by self-deception and a
denial of responsibility (1955, 7). Beauvoir explores these bad faith modes
of thought in the most detail in the longest of the essays, "La pensée de
droite, aujourd'hui" ["Right-Wing Thought Today"].[1] The essay describes
the many and devious ways in which "right-wing thought" works to mask
and legitimize "bourgeois" interests and to protect ruling-class privilege.
Abstract humanism is not the sole "ruse" of the bourgeois "illusionist," but
it is an essential one. Fearful of those he oppresses, this illusionist "arms
himself against them with abstract principles: all human life must be

---

1. The essay was written for a special issue of *Les Temps modernes* in 1955 on the
present condition of the French Left. Beauvoir's piece, the lead essay in the issue,
set out her account of "right-wing thought," an account regarded as a necessary
prolegomenon to the various analyses of the Left that followed. The other essays
republished *Privilèges* included "Must We Burn Sade?" (originally published in *Les
Temps modernes* in December 1951 and January 1952) and "Merleau-Ponty and
Pseudo-Sartrism" (first published in *Les Temps modernes* in June and July 1955).
This last was her angry response to Merleau-Ponty's recent critique of Sartre's politics
and philosophy, and she accused her former colleague at *Les Temps modernes* of having totally sold out to the bourgeoisie in his recent book, *Adventures of the Dialectic.*
She described his new position of "a-communism" and his appeal for a "new liberalism" as being in bad faith and as evincing "a revolting hypocrisy" (1955, 265).

respected, respect mine! He speaks in the name of the universal because he dares not speak in his own name" (1955, 199). Beauvoir's explicit focus in this essay is on the masking of class privilege. However, her analysis also resonates with more recent critiques of the self-deceptions inherent in masculine, white-race, and other forms of privilege.

Privilege, as considered here, consists in a benefit that redounds to the members of one group through the oppression of those of another. Privilege is *intrinsically* a scarce resource: For some to enjoy a privilege entails a structural relationship in which the benefits they enjoy are denied to others and may come at their expense,[2] and such benefits are often obtained through the systematic exploitation of one group by another. In "Right-Wing Thought Today" Beauvoir's project is to dissect the ideas that serve to obscure privilege and that enable those who benefit from it to claim either that their privilege does not exist or else that it is justified. Her concerns are with what has more recently been described as the embrace of "willful ignorance" on the part of the beneficiaries of privilege. "Willful ignorance," as Nancy Tuana describes it, is "a deception that we impose upon ourselves, but is not an isolated lie we consciously tell ourselves. . . . Rather, willful ignorance is *a systematic process of self-deception*, a willful embrace of ignorance that infects those who are in positions of privilege, an *active* ignoring of the oppression of others and one's role in that exploitation" (2006, 11).[3]

---

2. However, I would not want to say that the young are "privileged" with regard to the aged or those with "normal" abilities with regard to those with disabilities. For even though society is organized for the convenience of the young and active, still these are not oppressions that provide a direct transfer of benefits to them from the oppressed group. As discussed in chapter 2, the "logic" of these oppressions derives more fundamentally from aversion and disgust.

3. Although Beauvoir refers to Marx's notion of "ideology" in the essay, her concern is with something a little different from the production of the ruling-class "illusions" that Marx discusses. In "The German Ideology," Marx describes these illusions as forms of "false consciousness" that both the oppressing and the oppressed classes accept (Marx 1978, 173). However, in instances of "bad faith," as in "willful ignorance," beliefs are not as passively received as Marx seems to suggest. Rather, they are actively (if not fully consciously) chosen, embraced, and perpetuated by a dominant social group so as to obfuscate or legitimate their position. See Gordon (1995) for an extended application of the notion of bad faith to antiblack racism. See also Mills (1997) and Sullivan and Tuana (2006, 2007) for further explorations of the how "ignorance" supports a diversity of forms of privilege. These arguments profoundly complicate the debate as to whether oppression must be intentional (Cudd 2006) or is better conceived as structural (Young 2005), mentioned in chapter 1. For neither view adequately captures the important role of bad faith or of willful ignorance in sustaining oppression and privilege.

It follows that a key task for those who aim to contest oppression is to unmask such willful ignorance in order to bring the possessors of privilege face to face with its injustices. Of course, many who benefit from privilege will still refuse to acknowledge it or will self-righteously defend their privilege as justified. But what of those among the privileged who desire to resist its benefits? Although privileges may be individually enjoyed, they are the effects of large-scale structures of oppression and constraint. Thus, awareness of one's privilege may not necessarily enable one to shed it. This is the dilemma faced by privileged would-be progressives,[4] and I turn to Beauvoir to help address it. My concern here is not with those who wish to remain willfully ignorant or else unapologetic about their privilege. Nor is my concern (at least directly) with the possibilities for resistance available to those who are subject to oppression. Rather, my focus is on the predicament that their own personal privilege presents for those who actively seek to diminish injustice and oppression. Not surprisingly, given the intense contestations over "difference," as well as the emphasis on the importance of the personal, in feminist politics since the second wave, most of the attention given to this dilemma has come from feminist theorists. They address it most extensively with regard to the white-race privilege enjoyed by many feminists (among whom I include myself), although sexuality and, to a lesser extent, class and nationality are also examined as sites of privilege. Thus, it is primarily through discussions in feminist theory that I explore the perplexities of being a privileged progressive.[5]

It is striking that many Western feminists, especially (although not exclusively) white feminists, are concerned with the question of privilege less as a matter of what they themselves are denied as women than as a

---

4. I use the term *progressive* here because it best serves as an umbrella for a wide range of politics that militates against injustice and privilege. I avoid using the term *radical* because I am not convinced that "radicals" and "liberals" are as distinct as is often claimed. Under the progressive umbrella one may also locate socialists and critics of globalization, as well many of those involved in single-issue politics.

5. As Martinez notes, very few white philosophers address race as a central topic of concern in their work (Martinez 2010). It is also striking that on those few occasions when white male theorists do consider race and race oppression, they do so in a distanced way and they tend not to reflect reflexively on their own positions of race and gender privilege. There are, however, some exceptions, and the "men in feminism" literature offers some parallels to the white feminist literature on race privilege. For example, Larry May makes an argument for the general responsibility of all men for rape insofar as they do not actively contest the culture that invites it (May 1998, especially chap. 5; see also Digby 1998).

matter of what they unjustifiably enjoy. Typical are the remarks of the white, feminist, legal scholar Stephanie Wildman: "The conflicts I have faced have not been about oppression or the privileges I do not have, being a woman in a male-dominated society . . . Rather, the conflicts are about the privileges I do have, including class, race, and heterosexual privilege, and how to live my life of privilege consonant with my beliefs in equal opportunity and inclusive community" (1996, 2). It is in addressing the dilemmas that their whiteness, their heterosexuality, their class benefits, or (increasingly in a globalizing world) their "First World" nationality pose that many feminists now discuss privilege; and they frequently identify themselves as oppressors rather than acknowledging their more ambiguous situation as at once oppressors and oppressed.

White feminists (notably in the United States) most commonly address the problem of their privilege through what I call a "politics of self-transformation." By a politics of self-transformation I mean a project in which one endeavors to discover how one has unmindfully and ignorantly accepted one's privilege and then proceeds to "work on oneself" in order to overcome it. Although such a politics has some value, especially in developing insight into the more invisible, quotidian qualities of privilege, it is also based on some problematic assumptions about the self and political agency. Thus, I want to suggest that we should consider another political repertoire in which privileged progressives may also appropriately engage. This is what I call a "politics of deployment," where one contests privilege not by "working on oneself" but by consciously using the advantages that stem from one's privilege in order to combat structures of privilege. Although the two political repertoires are not in principle mutually exclusive, proponents of a politics of transformation tend to be uncomfortable about deploying their privilege even though this may sometimes be the more efficacious approach. Beauvoir provides resources to demonstrate the limits of a politics of self-transformation; through her own political activities she also provides an example of a politics of deployment. But, of course, "there is an element of failure in all success" (EA 152; PMA 213). Thus, in addition, Beauvoir's own interventions also confirm her warnings about the impossibility of moral purity, or a purity of ends, in politics.

White Feminism: The Politics of Self-Transformation

It is only since the era of the "rights of man" and the advent of liberalism, with their abstract claims about the universality of human rights and demands for equal treatment under the law for "all" (however narrowly

that "all" has been defined), that privilege by birth has come to be viewed as
at all morally suspect in the West.[6] However, the liberal tradition has always
maintained an acceptance of ostensibly "earned" privilege, which it has
tended rather to label as "just reward" or "just entitlement." Why may not
property acquired, as John Locke put it, through "industriousness"—be it
one's own or that of one's forbears[7]—entitle one to enjoy the kinds of benefits that money can buy (Locke [1690] 1988, especially paragraph 34)? Or
why, today, may not the effort one puts into becoming highly educated
entitle one to the economic rewards and social privileges still conferred by
formal professional status?[8] Here, Alison Bailey has complicated (but not
eliminated) the distinction between what she calls "earned advantage" and
"unjust" privilege by pointing out that often "privilege places one in better
a position to earn more advantages" (Bailey 2004, 307). For example,
although one might work hard to benefit from one's education at an expen-
sive elite school, one's access to such a school will probably depend on
chance of birth.

In 1955 Beauvoir was primarily concerned with the privileges of a small,
elite economic class. However, today privilege is conceived as more widespread. It is said to accrue to very wide sections (indeed, even to majorities)
of the population, as in the notion of "white privilege" in the United States

---

6. Historically, the term *privilege* was initially used to denote individual ex-
emptions from the law. The term derives from the Latin *privus* (private) and *legis*
(laws). In Rome, a "privilegium" was a special ordinance referring to an individual and often providing an exemption from the normal requirements of the law.
Within medieval and premodern Europe, the term continued to have strong legal
connotations. However, insofar as entry to certain privileged groups (notably to
the nobility and the upper echelons of the clergy, as well as to guild membership
or citizenship in a free city) came by virtue of one's birth, privilege also came to
denote an exclusive and advantageous *social* status, albeit one still subtended by
legal distinctions. Here, privilege began also to acquire the meaning of an *ascribed*
social status, which it most frequently connotes today. One's entitlements (or lack
of them) usually depended on where, to whom, and with what set of apparent or
attributed qualities one was born.

7. Locke's silent elision of the right to property earned through labor and the
right to enjoy inherited property has effectively remained unchallenged within the
modern liberal tradition.

8. Thus, for example, although developing (through the device of the "veil of
ignorance") principles of justice that initially disregard accidents of birth, John
Rawls still argues that "inequalities of wealth and authority" may be just "if they
result in compensating benefits for everyone, and in particular for the least advan-
taged members of society." Degrees of disadvantage and privilege will, it seems, always be with us, and certain ones will be acceptable even in a "just" society (1971,
14–15).

or Britain. Thus, "privilege" no longer necessarily retains its traditional connotation of a very narrow exclusivity. The notion has also been extended to refer to benefits other than material and status advantages. One important extension (anticipated by Beauvoir) concerns the power to define "knowledge" and "truth." What is now often referred to as "epistemic privilege" has become a focus of considerable concern. Theorists now ask: Who may know? Who may speak? Who is silenced? And so also: Who is objectified? Whose experience is ignored or appropriated by whom?[9]

However, a peculiar contradiction pervades many of the recent feminist analyses of privilege, for they tend to reinscribe a certain kind of individualism of which not only Beauvoir but also much recent feminist theory has itself been critical. There are numerous and highly sophisticated feminist analyses of the structures, institutions, practices, and norms, of the forms of discursive representation and performance that give rise to privilege. Most feminist theorists concur that individuals are in large measure socially constituted, and they do so irrespective of whether they emphasize the material, the cultural, or the discursive as the most significant site of this constitution. However, what is striking is that, when feminists (and notably white feminists) come to reflect on their *own* privilege, a peculiar analytical shift often takes place. Then privilege generally ceases to be thought about as structural. Instead, it is presumed to be the personal "possession" of an autonomous self, a self that is also tacitly assumed (as in abstract humanism) to be the bearer of strongly neo-Kantian qualities of reason and will. This self is then conceived as one that must be held individually accountable for how it acts.

Thus, where feminists' own individual privileges are the issue, the discourse on privilege generally shifts away from structural (or poststructural) analysis, "inward" toward a discourse of personal self-discovery, which is to be followed by guilt and confession, and from thence to the moral imperative to engage in a politics of self-transformation through "working on oneself" (McIntosh [1988] 2011; Frye 1992).[10] Most frequently, so these narratives go, the white (and/or wealthy, well-educated, or heterosexual) woman who is in possession of privilege claims to be ignorant of the fact and she simply takes for granted the benefits she enjoys. She is oblivious to the ways in which she reproduces racist (or other) stereotypes. In willful

---

9. The locus classicus of such concerns is, of course, Spivak (1988).

10. I have found a similar shift also among my white students. Although eager to engage with the theoretically sophisticated work of Butler, Spivak, Foucault, and so forth, they quickly revert to a rather simplistic and self-referential discourse of individual guilt when matters concerning their own privileges are discussed in class.

ignorance, if not worse, she objectifies (or contributes to the objectification of) women who are different from herself. Because privilege is generally invisible to the privileged, the necessary, if not sufficient, condition for overcoming one's privilege must be to reveal the truth about it.

Many contemporary writers thus offer echoes of Beauvoir's remarks about the bad faith in which the privileged obscure the sources of their benefits from themselves. For example, in *Invisible Privilege: A Memoir about Race, Class, and Gender*, Paula Rothenberg moves back and forth in time between her youthful, ignorant self and her now-mature and more insightful one, "sometimes using the voice of one who fails to understand that the world she takes for granted is riddled with 'privilege,' and sometimes using the voice of the narrator years later, when she is capable of making this distinction and commenting on it. At times the early voice may sound prideful, insensitive, cruel—even racist to some people" (2000, 5). The memoir tells of Rothenberg's personal struggles to achieve what she believes is an adequate critical consciousness of her own privileges. Through her own story she wants also to explain the privilege blindness of others, notably white liberals. She especially wants to show how privilege continues to remain invisible to those whom she calls "*basically decent people who should know better*" (8; my emphasis). Within this telling—and many similar ones—privilege comes to be addressed primarily as a problem of individual willful ignorance, and the struggle against privilege becomes cast as the struggle to reveal a truth that may (it is assumed) help to set us free.[11]

---

11. The titles of some recent books and articles on white women's privilege are indicative here. In addition to *Invisible Privilege* (Rothenberg 2000) and *Privilege Revealed* (Wildman 1996), see, for example, *Revealing Whiteness* (Sullivan 2006) and the articles "Resisting the Veil of Privilege" (Ferguson 1998) and "Locating Traitorous Identities" (Bailey 1998). See also the now near-classic "White Privilege: Unpacking the Invisible Knapsack." Originally published in 1988, this essay, which provides a laundry list of the invisible benefits that whiteness may bring (irrespective of gender), continues frequently to be republished and is widely used in teaching (McIntosh [1988] 2011, 235–38). Invisible benefits that McIntosh lists include being able to reside where one wants; finding food, music, magazines, children's toys, and so on that align with one's race and culture; being able to buy bandages that match one's skin color; being sure that one is not being singled out because of one's race if pulled over by a traffic cop or audited by the IRS, and so forth.

Minnie Bruce Pratt's early and pathbreaking autobiographical reflections on white feminist privilege also take as central the project of revealing truth: "I am learning that what I think I *know* is an accurate view of the world is frequently a lie. . . . So I gain truth when I expand my constricted eye, an eye that has let in only what I have been taught to see" (1984, 17). See also Frankenberg (1993) for an important analysis of the invisibility of whiteness.

Various strategies are suggested for revealing the truth about one's privilege, including among others conversations, encounter groups, and "sensitivity" trainings. However, the emphasis always remains on shifting the *self*-understanding of the individual. Thus, such strategies are all variants of what I am calling a politics of self-transformation, for they assume that one attains awareness primarily through one's own individual endeavors. They require actively addressing one's own ignorance, trying to be more sensitive, using one's imagination to grasp the reality of others. In one of the stronger versions of this politics, María Lugones argues that, by renouncing "arrogance" and instead engaging in "loving playfulness," it is possible deliberately to make the experiential shift that she calls "world"-traveling. We may, with effort, suspend our taken-for-granted world and so cease unmindfully to objectify others. "Travelling to someone's 'world' is a way of identifying with them . . . because by travelling to their 'world' we can understand what it is to be them and what it is to be ourselves in their eyes. Only when we have traveled to each other's 'worlds' are we fully subjects to each other" (1990, 401).

However, to address one's privilege adequately also requires that one move beyond this initial epistemological project—to a transformation of self. For as one's privilege becomes revealed it is presumed to become subject to one's own personal volition and control. The claim is not that privilege can be shed or renounced completely but rather that we are free radically to reconstruct ourselves and that, in doing so, we will come to act in ways that are significantly resistant to it. Thus, for example, Marilyn Frye suggests that, even though "we" cannot fully separate ourselves from the "white club" since "membership in it is in a way, or to a degree, compulsory" (1992, 150), still we can through our own efforts unlearn many of the tacit assumptions and behaviors, the "ways of being," which she calls "whiteliness." Similarly, Sandra Harding has argued that it is possible for whites, like men or heterosexuals, to effect a shift in standpoint that undermines their privilege and enables them to take up what she calls "traitorous social locations" (Harding 1991, 288–95). Entering such locations does not involve literally shedding whiteness (or masculinity or heterosexuality) but rather seeing the world from the perspective of the less privileged and developing a political practice from the perspective of the marginalized. It is a matter of free choice. We can "*choose* to become 'marginalized,' " Harding claims, not in the sense of actually leading marginal lives "in the ways that women and people of Third World descent are forced to do," but rather by learning "to think and act *not* out of the 'spontaneous consciousness' of the social locations that history has bestowed on us but out of the traitorous ones we choose with the assistance of critical social theories generated by the emancipatory social movements" (295).

Projects that aim to develop self-awareness and endeavor to overcome race (or other) privilege through self-transformative projects by "working on oneself" are important. They have developed a more widespread awareness among progressives of their still-pervasive forms of privilege and how these permeate daily life. Taken collectively, such individual efforts may help to shift (though probably not to eradicate) societal norms that continue to legitimize various types of privilege. However, the emphasis on individual *self*-transformation also encounters significant practical and theoretical difficulties.

One difficulty of a politics of self-transformation is that it may too easily collapse into a rather self-referential, even self-indulgent, concern with one's own feelings, attitudes, and actions, a kind of "care of the self" or a personal therapeutic. Indeed, as Marilyn Frye herself has noted, "projects of consciousness-raising and self-analysis are very susceptible to the slide from 'working on yourself' to 'playing with yourself' " (1992, 148). More often, however, working on oneself, "unpacking one's invisible knapsack" stuffed with the subtle benefits of privilege, leads to a guilt-ridden focus on the self. But this too may be unproductive. Thus Frye also talks of experiencing all her thoughts and actions as being "poisoned" with privilege (147), and in *Privilege Revealed* Stephanie Wildman writes that, however hard she struggles against it, "I fear that my own racism will make things worse, causing me to do more harm than good" (1996, 20). Since the attempt to expunge one's own last vestiges of race blindness or insensitivity can never be brought to an adequate closure, "working on oneself" may heighten one's feelings of guilt in ways that lead only toward despair, self-hatred, and demobilization.[12]

Sandra Bartky has helpfully argued that one should distinguish between guilt as an "emotion" and guilt as "an existential-moral condition." The latter arises simply by virtue of who one is (white, middle class, heterosexual, and so on). She points out that one may be guilty in this existential-moral sense, since one is implicated in a system of privilege and exclusion, irrespective of whether one feels guilt as an emotion (Bartky 2002, 142). However, I want to suggest the converse: Those practices that heighten guilt as an emotion may not always be the best way to go about addressing the "existential-moral" condition of guilt in which we find ourselves. Guilt as an emotion may well be an important moment of an initial "conversion" process, in

---

12. I am not, of course, accusing any of the specific feminist theorists I discuss of excessive self-referentiality or of being politically demobilized. My point is that these are general tendencies inherent in the practice of a politics of self-transformation.

which one becomes aware of one's privilege, but it may become quite crip-
pling as a basis for effective, long-term political action.

In addition, a politics of self-transformation runs up against the limits
that pertain to any politics primarily focused on individual consciousness
and conscientization. In a world whose circumstances are often beyond
our own making, we always find ourselves already in possession of social
attributes that we did not choose and yet which are profoundly integral
to who we are. This is not to say that we lack all possibilities of choice or
volition but that we may discover that our possibilities are severely constrained. In some areas, including being white, privilege will not cease to
exist no matter how well we become aware of it or how much we endeavor
to reform our previous styles of personal behavior. For the world will continue actively to reinscribe our privileged status upon us. Even if we act
as "traitorous" whites, we will still be seen and treated as whites, albeit
deviant ones. The structural asymmetries of privilege and our implication
in them may perhaps be mitigated, but it cannot be expunged through
our own individual volition.[13]

A politics of self-transformation presupposes, in short, a conception of
the self as more autonomous than is plausible. Moreover, such a conception
is usually accompanied by a tacit neo-Kantianism, a certain "intransigent"
moralism, in which it is demanded that we treat all others as "ends in themselves": We are always to respect the dignity of each person as the bearer of
freedom, to recognize each as an autonomous rational will. Thus, we are
judged to be morally at fault if the effect of our attitudes or actions is (as it
often must be) to objectify others. For, it is assumed, if we would only
purge ourselves of our privileged attitudes we would all be able to treat
each other as ends; we would all unambiguously come to be (as Lugones
puts it) "fully subjects to each other."

Such conceptions of the self are, as Beauvoir argues, problematic. They
also fly in the face of a now voluminous and persuasive feminist literature

---

13. Linda Alcoff has rightly warned about the dangers of reinforcing white
privilege that inhere in personal lifestyle projects of "crossover," where individual
young white Americans choose to "act black." She remarks that "the core of white
privilege is the ability to consume anything, anyone, anywhere," and so crossover
often ends up by erasing difference and becoming "coterminous with a coloniz-
ing desire of appropriation, even to the trappings of social identity" (1998, 19).
See also Alcoff (2006), where she again asks, "When does the transcendence of
cultural chauvinism merge into cultural appropriation?" She argues that forms of
cultural "hybridization" do not eliminate racism: "Racism has not, on the whole,
slowed cultural hybridization. This means that hybridization is not a sufficient
cause or even a necessary indicator of antiracism" (217–18).

that effectively criticizes the masculinism implicit in notions of the self as "sovereign," as a bounded, rational, freely willing entity. Yet in the works of the white feminists I have been discussing the self is presumed, yet again, to be such a sovereign, autonomous agent. For even if it was initially shaped by its circumstances (whence it derives its original, spontaneous, or unreflective stance on its own privilege), *once* it becomes aware of them, *once* it attains consciousness, then this self becomes free; that is, it becomes able to transcend its circumstances and radically to remake itself through its own individual efforts. Harding, for example, insists that the privileged should not be allowed to "get away" with claiming they cannot help being who they are: "We should refuse to believe that there are no ways for overly privileged white men to take responsibility for their identities. Most of them may not *want* to do this, but they *can*" (1991, 290). However, while to *want* to do something is necessary, it is not in itself sufficient for success, and even when white men (or others) do want to take responsibility for their privilege, their ability to do so effectively may be sharply delimited by societal structures and processes beyond their control.

The tone of Harding's comments points to another problematic tendency that may inhabit a politics of self-transformation: self-righteousness. For having laboriously and painfully "worked on oneself," one may feel inclined to be overly judgmental about those who do not appear to have done so as diligently. One's newfound consciousness may then provide a facile platform from whence, on high, to pronounce others guilty of failure. Thus Rothenberg's moralizing remarks about the failings of those white liberals "who ought to know better" often finds echoes among other antiracist white feminists. Anger at and criticism of the willfully ignorant certainly have their place, but when the emotional guilt white people feel as they work on their own racism simply gets displaced onto others, it may be counterproductive.

A more nuanced version of the politics of self-transformation, one more attuned to its ambiguities, is provided by Shannon Sullivan in *Revealing Whiteness* (2006). Sullivan rightly insists that something more than a conscious epistemological shift is necessary to transform the self since racial privilege is instantiated in a host of unconscious habits, many of which are embodied. She writes: "White privilege is not just 'in the head.' It is also 'in' the nose that smells, the back, neck, and other muscles that imperceptibly tighten with anxiety, and the eyes that see some but not all physical differences as significant" (2006, 188). It follows that we cannot easily reconfigure our habits simply through revealing them, or through a purely intellectual "knowing." Instead, we need to work at transforming them at an embodied level. To do this, Sullivan argues, requires shifting the environment in which we act. Stressing an interactive, or "transactional," relationship between self and surroundings, in which each may modify the other, she argues: "Changing unconscious habits of white privilege requires altering the political, social, physical, economic, psychological, aesthetic, and other environments that 'feed' them. Correspondingly, a white person who wishes to try to change her raced and racist habits would be better to change the environments she inhabits than (to attempt) to use 'will power' to change the way she thinks about and reacts to nonwhite people. . . . A person cannot merely intellectualize a change of habit by telling herself that she will no longer think or behave in particular ways" (9).

But how is one to change one's environment? Here Sullivan does discusses the possibility of deploying one's privilege. She talks, as an example, about a white couple living in a segregated area who bought a house in order to deed it over to a black couple. Their act, a challenge to the residential segregation of their community, constituted an attempt to modify their own environment.[14] However, even in this example of the deployment of privilege, Sullivan's primary focus still remains on the *self*-transformation of the white individual. It is because unconscious habits are not amenable to change through intellection that one must struggle to change one's environment as an indirect strategy for modifying them. Thus, in concluding the book she writes: "Change can occur and habits of resistance can be developed, but only if a person takes responsibility for her unconscious life" (197).

In what follows, I propose to shift the ground and to suggest that in some instances it will be preferable to adopt another politics. Rather than investing great amounts of energy in the self-referential labor of disclosing and resisting the subtle benefits that accrue from one's privilege, it may be preferable to acknowledge that one is privileged but then to act *from* one's privileged location: to deploy one's privilege as effectively as possible. There is, of course, a risk that in doing so one will also be reinscribing privilege, but even so this may still be a more effective way of contesting it. A politics of deployment is less focused on self-transformation and more concerned with a transformation of the social structures that support oppression.

It is here that I return to Simone de Beauvoir. Several key postulates, already set out in chapter 1, frame Beauvoir's approach to privilege. To

---

14. She also rightly warns that privilege is not easily shed through such an action. For although the white couple were ostracized and subject to threats, they "continued to be thought of as white by those who did not know about their traitorous act, and they retained their whitely privileges accorded to them through others' perception and treatment of them . . . . [They] used, rather than gave up, their privilege of being allowed to enter the space of the neighborhood in question to help dismantle the racist magnetization of that space" (Sullivan 2006, 166).

recall: she argues that because human beings are always "in situation," their actions are at once constrained and free; that situated human action is always *ambiguous* in its practical and moral import; and that what we do always has multiple meanings and effects. Consequently, we must accept that our best intentions may not lead to the outcomes we intend and that it is dangerous to "insist at any cost on keeping [one's] conscience pure" (MIPR 175; IMRP 55). We must always navigate between "moral idealism and political realism," acknowledging that human action is beset by imperfections and failure.

Beauvoir and Privilege

To begin, I briefly return to *The Second Sex*. For this is where Beauvoir begins explicitly to formulate her ideas about privilege—here, sex privilege—as involving social ascriptions usually acquired at birth. The ascription of anatomical sex to an individual at birth, like the ascription of noble or servile "blood" at birth, instantly confers a situation of privilege on some and of concomitant exclusion and oppression on others. Beauvoir thus describes the young girl who discovers in her femininity a ready-made "destiny," an ascribed status "imposed on her from the exterior" that she must necessarily assume in one way or another (TSS 312; DS II 52). But if women's inferior status is socially ascribed, so also is the privileged status of men: "He is the Subject, he is the Absolute" (TSS 6; DS I 15). Thus, even should they wish to do so, men, the members of the "first" sex, find that they are unable fully to shed the privileges of masculinity. Beauvoir writes: "A colonial administrator has no possibility of acting well towards the natives, nor a general toward his soldiers; the only solution is to be neither colonialist nor military chief; but a man could not prevent himself from being a man. So there he is, guilty in spite of himself and oppressed by this fault he did not himself commit" (TSS 759 TA; DS II 652–53). This passage raises a complex set of questions about what degrees of freedom, complicity, and responsibility exist when individuals benefit from unchosen privileges.

Where a clear choice of entry to and exit from a situation of privilege exists—nobody has to become a colonial administrator, just as nobody has to become a corporate executive—a fairly clear-cut moral judgment is possible about a person's actions. But more often—not only when privileges inhere in sex differences but also when they arise from distinctions such as race and nationality, or from the advantageous location in the global economy enjoyed by most "working-class" individuals in Western societies today—matters are far more ambiguous. For just as one "becomes" a woman or a man, so one also "becomes," for example, white, French, or American in ways that are both inescapably given to one and yet also self-created. Just as Beauvoir says "I am my [sexed] body," so one may also say "I am my race, my ethnicity, my nationality," even perhaps (though it is less straightforward) "I am my class."[15] For these social ascriptions, usually acquired at birth, are instantiated over the course of a life history, and they become integral to one's way of being in the world. They become elements of a lived experience that is significantly constitutive of a self.[16] Although Beauvoir continues to insist that we are responsible for our own actions, still this responsibility may be mitigated by our situation: We cannot fully jump out of our skins; nor can we fully shed our "personal" histories, for they are never purely "our own."

Thus, it is important to recognize that the *degree* of responsibility we have for injustices and oppressions in which our privilege implicates us may also vary significantly. As Larry May has argued, responsibility is a "scalar" concept, and how far we are responsible will depend on the extent to which we act as autonomous agents in any given case (May 1992, 120). In many instances we may be implicated in oppression in a less than voluntary manner. Then what is at issue is not our individual culpable actions so much as the effects of our social or even national identities. May suggests that in instances where we have not committed an identifiable wrong, rather than talking of "moral guilt," we can more usefully talk of "shame" or "moral taint." To give an example, a white person who knows that, simply given the statistical probabilities, she (or he) is likely to be promoted ahead of an equally qualified African American colleague, is not "morally guilty" of racism in accepting her promotion, whereas a Klan member burning a cross in

---

15. Of course, especially in our increasingly fluid world, these ascriptions are rarely fully stable or unambiguous. Social class is perhaps the most malleable ascription in Western societies. But even so, class may become integral to one's way of being in the world, suffusing one's habits, one's style of comportment and expression, and so forth.

16. It may be the case that these lived ascriptions give rise to a more stable experience of the self for the privileged than for more marginalized people. Some feminists of color have argued that, for them, tensions among the many ascriptions that they have to negotiate give rise to a more "mobile" experience of the self (Anzaldúa 1987; Sandoval 1991; Lugones 2003).

I leave out of consideration here the special case of acquiring nationality through naturalization. Naturalization (and sometimes immigration) imposes new demands and offers new possibilities that may require that we profoundly reorganize our previous ways of being and our sense of self. Likewise, transgendered selves must, in significant ways, start out anew.

front of an African American church is. Even so, this person may experience shame when the promotion letter comes; and when she learns of the cross burning she may, as a white person, experience a certain "guilt by association" or a feeling of "moral taint" even if she is not in a position to do anything directly about it. She is not directly culpable in either of these two instances, and yet she is implicated in a white-supremacist system that preferentially rewards her and in which Klan terror mechanisms play a part. These lesser levels of complicity may place us under a degree of moral obligation to address wrongs that we did not ourselves commit. However, although in such cases we may experience what Bartky calls "emotional guilt" and engage in self-blame (we may, for example, feel, as Frye does, that all we do is "poisoned" or, as Wildman says, that whatever we do, our own racism "will make things worse"), these are hardly the most productive responses.

In 1955, in *Privilèges*, Beauvoir did not include herself among the ranks of the privileged. Rather, "they," those obfuscators who mask class privilege in the language of the universal, were at fault—not she. But she was shortly to learn that she enjoyed many privileges (and not only those of class) of which she still remained perhaps surprisingly unaware. For by 1955 a violent struggle had already begun in Algeria between a movement for national independence (the Front de Libération Nationale, known as the FLN) and the French colonial regime. This war was to arouse in Beauvoir a profound sense of guilt, overwhelming feelings of shame and moral taint. Indeed, it was to shatter her world. In time, it also induced Beauvoir to reflect profoundly upon her privileges as French and as a prominent member of the French intelligentsia.

Beauvoir, along with Sartre, had long held a principled objection to colonialism and had earlier been critical of French policy in Indo-China. Even so, it was only in 1957 that the war in Algeria truly burst in upon her life. French atrocities and the widespread, systematic use of torture against Algerians, militants and civilians alike, had become increasingly well documented, and *Les Temps modernes* published some of this evidence.[17] In her autobiography, Beauvoir later described the war as invading "my thoughts,

---

17. The extensive use of torture in Algeria had begun to be documented in early 1957. Sartre published an editorial in *Les Temps modernes* in May 1957 in which he referred to already-published accounts and drew an analogy between the "collective guilt" of Germans who claimed "not to know" about the concentration camps and the French who now claimed "not to know" what was being done in their name (Sartre 1957, 1642–47). *Les Temps modernes* also published its own exposés: reports by French soldiers who had returned from Algeria and were prepared to risk writing about what they had seen. See Pucheu (1957) and Tahon (1958).

my sleep, my moods." She added, surely without exaggeration, "my own situation in my country, in the world, in relation to myself, was shattered by it all" (FC II 87 TA; FC Fr II 120). The second volume of *Force of Circumstance*, published in 1963, covers the period from 1952 to 1962. Beauvoir began to write it in 1960, while the war was still going on, and Algerian independence was declared in July 1962, only eight months before she completed her narrative. Her account of her life from 1957 onward dwells almost continually on the war and its ramifications, both personal and political. Beauvoir was haunted by the ungraspable brutality of what was going on in Algeria, by the systematic use of torture as a tactic against a whole people—and above all by her sense of her own complicity in it as a French citizen. She began to see herself through the eyes of others, as one of the oppressors, and to realize that, in spite of herself, she really was! Experiencing the radical decentering of self and the shift to the perspective of the other that Harding, Lugones, and others urge, along with the overwhelming feelings of guilt that so often initially accompany it, Beauvoir writes the following:

> In 1957, the broken bones, the burns on the faces, on the genitals, the torn-out nails, the impalements, the cries of pain, the convulsions, they hit me. . . . I could no long bear my fellow citizens. . . . Whether I wanted to be or not, I was an accomplice of these people with whom I couldn't bear to jostle in the street. . . . I needed my self-esteem [*mon estime*] to go on living, and yet I was seeing myself through the eyes of women who had been raped twenty times, of men with broken bones, of crazed children: a Frenchwoman. . . . I wanted to stop being an accomplice in this war, but how? (FC II 89–91 TA; FC Fr II 122–26)

How indeed? As well as feeling intense personal guilt (far stronger than what Bartky calls "existential-moral guilt"), Beauvoir clearly experienced an immediate, indeed visceral, empathy with the acute physical suffering inflicted on others in the name of France, in her name. But her sense of her own complicity was overwhelming and thoroughly unproductive. Until 1960

Pucheu emphasized that torture became so routine that it seemed "normal" and that "indifference" became the soldiers' main attitude to it. However, while such reports circulated among the sections of the intelligentsia that read *Les Temps modernes* and similar journals, the mainstream media continued either to cover up torture and other atrocities or to treat them as the minor aberration of a few bad soldiers. Under emergency censorship laws several issues of *Les Temps modernes* were proscribed in Algeria, and the December 1957 issue, containing a report on the Algerian Resistance, was also banned in metropolitan France.

she found herself depressed and demobilized, and she felt she could not do much about the war. Later she criticized herself for her inactivity, commenting in *Force of Circumstance* that "today, however little I might effect the outcome, I could only throw all my weight into the struggle" (FC II 91–92 TA; FC Fr II 126). She also later criticized, as an "absurd maneuver," her initial dismissal of the clandestine support work that she knew Francis Jeanson, a former colleague at *Les Temps modernes*, was organizing. She told herself that people were engaging in underground activities only for dubious motives, such as a self-indulgent desire to assuage their own guilt (FC II 92; FC Fr II 127). She also says that she was not yet ready to appear a "traitor" in the eyes of her compatriots: "Something inside me—timidity, vestigial ideas—still prevented me from contemplating such a thing" (FC II 93 TA; FC Fr II 128).[18]

One might reasonably suggest that Beauvoir was guilty of bad faith in the late 1950s, of the self-evasion and "flight" from freedom and responsibility that she had criticized in others. By claiming that no appropriate action was open to her she was deliberately veiling from herself her refusal to act. And yet it is not that simple. For her case also bears out her own insistence that one's situation may profoundly suffuse one's subjectivity. One's situation, including one's privilege, may shape the self so profoundly that action that destroys it becomes threatening, perhaps even dangerously destructive, to self-identity. This may be one explanation—though certainly not the only one—as to why people so often cling to privilege. "I needed my self-esteem to go on living," Beauvoir had written. She was surely right, and her self-esteem was seriously undermined. However, if, as Beauvoir argues, our freedom is not sovereign or absolute, it follows also that bad faith is not an all-or-nothing affair but also a matter of degree.

Without embracing a crude chauvinism, Beauvoir was profoundly and consciously "French."[19] Born and raised in Paris, she lived there her entire life; the city, as built, social, and cultural space, was tightly woven into her existence. For Beauvoir's generation, the German Occupation during World War II had also heightened a positive sense of Frenchness. Under the eyes of the Germans, to be French was to have a despised identity that one needed proudly to affirm. Moreover, "France" stood in this context (its own

18. The name "traitor" of course had a very specific connotation in France for Beauvoir's generation: those who had collaborated with the Germans during the Occupation.

19. "It's a question of my country and I used to love it. . . . it's pretty hard to be against one's own country," she observed (FC II 130 TA; FC Fr II 177). While in a 1959 letter to her American lover, Nelson Algren, she wrote: "Now we don't feel we belong to this new kind of France; we are strangers in our own country" (1998, 528).

warts now paling into insignificance) for freedom and civilization, as the antithesis of Nazi brutality. Beauvoir's world was saturated with French culture, philosophy, history, and politics. After 1945 it revolved largely around *Les Temps modernes* and the people associated the journal. Although the sweep of *Les Temps modernes'* concerns and coverage was truly international, it saw its task primarily as engaging a *French* public and intervening in *French* public discourse. Thus, the degree of alienation Beauvoir felt from her compatriots over Algeria, as well as her simultaneous reluctance to be cast out as a "traitor," should not be dismissed as simply bad faith or as neurosis.[20] She was in the process of making the startling discovery that she was complicit—and it was initially overwhelming.

For now being French meant she was part of the oppressor nation.[21] It also meant that she was protected by privilege of birth from the risks of torture and death to which every Algerian woman, man, and even child was now subject. Like her compatriots, she also had the freedom to ignore what was being done and to distance herself from the suffering of others inflicted in her name. "I deserved their [Algerians'] hatred," she writes, "because I could still sleep, write, enjoy a walk or a book" (FC II 106; FC Fr II 145). She repeatedly made comparisons with the experience of the German Occupation. "I could feel the lump forming in my throat, the old impotent, raging disgust: exactly what I used to feel when I saw an SS man. French uniforms today were giving me the same shudder that

---

20. Toril Moi, for example, attributes the intensity of Beauvoir's feelings in large measure to the termination of her affair with Claude Lanzman in 1958 (Moi 1994, 240–41). But Beauvoir's crisis over Algeria began earlier than that and is explicable without adducing such extraneous factors. For a critical overview of claims that Beauvoir's reaction to the war was excessive, neurotic, or actually about something else, see Julien Murphy (1995, 276–79). It is important to understand how profoundly Beauvoir's previously stable sense of her world and of her place within it were being shattered at this time. This was a "metaphysical," or an "existential-moral," but not a neurotic crisis. Beauvoir was effecting the kind of displacement of self, the shift to the viewpoint of the other, that many later feminists have applauded—and it was acutely debilitating.

21. However, Beauvoir does not seem to have recognized her Frenchness as a form of whiteness. As we saw, she had been acutely aware of the privilege imparted by her white skin when traveling in the still-segregated American South in 1947 (ADD 202ff; AJJ 284ff). But once back in France, she did not engage reflexively with race as integral to her own identity even though she recognized racism as an element in the French treatment of Algerians. But, of course, when Frantz Fanon arrived in France in 1947 to study, a young black man who had French nationality and who thought of himself as "French," he very quickly discovered how white-raced "French" identity was (Fanon [1952] 1967)!

swastikas once did. . . . Yes, I was living in an occupied city, and I loathed the occupiers with more troubled intensity than those of the forties *because of all the ties that bound me to them* (FC II 106–107 TA; FC Fr II 146; my emphasis).[22]

These ties were real, and they were strongly constitutive of who she was. By this time Beauvoir could no more say "I am not French" than she could say "I am not a woman." But Beauvoir was not any or every French woman: She was a highly visible, intellectual French woman and a writer. In the opening pages of *The Second Sex* she had declared, "I am a woman." Now, in the epilogue to *Force of Circumstance*, she affirms, "I am a writer—a woman writer," continuing: "somebody whose whole existence is governed by her writing" (FC II 370; FC Fr II 495). The privileges of Beauvoir's status were considerable. They included not only material benefits but also the recognition and respect accorded to prominent intellectuals in France, and the epistemic privilege that accompanied this status.[23] As she became increasingly clear about her identity Beauvoir did not try to renounce these privileges. In spite of her ambivalence, did she not "work on herself" in an effort to become less "French," or to reject her own privileged culture, or her privileges as an intellectual.[24] Nor (as far as I know) did she attempt to "world"-travel. Her outrage at French violence and abuse did not move her to try to immerse herself in the lived experience of Algerians. Her strategy was very different. Aware of her privileged status, she instead learned to deploy it as a basis for effective, public, political intervention.

---

22. In his essay, "Albert Camus's Algerian War," Michael Walzer says he finds the depth of Beauvoir's reaction "slightly comic," and he argues that her attempt to "detach" herself from the French people was dangerous, leaving her uncaring about French casualties and indifferent to FLN-inflicted violence. "Wrenched loose from bourgeois France, unable to become Algerians, Sartre and Beauvoir see an ideologically flattened world. The FLN represents liberation, the French are fascists. . . . Reading the account of her Algerian years, one feels the force of E. M. Forster's injunction: 'Only connect!'" (Walzer 2002, 141–42). However, Beauvoir never wanted to "become" Algerian, and she recognized that she could not break the ties that bound her. Hers was the anguish of having a connection that one at once hates and loves.
23. In France, intellectuals have long been held in much higher esteem than in the United States or Britain. Beauvoir was what Foucault later dismissively called a "universal" intellectual— but such people were, and still remain, important in the shaping of French political discourse (and, arguably, Foucault was also one).
24. Later, in *All Said and Done* [1972], she remarked: "I do not believe in the universal and everlasting value of Western culture, but I have been nourished by it and I still love it. I hope it will not become obliterated but will, for the greater part, be handed on to rising generations" (ASD 209 TA; TCF 286).

By 1958 Beauvoir had overcome her earlier doubts about the importance of clandestine work, but she remained clear that she could not herself
participate in it. With considerable candidness she observed:

> If one wanted to remain faithful to one's anticolonialist convictions and break
> free of all complicity with this war, then underground action remained the only
> possible course. I admired those who took it. But to do so demanded total com-
> mitment, and it would have been cheating to pretend that I was capable of it. I
> am not a woman of action; my reason for living is writing; to sacrifice that I
> would have had to believe myself indispensable elsewhere. Such was not at all
> the case. (FC II 182–83 TA; FC Fr II 245–46)[25]

Now, however, one may not accuse Beauvoir of bad faith, for she is very
conscious of who she is and what she values. But she is also clear that in
making our decisions we do so as who we have "become." In her later autobiographical volume, *All Said and Done*, Beauvoir emphasizes the continuity of her life: She has lived for most of it, she says, "on rails" [*sur des rails*]
(ASD 12; TCF 24), for what she had done previously always seemed to propose her future actions to her. She writes: "I have never had to *ponder* over
important things. My life has been the fulfillment of an original project
and at the same time it has been the product and expression of the world in
which it has unfolded. . . . The past dwells in me and suffuses me" [*Le passé*

---

25. There were also practical reasons why Beauvoir could not engage in clandestine work: She was far too well known. By this time she could even not sit in a café
without being recognized; she was far too visible easily to shelter FLN militants or
to transport money or materials for them, as the "Jeanson Network" and others
were doing. Even so, Beauvoir did at times offer practical support to the "Network": She lent members her car and allowed her apartment to be used. On at
least one occasion, she helped to find a secure hiding place for a fugitive (Hamon
and Rotman 1982, 158, 283). The Jeanson Network consisted predominantly of
middle-class professionals whose engagement in clandestine support work was
motivated by a combination of moral outrage at French policies and commitment
to anticolonial struggle as a means of revitalizing the French Left. As Martin
Evans remarks in his history of the network: "It was not . . . French people who
ran the risk of being tortured. This was the plight of Algerians alone. For French
people, therefore, the dynamics of resistance to the Algerian war were more intellectual than experiential. Taking a stand against the war was a moral choice which
involved a long process of reflection. Central to this process was an ability to sym-
pathise with an experience which was not their own" (1997, 208–209). Beauvoir
would not be alone in developing a political commitment that was stimulated by
empathy with torture victims but which did not depend on (or inspire) an intensive politics of self-transformation.

m'habite et m'investit] (ASD 30–31 TA; TCF 47–49). How then, at fifty years of age, could she not have "chosen" herself as she now was, as a writer and public intellectual rather than a clandestine activist? Nothing had prepared her for the latter role. However, it was as a writer, with all the privileges of recognition and authoritative voice that it brought, that she began to develop effective forms of public political intervention.

The Politics of Deployment: Algeria

A call from Gisèle Halimi, anticolonialist, feminist, and an attorney, opened the path. Halimi was of Jewish Tunisian birth but a French national. She had already been involved in the defense of several Algerian torture victims. In May 1960 she contacted Beauvoir about a young woman FLN member called Djamila Boupacha. After her arrest on charges of planting a bomb in a café in Algiers, Djamila Boupacha had been repeatedly tortured over a period of several weeks and raped with a bottle before confessing to a crime she afterward said she had not committed. Halimi's main goals were to have Boupacha's case deferred and moved to France, where it might be heard more fairly than in Algeria, and to get her acquitted on the basis that there was no evidence against her other than her own extorted confession. With Halimi's encouragement Boupacha also filed countercharges against her (unknown) captors for illegal confinement and "corporal torture": The aim was not only to get Boupacha acquitted but also to bring a counterprosecution that would definitively prove in a court of law that torture was being used in Algeria. As it turned out, the counterprosecution was unable to proceed, and it was dropped when Boupacha was finally released after the war ended in 1962. Still, her case helped to shift the issue of torture from a matter that the public could choose, in willful ignorance, to disbelieve to one of indubitably established fact.

In order to pressure the French government, Halimi wanted to mount a highly public campaign. It was here that Beauvoir came in: Here was how she could use her privilege as a source of resistance. When Halimi contacted her and asked her to write about the case, Beauvoir immediately agreed. She simply tells us in *Force of Circumstance* that "I limited myself, more or less, to transcribing Djamila's own account of the affair and sent the article to *Le Monde*" (FC II 222; FC Fr II 299). She describes receiving a reproachful phone call from the newspaper: Boupacha looked to be a pretty suspicious character, and would Beauvoir mind not using the word "vagina" when talking about the rape "in case adolescents should read the article"? But Beauvoir does not appear to have been concerned that *Le Monde* might actually refuse to publish her article, and perhaps the thought did not even cross her mind. For access to this major national forum was self-evidently part of her privilege: Who would refuse to publish Simone de Beauvoir and run the risk of the uproar that would ensue? In the event, the June 3, 1960, issue of *Le Monde*, carrying her article, was seized and confiscated by the government in Algiers. The ensuing controversy and international outcry gave yet more publicity to the case.[26]

Beauvoir's article was, as she noted, primarily a summary of Djamila Boupacha's own legal deposition. However, Beauvoir's privileged position meant that her retelling of the tale functioned as a significant intervention in the formation of French political discourse. She reframed what many (if they even believed it) saw as an uncomfortable but peripheral "fact" of the Algerian war, the "regrettable" but perhaps "necessary" use of torture, as an issue that members of the reading French public had personally to confront.[27] In the final paragraphs Beauvoir bluntly asserted her readers' responsibility to pressure their government to end it. With an ironic inversion of the colonial trope, she insisted that it was inexcusable that Algeria be abandoned to the "savage caprices" of enraged settlers. If the law of France continued to be defied with impunity, she wrote, "it is France as a whole that would be betrayed; it is each one of us, it's me, it's you. For whether we have chosen those who rule us willingly or submit to them grudgingly, willy-nilly we find we are their accomplices" (1962a 197 TA; 1962b 223). By affirming her own complicity along with theirs, Beauvoir was appealing to her readers to join with her in collective opposition.

Beauvoir threw herself energetically into political activity. She was the moving force in immediately forming the "Committee for Djamila Boupacha."[28] She chaired its meetings, spoke in public. She was a member of the delegation that went to talk with the minister of justice, who alone had the power to

26. The case also received widespread international notice. There were articles in *Time-Life* in the United States and in the *Observer* in Britain.

27. Plus ça change! In the wake of the disclosures in spring 2004 of the "abuse" of Iraqi prisoners by U.S. soldiers, earnest discussion also ensued about whether the use of torture (although regrettable) might be justified. See, for example, the article "What's Wrong with Torturing a Qaeda Higher-Up?" in the *New York Times*, May 14, 2004, section 4, p. 4. Since then the debate about the alleged line between "harsh treatment" and "torture" in Guantanamo has been earnestly enjoined by pundits. Beauvoir's article was republished in Beauvoir and Halimi (1962a, 1962b), from where I cite it.

28. This is according to Halimi (2002, 294). As she presents it in *Force of Circumstance*, Beauvoir is more modest about her role.

move Boupacha's case from Algeria to France (which was later done). As in the instance of the *Le Monde* article, Beauvoir could use her privilege to help open doors. However, her goal was not simply to obtain the release of this one young woman or even to end the use of torture. She also wanted to help shift opinion in France against the war in Algeria and in favor of full independence. By 1961 Boupacha had been moved to France but was still in prison awaiting trial. It was decided that Halimi would write a book about the case, and Beauvoir agreed to serve as its coauthor.

The book, in French simply titled *Djamila Boupacha*, appeared in January 1962. It provided a damning exposé of the failures of the French legal system, as well as documenting the atrocious physical abuse to which Boupacha had been subjected. Under the emergency laws then in place the publication of such material was in fact illegal. Thus, although she had written only the introduction, Beauvoir agreed to assume full coauthorship with Halimi "in order to share the responsibility" (FC II 336; FC Fr II 449). Yet again she would use her privilege, here both to protect Halimi from prosecution and to ensure a wider audience for the book: an audience who now would have to confront the question of torture and the policies that allegedly "necessitated" it (Halimi 2002, 294).[29] The significance of the book, Beauvoir wrote in her introduction, was that it exposed "a lying propaganda machine so well constructed that during the past seven years it has let only a few faint glimmers of truth slip by it." Thus, she went on to say, it would enable the reader to understand "why these groans, these cries, these howls of agony that have so long been going up from Algerian soil—and indeed from France as well—have failed to reach your ears or, if they have, have been so faint that it took only a little bad faith [*un peu de mauvaise foi*] on your part to ignore them" (Beauvoir and Halimi 1962a, 10–11 TA; Beauvoir and Halimi 1962b, 2–3). The case did indeed stir up public opinion. Becoming a *cause célèbre*, it certainly contributed (although one cannot, of course, say how much) to the shift in public opinion that finally led to the positive referenda votes in support of Algerian independence.

---

29. In addition, from 1960 Beauvoir also began to engage in acts of highly public illegality. In 1960 she signed the "Manifesto of the 121." Planned to coincided with the trial of members of the Jeanson Network, this benchmark document signed by many prominent intellectuals ran afoul of emergency laws as it supported those being prosecuted for refusing to serve in the French army, as well as those assisting the Algerian independence movement. She also attended banned demonstrations. In addition to the threat of prosecution, Beauvoir also faced death threats, including one telephoned to the concierge at her apartment building the day after the book appeared.

The Ambiguities of Acting for Others

Elizabeth Spelman has argued (within the U.S. context) that white wom-
en's attention to the suffering of black women has often had an appropriat-
ing and self-serving strain. The "compassion" of the privileged for those at
whose expense their privilege has come threatens further to reproduce the
existing dynamics: "People [who are] enjoying being in the saddle of compassion may have disincentives to cancel the suffering that provides the
ride. . . . [T]he means by which attention is brought to suffering may prolong or deepen it rather than alleviate it" (1997, 158–59), she warns.[30] She
is critical of those "whose interest in excelling at being empathetic or compassionate dwarfs careful solicitude for the objects of their care" (161). This
may well be the case on some occasions, but what conclusions should one
draw from Spelman's warning? Should white women (or members of other
privileged groups) then refrain from acting on behalf of others lest they
become guilty of reaffirming their own privilege? In some instances, silence
and inactivity may well be the best course for the privileged to follow, especially when an underprivileged group has become capable of articulating its
own demands. In other instances, however, when the oppressed cannot
speak or cannot speak as effectively, or when one is asked to be an ally, the
better use of privilege may well be to deploy it in order to speak and act for
others. Spelman rightly draws our attention to the dangers of yet another
form of possible self-referentiality on the part of the privileged progressive. However, it is not *necessarily* the case that acting for self-referential
motives will "prolong or deepen" the oppression of others. Sometimes the
purity of our motives may not greatly matter as long as our actions are (on
balance) likely to be of benefit to those we support.

We often act from multiple motives, some self-serving, some principled,
some compassionate, some habitual, and so forth. Moreover, our actions
are likely to contribute to multiple events and processes and to carry multivocal significations. A reluctance to acknowledge such ambiguities—what
Beauvoir had called the "dream of purity"—inhabits Spelman's critique of
white women's actions, as well as the exhortations of others that we "work
on ourselves" to expunge our privileged ways of being. Such purism is based, as I have argued, on views of agency, guilt, and responsibility that are

---

30. Beauvoir perhaps voices some similar concerns in her remarks on the dangers of charity: "There is nothing more arbitrary than intervening as a stranger in
a destiny which is not ours: one of the shocking things about charity . . . is that it
is exercised from the outside, according to the caprice of the one who distributes
it and who is detached from its object" (EA 86 TA; PMA 121).

too all-or-nothing, too ambiguity-averse; and these are, in turn, grounded in problematic assumptions about the autonomy of the self.

Beauvoir had argued in *The Ethics of Ambiguity* and elsewhere that it is not always possible to treat others as "ends in themselves." Against the abstract humanist and the moral idealist, she had argued that, in the imperfect world of politics, objectifying others—even those whom one aims to support—may be unavoidable. Boupacha was objectified by Beauvoir and Halimi throughout their campaign on her behalf. For, although Halimi says she consulted with Boupacha, she and Beauvoir were the ones who made the final decisions about how Boupacha would be represented to the French public. Speaking for her from their position of privilege, they carefully chose how to portray Boupacha, selecting the tropes that would most arouse public empathy and concern. In the book they present her as a violated young virgin; a loving member of a loving family; a "modern" young Algerian woman. A sketch by Picasso (the frontispiece of the book), followed by a full-page photographic portrait, presents her with her head uncovered and looking directly at the viewer: She is no veiled "Oriental" woman but rather, it is implied, could be the French reader's own daughter.[31] Of course, locked away in jail and awaiting trial, Boupacha had to rely on others to speak for her. We do not know what Boupacha thought about the ways in which Beauvoir and Halimi chose to represent her, and she may for all we know have been quite uncomfortable with them. Yet even if she was, theirs was a reasonable strategy to help secure her release, as well as to mount a wider critique of French policies in Algeria.[32] To speak for others is

---

31. The photographic portrait is absent from the U.S. English translation, as are some smaller photos, including one of Boupacha in her nurse assistant's uniform. Other artwork is also omitted from this translation, while a photo of her stroking a camel against a desert background has been added! For the most part, women who were FLN militants chose not to wear a veil.

32. See Murphy (1995) for an excellent (and a fuller) discussion of the complexities of how Boupacha was represented. As the case progressed, the press (in both Algeria and France) presented Boupacha not only as a "native" and a violent "terrorist" but also as a fallen, promiscuous Muslim woman (for whom the alleged rape would not really matter since she was not a virgin anyhow). Thus, Beauvoir and Halimi needed to work against both Orientalist and sexist stereotypes to make Boupacha's humanity "visible." They needed to communicate the horrendous nature of her ordeal in ways that did not reduce her to an Oriental "Other" but drew sympathy for and a sense of connection with her from the (male, middle-class) French reader. To do so they emphasized her middle-class background, her youth, and her attractiveness. Thus, Murphy perceptively observes, "the subtext of Beauvoir's writings played upon class solidarity and paternalism (the sufferings of a young girl) to attack racist imperialism and misogyny" (1995, 288). This was hardly an "ideal" strategy—but then no ideal strategy was possible.

sometimes necessary, but it is naïve to think that in doing so one will be merely a transparent medium or a simple mouthpiece: Who one is and to whom one communicates will shape the import of the message one transmits.

However, Beauvoir also engaged in a form of objectifying appropriation that may have been more problematic. Frantz Fanon had bitterly complained about French intellectuals who protested about atrocities in Algeria only because of the corrupting effect they were having on the *French*: "The gravity of the tortures, the horrors of the rape of little Algerian girls, are perceived because their existence threatens a certain idea of French honor," he wrote. In the process, the Algerian victims were shut out of consideration in "that form of egocentric, sociocentric thinking which has become a characteristic of the French" ([1964] 1988, 71). Although these accusations were not aimed at Beauvoir's role in the Boupacha affair—and arguably would have been wide of the mark had they been—still a certain appeal to restoring French moral integrity was a part of Beauvoir's strategy. Thus, as we saw, at the end of her article in *Le Monde*, Beauvoir's appeal for action was also cast as an appeal to rescue *France*. The government must not be allowed to "betray" France—that is, to betray all the good that "France" signifies—by its failure to curb the atrocities. Beauvoir's appeal to patriotic ends in order to engage her readers was a deliberate rhetorical strategy on her part. It may also have been an expression of her own feelings since, as we saw, her own self-esteem was at risk. Irrespective of her motives, it was surely a highly effective strategy to mobilize public opinion, yet it did also function in the self-referential way that Fanon had described. It appropriated Boupacha and Algerians more generally insofar as it deflected attention away from them and back to the needs of France: It did center attention on the lost virtue of France. In an ideal world, Beauvoir surely would not have used such a strategy. However, in the context of the Algerian War, where the government was using a rhetoric of patriotism to justify its policies, to take up this patriotism and turn it against itself was, at the least, a defensible move on her part. I do not want to say that Beauvoir was "right" or, of course, that the end routinely justifies any means. Rather, my point here is that her own political interventions bear out her insistence on the necessary ambiguity of action in politics.[33]

---

33. Mary Caputi has considered whether the charges of "egocentrism" and self-referential patriotism that Fanon made against "concerned" French intellectuals also apply to Beauvoir and she concludes that they do not. Caputi argues that her actions on behalf of Boupacha "reveal Beauvoir's desire to come to the latter's aid for her own sake" (2006, 125). I am less convinced than Caputi that Beauvoir did greatly care about assisting Boupacha for the latter's "own sake." However, this

There was another tension that arose, one that was to divide Beauvoir and Halimi. For Beauvoir's concerns were not only to bring about Boupacha's release and to shock the French public out of their willful ignorance of the use of torture. Far more than Halimi, Beauvoir also saw this as wider political intervention; it was an act of solidarity in support of the FLN, which was the main anticolonial resistance movement (and, by July of 1962, the official government) in Algeria. However, if Beauvoir felt entitled to use her privilege to intervene as a French citizen in French politics, she did not consider she was justified in intervening in the internal affairs of the FLN. According to Halimi, (who later wrote of these events in her own autobiography), after Boupacha was released from prison later in 1962, FLN militants in France ordered her to go back to Algeria, and they threatened to take her there by force if she refused. Boupacha was emphatic that she did not want to go. She did not want to be sent back to her "woman's life" there, she said; the "brothers" would not allow women in the new government and would give women no power, and she herself would have no possibility to continue her education there (Halimi 1988, 319). Shortly afterward Boupacha was entrapped into a meeting with FLN members, and was indeed abducted and forcibly returned by them to Algeria. Halimi, horrified, asked Beauvoir to intervene. But Beauvoir refused. The FLN had the right to tell its militants what to do, she said. It was not appropriate for her and Halimi, as French women, to interfere (321). Upset by Beauvoir's indifference to Boupacha's plight, Halimi later complained that Beauvoir had merely used Boupacha to further a wider political agenda. She wrote that Beauvoir "considered Djamila as one victim among thousands, a useful 'case' to conduct the battle against torture and the war" (317); she said that Beauvoir did not "care" about Boupacha as an individual who had suffered greatly, and that she did not even show any interest in meeting her.

Halimi's diagnosis of Beauvoir's priorities was probably accurate. Beauvoir, in turn, was clear that Halimi's compassion for and personal attachment to Boupacha could not justify overriding the boundaries of their appropriate sphere of action. Beauvoir would speak out for Boupacha against her own government but not against an independence movement that she supported, since to create an outcry over Boupacha's treatment by the FLN might have played dangerously into the hands of the French Right. Here, care for the well-being of a particular individual became pitted against support for a

---

does not mean that Beauvoir's goals in involving herself in Boupacha's case were egocentric. Rather (as I discuss below), it means that she was more concerned about broader political issues than about the fate of one particular individual.

movement for social and political liberation.[34] Before Boupacha's release
the two had aligned easily, but now they split apart. It is interesting in light
of later feminist advocacy of an "ethics of care," as well as Beauvoir's own
insistence on the importance of attending to selves in their particularity,
that her choice was that of solidarity with the wider political movement
rather than concern for the individual. She aligned herself with a movement of the oppressed against an oppression in which she herself was complicit; her project was only to use her privilege on their behalf. But there
were paradoxes here, too. As Boupacha had noted, the FLN "brothers" were
not exactly attuned to the issue of women's equality.[35] Nor were they sensitive to the fear of going back to Algeria experienced by a young woman
militant who felt herself to be defiled after her rape by French soldiers.[36] In
supporting the FLN Beauvoir was remaining silent about oppressive gender
relations. Yet again we see how failures inhabits action and how judgments
must often be made among incommensurable ends.[37]

---

34. By the time of the Boupacha case the FLN was the main movement in the
struggle for independence in Algeria, and Beauvoir regarded it as a force for freedom and justice. Others have criticized the FLN for its use of violence not only
against the military but also against French civilians in Algeria. Beauvoir defended
such violence as necessary in the face of French intransigence and violence, as did
Sartre and Fanon. However, she does not appear to have shared the belief in the
creative qualities of revolutionary violence that Fanon affirmed in *The Wretched of
the Earth* ([1961] 1963) and that Sartre endorsed in his preface to Fanon's book.

35. Many women participated in the struggle for independence, mainly in noncom-
batant roles. Frantz Fanon's optimism that the war would contribute to the eman-
cipation of Algerian women (Fanon [1959] 1989) was not, in the event, justified.
Beauvoir later expressed her anger at the condition of women in post-independence
Algeria, commenting that "Fanon thought they would become emancipated after the
Algerian war. On the contrary, they have been crushed" (cited in Moorehead 1974).
For a detailed study of the Algerian women during and after the independence strug-
gle see Lazreg (1994).

36. Halimi recounts how concerned with this question Boupacha was during
their first meeting: "She came closer and said: 'my parents don't know. I mean,
they *know*, but they don't know everything. Not about the bottle. I haven't said
anything about that to them. For people like us it's such a dreadful thing—'. . . .
Then she asked me a question she must have asked herself already, a hundred
times over: 'What do you think? That I'm no longer a virgin? Tell me frankly—
what's *your* opinion?'" (1962a, 31; 1962b, 24).

37. In the event, Beauvoir's refusal to help Boupacha turns out not to have had
such negative consequences as Halimi anticipated. Although Boupacha feared she
would be regarded as sullied and would never find a husband, according to Halimi
she met and married an FLN militant shortly after her return to Algeria. She had
children and seems to have lived a satisfying life (communication from Halimi at

"I Am a Profiteer"

Reflecting back over her life, in the epilogue to *Force of Circumstance* Beauvoir meditates on the privileges she enjoys. She focuses here less directly on her Frenchness than on her wealth, social status, and enjoyment of the fruits of high culture. "Economically I belong to a privileged class," she writes (FC II 373; FC Fr II 500), and even more bluntly, "I am a profiteer" (FC II 374; FC Fr II 501). Beauvoir has earned a great deal of money from her books, and she lives in comfort and financial security. On the one hand, this is a reward for her own talents and efforts, but on the other hand she realizes that she was able to develop these talents only because of her class privilege and other accidents of birth: "I am a profiteer primarily because of the education I received and the possibilities it opened up for me" (ibid.). For Beauvoir, what some would straightforwardly regard as their just entitlement is not unproblematically so. For, in becoming who one is, one always takes up, in one way or another, the ascriptions given to one at birth and the possibilities assigned to one in childhood. In Beauvoir's case, although of course the extensive education she received did not by itself make her a "well-known writer," she recognizes that without it she would not have become one: "Earned reward" and "privilege" cannot easily be separated.

Faced with her own privileges, Beauvoir addresses questions about the responsibility and complicity of a "situated" self. She concludes that, in an unjust world, the privileged are unable to avoid elements of complicity. She writes: "When one lives in an unjust world there is no use hoping by some means to *purify* oneself of that injustice; what is necessary is to change the world, and I don't have the capacity. To suffer from these contradictions serves no good purpose; to forget about them is to lie to oneself" (FC II 374–75 TA; FC Fr II 501; my emphasis). Lying to oneself, the bad faith refusal of the willfully ignorant to acknowledge their complicity is unacceptable to Beauvoir: We should indeed try to see the world from viewpoints beyond the confines of our own privilege. However, to engage in a politics that aims at doing so primarily in order to "purify" ourselves, in the hope of ridding ourselves of our privilege, is problematic.

---

the conference "De Beauvoir à Sartre: de Sartre à Beauvoir," Paris, June 2003). When a special issue of *Les Temps modernes* was being prepared to commemorate the centennial of Beauvoir's birth in 2008, Boupacha was contacted in Algiers by Wassyla Tamzali. Tamzali requested an interview with her to discuss her experiences and her views on Beauvoir. However, Boupacha refused, saying: "I don't want to talk about that period, I want to forget, it is too painful" (cited in Tamzali 2008, 290).

And what of "changing the world"? Beauvoir said she did not know how to do so, and of course nobody produces change alone. In actuality, Beauvoir supported a project of decolonization that did bring about very significant changes in the world (not all of them perhaps for the best). Furthermore, without "working on herself" or attempting to shed her privileges, she did also change herself in the process of working with and for others. Not only was she now aware of her privileges in a way she had not been in 1955, but after Algeria she also went on to use them in support of a range of other movements. She would directly lend her voice and status to a variety of international and domestic struggles. These included (among others) participation in 1967 in the Russell Tribunal on U.S. war crimes in Vietnam; supporting Maoist groupings after May 1968; and assuming the editorship of their periodical, *L'Idiot international* (threatened with government suppression) in 1970 and 1971. During the 1970s Beauvoir participated extensively in the growing women's liberation movement in France, notably with regard to the struggle for reproductive rights.

Beauvoir's feminist activities included assuming the presidency not only of the reproductive-rights organization Choisir [To Choose] but also that of the Ligue des droits des femmes [League of Women's Rights], writing, speaking, and organizing on behalf of both. She signed the "Manifesto of the 343," in which she and many others announced that they had undergone illegal abortions, again offering protection from prosecution for those who did not have her stature. She also opened the pages of *Les Temps modernes* to a group of younger feminists who, from 1973 to 1979, ran a monthly column titled "Le sexisme ordinaire" [Ordinary Sexism], in which sexist and discriminatory items from the press, government sources, and so forth were published and ridiculed.[38] In 1979 she offered public support for Iranian feminists when the newly successful Islamic revolution (much celebrated by Foucault and other leftist intellectuals in France) demanded that women wear the veil. Even during the last few years of her life, years deeply marred by Sartre's death in 1980, quarrels over his literary estate, and her own ill health, she remained politically active. She continued to write in support of numerous radical causes internationally, gave financial support to battered-women's shelters, and served as the honorary chair and was an active member of the Commission Femme et Culture [Commission on Women and Culture] of the new Ministry for the Rights of Women, established by the Mitterrand government in 1981 (Bair 1990, 602–604).

---

38. On Beauvoir's supportive role in this endeavor see Kandell (2008).

Of course, Beauvoir's life was far from typical. But what her story teaches is that the tendency of privileged progressives to fixate on disclosing and overcoming their personal privilege needs to be complemented, or sometimes even countered, by another politics in which privilege is usefully deployed rather than introspectively dissected and "worked on." White civil-rights activists in the South in the 1960s, men who defend abortion clinics against threats of violence, and educated middle-class activists who put their writing skills at the service of less-educated, underprivileged groups offer some other examples. In each of these instances, however, there are ways in which the actions of the privileged are ambiguous in their benefits. They may, for example, risk casting blacks, women, and/or the less educated as inferiors and as objects of condescension.

As Beauvoir's actions indicate and her writings argue, there will always be risks to progressive political action: risks that one will reinscribe one's own privilege, objectify those one supports, or be required to prioritize one valued goal at the expense of another. The "dream of purity," whether it be the moral purity of the self or the purity of the ends pursued, and whether within a politics of self-transformation or one that seeks to deploy privilege in support of others, is a dangerous chimera. It may overwhelm us with guilt, make us become self-righteous, or demobilize us because we fear our inevitable failures. Thus, Beauvoir returns us yet again to the importance of acknowledging the ambiguity of politics. In doing so she also raises questions about how we arrive at our political choices in a world where right and wrong are not always clear-cut and where good intentions may have harmful outcomes. Such questions concerning political judgments are taken up more fully in the next chapter.

4

Dilemmas of Political Judgment

"Surely politics is made with the head, but it is certainly not made with the head alone," insisted Max Weber.[1] Contrary to Weber, most accounts of what constitutes political judgment presuppose that it must be made with the head alone. Judgment is deemed to be, par excellence, a matter of cognition, of cool, dispassionate reasoning, uncontaminated by the nonrational elements of the human psyche. For example, Peter Steinberger writes that effective political judgment endeavors "to cast upon the dim, disorienting landscape of the public realm the cold light of critical reason" (1993, 304). It follows that decisions in which emotions, affects, dispositions, habits, and so forth play a significant part are not considered to be judgments "proper." For such nonconceptual elements are deemed to be but unfortunate intrusions that contaminate and destroy judgment unless cold reason rightly overcomes them.

Chief among rationalist models of political judgment are those that build on Kant's account of "determinate judgment," where judging is conceived as an inferential process that correctly subsumes particulars under a universal. This is an account of judgment upon which (as we saw in chapter 1) Beauvoir casts profound doubt, especially as it purports to explain how we should resolve ethical and political dilemmas. For, like the abstract humanism that it so often accompanies, it is inattentive to the nonconceptual, embodied, and factic qualities of the self that must also enter into making such judgments. In addition, because the ends we value will often be incommensurable, conflicts among them cannot be resolved by subsuming

---

1. In "Politics as a Vocation." The essay was based on a lecture Weber gave in Germany in 1918, as attempted revolution swirled around him (1958, 127).

them under a more universal principle such as the categorical imperative or even under some less rigorous regulative ideal.[2] However carefully we deliberate we will still ultimately have to make a choice that cannot be arrived at by inference alone. This is to say that since judgments are, in the final analysis, acts of situated freedom they must exceed the application of principle. To recall, Beauvoir had written in *Pyrrhus and Cinéas*:

> What is good for different men differs. Working for some often means working against others. One cannot stop at this tranquil solution: wanting *the* good of *all* men. We must define *our* own good. The error of Kantian ethics is to have claimed to make an abstraction of our own presence in the world. Therefore, it leads only to abstract formulas. *The respect of the human person in general cannot suffice to guide us because we are dealing with separate and opposed individuals.* (PC 127; PC Fr 91; my emphasis in the last sentence)

Neo-Kantian accounts of judgment have become less pervasive since Beauvoir was writing, but they still widely persist. Thus, in his much-cited work, Steinberger defines judgment as in general "the mental activity in virtue of which we predicate universals of particulars," and he argues that *political* judgment is but a subset of this kind of activity: "When an activity occurs in a political setting with respect to universals and particulars of a political nature, then we have political judgment" (1993, vii). Steinberger offers what one might call a "soft" version of determinate judgment in politics, however, since he acknowledges that we do not always go through such a formal procedure of inference when we are actually in the process of arriving at a political judgment. Frequently (as Aristotle had observed of "practical wisdom") we rely instead on a stock of "common sense" or even on what we might call "intuition" as we arrive at a judgment. However, Steinberger insists that for a decision to have the status of a judgment "proper" it must be an instance of what he calls "intelligent performance" such that, if asked to do so, we could fully and coherently reconstruct it *post festum* on the determinate model. If a decision cannot be so justified after the event, then it is, he says, "more like a nervous tic, a biochemical reaction, a mechanical response to an external stimulus; it is the behavior of an

---

2. As Beiner points out, "One cannot 'prove' one's judgment was the right one; if one could furnish a proof, one would have a patent case of determinant judgment. But while one does not possess such a proof one can point to various features of the particular situation that justify one's choice . . . since the range of possible features that can be appealed to is virtually boundless—or generally so—the meaning of the situation is not univocal, but rather, multivocal" (1983, 132).

animal or a machine, not an intelligent performance" (238). Such a claim presumes a mind-body dualism and a conception of the self as the sovereign bearer of rational autonomy, which Beauvoir's account of the ambiguity of embodied subjectivity rightly challenges.

Similarly rationalistic assumptions subtend other commonly held views of political judgment. Those premised on rational choice theory or on utilitarian principles generally posit judgment as a process of correct inference about the best means to attain already-given ends such as self-interest or well-being. While Habermasian and Rawlsian accounts of "communicative action" and "public reason," respectively, both demand that we exclude what they consider to be nonrational elements from political deliberation and judgment proper. For Rawls, for example, the proper exercise of political power must accord with determinate constitutional principles, and its exercise should consist in actions that "all citizens as free and equal may reasonably be expected to endorse in the light of principles and ideals acceptable to their common human reason" (Rawls 1993, 137);[3] while, for Habermas, ideal, illocutionary speech must be devoid of passions and interests, and he explicitly excludes from communicative "action" proper what he calls the bodily "movements" that may accompany it.[4]

---

3. In his plea for a more "realist" style of political theorizing, one that is more attentive to context, contingency, and power, Geuss especially criticizes Rawlsian liberalism for its commitment to "ideal" theory and for what he calls an "ethics first" orientation to politics. He objects to what is still the preeminent commitment among political theorists and philosophers: to start thinking about politics by establishing determinate principles of equality, justice, and so forth, against which particular judgments and actions may then be evaluated. A more realist approach, he writes, would instead acknowledge that "politics is a craft or a skill, and ought precisely not to be analysed, as Plato's Socrates assumes, as the mastery of a set of principles or theories" (2008, 97). In contrast to Geuss, Ferrara is more sanguine that a new and better configuration is now emerging between the old "subsumptive" model of political judgment as "context transcending" and more recent postmodern theories that do not accept notions of "trans-contextual validity." Ferrara is surely right that poststructuralist critiques offer a serious challenge to the foundations of ideal theory. However, few ideal theorists actually engage with poststructuralism, and I think Ferrara underestimates the persistence of "context transcending" theories of judgment such as Rawls's (Ferrara 1999, especially x).

4. Positing a strong mind-body dualism that denies a place for embodied intentionality, Habermas writes:

Under the aspect of observable events in the world, actions appear as bodily movements of an organism. Controlled by the central nervous system, these movements are the substratum in which action is carried out . . . In a certain sense, actions are realized through movements of the body, but only in such a

What all of these accounts presume is that a definitive boundary exists between mind and body, between cognition as a transcendent rational faculty and those elements of human life that are less conscious, more embodied, more affective. They all espouse, whether explicitly or not, what Elizabeth Spelman has nicely characterized as the "dumb view" of emotions: the view that emotions are simply lacking in any cognitive significance.[5] However, as Weber insists, far more than "the head" is involved in arriving at political judgments. Indeed, we most often "think" with our entire being, and our judgments are, de facto, affectively inflected. Furthermore, even if we were able to make fully dispassionate judgments, we would still not be able definitively to resolve many of the issues about which we must arrive at decisions, for alternative conclusions may often be equally reasonable. Thus (in addition to being inflected by emotion, affect, and so forth), insofar as they are rational cognitive practices, judgments must more often be described as *informed and reasonable guesses* than as strictly rational inferences. We must consider political judgment—the process of arriving at such reasonable guesses—to be an *essentially* ambiguous activity and one that, like all human action, is open to failure. Beauvoir's comment, "without failure, no ethics" (EA 10; PMA 16) equally applies to political judgments—hence, the significance of her claim that the judgments we make in politics are a "wager" *as well as* a "decision" (EA 148; PMA 207).[6] But *how* we come to arrive at these wagers is the question I want to explore.

---

way that the actor, in following a technical or social rule, *concomitantly executes* these movements. Concomitant execution means that the actor intends an action but not the bodily movement with the help of which he realizes it. *A bodily movement is an element of an action but not an action.* (1984, 96–97)

5. Spelman describes the "dumb view" as one for which "emotions are like feelings of dizziness or spasms of pain since they do not involve any cognitive state. According to this view emotions are, quite literally dumb events" (1989, 263–73). Steinberger, it should be recalled, described those decisions that cannot be wholly rationally reconstructed as "more like a nervous tic, a biochemical reaction" (1993, 238). Against the "dumb view" Spelman defends an enlarged "cognitivist" approach. She argues that emotions do not only involve their own kinds of cognition but also carry moral judgments. For example, she notes, we deem anger to be an appropriate emotional response to an injustice; grief to a death, and so forth.

6. Merleau-Ponty, in an allied vein, refers to this wagering as "faith": "Faith—in the sense of an unreserved commitment which is never completely justified—enters the picture as soon as we leave the realm of pure geometrical ideas and have to deal with the existing world." He adds, however, that "If commitment goes beyond reason, it should never run contrary to reason itself" ([1945] 1964a, 179).

Hannah Arendt's account of political judgment, which has received considerable attention of late, goes some way toward acknowledging the ambiguity of judgment. Drawing on the idea of "reflective judgment," which the later Kant developed with regard to aesthetic evaluations, Arendt argues that political judgment is a faculty of discrimination akin to "taste."[7] Political judgments, analogous to those of aesthetic taste, are "opinions," she says. However, they are not purely subjective opinions because they must also have the potential to persuade others. As such they must be validated not by the criteria of abstract reason but, potentially, by the specific "public" to which they are addressed. She writes: "The power of judgment rests on a potential agreement with others, and the thinking process which is active in judging something is not like the thought process of pure reasoning, a dialogue between me and myself, but finds itself always and primarily, even if am quite alone in making up my mind, in an anticipated communication with others with whom I must finally come to some agreement. From this potential agreement derives its specific validity" (1977, 220). Judgment is not, then, arbitrary or wholly subjective, but neither is it, *pace* Steinberger and others, one and the same as formal inference, or "pure reasoning." Arendt also argues that, in judging, one discloses one's particular self: In a person's manner of judging, she says, the *"who one is"* becomes manifest (1958, 223; my emphasis). Judging is an important aspect of what Arendt calls "action": "In acting and speaking, men show who they are, reveal actively their unique personal identities and thus make their appearance in the human world . . . this disclosure of 'who' in contradistinction to 'what' somebody is—his qualities, gifts, talents, and shortcomings, which he may display or hide—is implicit in everything somebody says or does" (179).

Here, then, we have a conception of political judgment that is far more concrete and situated than those previously discussed. It is also intrinsically bound up with freedom, and Arendt, like Beauvoir, insists that freedom is possible only through our being in the world with others. For Arendt, as for Beauvoir, freedom is not to be equated with autonomy or the "sovereign" self: "If it were true that sovereignty and freedom are the

---

7. Arendt treated the question of judgment on many different occasions and with differing framings and emphases. There is a difference in stance between her earlier work, which dwells on judgment from the perspective of the political actor, and her later work (notably her 1970 "Lectures on Kant's Political Philosophy"), which operates primarily from the stance of the spectator. My concern here, of course, is with the judgment of the political actor, and I draw on essays collected in *Between Past and Future* (1977).

same, then indeed no man could be free, because sovereignty, the ideal of uncompromising self-sufficiency and mastership, is contradictory to the very condition of plurality. No man can be sovereign because not one man, but men, inhabit the earth" (234). For Arendt, freedom (the initiating of new beginnings, which she calls "natality") is possible only within the human multiplicity, which she describes as "the paradoxical plurality of unique beings" (176). Arendt repeatedly tried to distance herself from "existentialism," which she dismissed as "at least in its French version . . . primarily an escape into the unquestioning commitment of action" (1977, 8). However, her notions of freedom and plurality share striking affinities with Beauvoir, when the latter insists that the world would be meaningless without others and that freedom becomes possible only in concrete relations among men. "It is not impersonal, universal man who is the source of values, but the plurality of concrete, particular men projecting themselves toward their own ends," Beauvoir writes (EA 17 TA; PMA 26), and "man can find a justification of his own existence only in the existence of other men" (EA 72; PMA 101–102).[8]

However, the "who one is" still remains overly identified with the intellect in Arendt's account. Political judgment, she argues, requires us to achieve what she called an "enlarged mentality." It requires us to engage in

---

8. Arendt took pains to distance herself from French existentialism, but what gives rise to such affinities is Heidegger's influence on the thought of both Arendt and the French existentialists. There are strong family resemblances here but also philosophical family quarrels—not to mention political ones. For Arendt in no way shared Sartre's and Beauvoir's sympathy for socialism or hostility to the United States. In her 1946 essay titled "What Is Existenz Philosophy?" Arendt explicitly excluded French existentialism from philosophical consideration, characterizing it as "a French literary movement of the last decade" (1946b, 34). She also treated it as only a literary movement in a short essay she wrote for *The Nation* at about the same time. Although she was positive about the literary merits of Sartre and Camus and the novelty of their ideas (she does not mention Beauvoir), she ended by warning that they risked nihilism (1946a, 228). Arendt personally disliked Sartre, describing him in a letter to Karl Jaspers as "too typically a Frenchman, much too literary, in a way too talented, too ambitious" (Arendt and Jaspers 1992, 66). She also told the editor of *Partisan Review*, when he met with Beauvoir while she was in New York in 1947, that "the trouble with you, William, is that you don't realize she's not very bright. Instead of arguing with her . . . you should flirt with her" (cited in Brightman 1992, 330). Arendt's dismissal of Beauvoir notwithstanding, much interesting work remains to be done in exploring both the affinities and the disparities in their thinking. For a thoughtful discussion of how both conceive of philosophy as a means of engaging daily life see Blanchard (2004).

"representative thinking," in "being and thinking in my own identity where actually I am not" (1977, 241). We must, as she also put it, be able "to think in the place of everybody else" (220), thereby encompassing more viewpoints and being able to appeal to a wider community to validate our judgments. Such an imaginative endeavor to think in the place of others is certainly an important component of political judgment.[9] However, as Arendt characterizes it, representative thinking remains located too much in the head, and it demands that we shed our particularities more fully than is often possible. "Such judgment," Arendt writes, "must liberate itself from the 'subjective private conditions,' that is, from the idiosyncrasies which naturally determine the outlook of each individual in his privacy and are legitimate as long as they are only privately held opinions, but which are not fit to enter the market place, and lack all validity in the public realm" (ibid.).

It is not the case that one can shed what Arendt here calls "idiosyncrasies." Nor may "who one is" in public as easily be detached from one's "subjective private conditions" as she assumes here.[10] This is certainly not to deny the value of representative thinking but rather to acknowledge that it will necessarily remain incomplete, unable fully to transcend the facticities that suffuse a particular life. Furthermore, it is misguided to regard such facticities as flaws that cause our judgments to "lack all validity in the public realm." To the contrary, as Beauvoir argues, they are constitutive of the very personhood without which we simply would not be able to engage in judgment at all. No, politics is not made with the head alone. But this being so, it is necessary to examine political judgment with regard not only to its explicit deliberative aspects but also its wider "lived" qualities. Political judgment needs also to be considered phenomenologically: as the unfolding of the lived experience of deliberating, deciding, and acting within the complex, shifting field of possibilities and constraints that is the world of politics. Such an account will reveal the activity of judging to involve far more than representative thinking; it is also an expression of a person's particular way of being in the world.

---

9. As Linda Zerilli argues, the "outsideness" of representative thinking may also enable us to form judgments about other cultures that will avoid the twin perils of a false universalism (where we fail to think outside ourselves) and a dangerous slide into relativism (where we cease to remain at all anchored in our own world and its values) (Zerilli 2009).

10. Arendt's much criticized insistence on a radical disjuncture between public and private worlds reemerges here, but now with specific regard to the judging self. She supposes such a self to be operating only in what, in *The Human Condition* (1958), she calls the world of "action."

Literature and Judgment

Beauvoir did not set out a systematic account of what she took political judgment to involve, although one is implied in her moral period essays (in her account of the ambiguities of ethical choice and her critique of abstract rationalism). However, she offers a rich phenomenology of political judgment in her novel *The Mandarins*. Published in 1954 and the winner of the prestigious literary award, the Prix Goncourt, *The Mandarins* presents in fictional and yet quasi autobiographical form a tapestry of the lives of a group of non-Communist but left-wing intellectuals in Paris, such as Beauvoir belonged to in the immediate postwar period. Against the backdrop of liberation from the Nazi Occupation, the emerging Cold War, and the consequent very real fear that a third world war would be fought on European soil, she sketches their lives and loves and—above all—their political dilemmas, the judgments they arrive at with regard to these dilemmas, and their subsequent actions. Although the political moment depicted in the novel is long past and the hopes and fears of the characters often seem (with hindsight) naïve, the work remains a rich resource for examining the ambiguities of political judgment.

My project here is not to offer a post hoc evaluation of the actual political positions that Beauvoir and her circle espoused in the postwar period[11] but rather to draw on what she called her "evocation" of the period in order to explore some of the complexities of how political judgments come to be made. For, as Beauvoir herself argues, literature offers a mode of "knowing" that is an important alternative to abstract rationalism. It can be, as she puts it, "a privileged site of intersubjectivity" that enables one to enter another "world," even as one remains within one's own. What distinguishes

---

11. Later evaluations of the political positions espoused by the *Temps modernes* group in this period have ranged from the sympathetic to the highly critical, depending on the evaluators' own political viewpoints. Thus, for example, McBride is sympathetic to their anti-Americanism, and he also concurs with the view put forward by Beauvoir's main protagonists in the novel (and that correspond to her and Sartre's own view), that there were no other realistic alternatives open to the French Left than to support the Soviet Union and the French Communist Party. For, even though flawed, they provided the main counterforce to American hegemony (McBride 2005, 37). By contrast, for an emphatic critique of the anti-Americanism of French leftists, including the *Temps modernes* group, see Judt (1992). He accuses them of "moral bifocalism" and a "double standard." Threats to liberty and even racism in the Soviet bloc were excused because the system was said to promise a liberatory future for humankind, whereas capitalist states were unrelentingly condemned (168ff).

literature, she writes, is that "another truth becomes mine without ceasing to be other. I resign my own 'I' in favor of the speaker's; and yet I remain myself" (1965, 82).[12] Viewed in this way, literature may have strong affinities with what Arendt calls "representative thinking," or "thinking from where I am not," while also acknowledging the significance of forms of less "rational" cognition.

Beauvoir insisted, contrary to what was often claimed by critics at the time, that *The Mandarins* was not a *roman à clé*. Neither *roman à clé* nor a "thesis-novel" (FC I 270; FC Fr I 369), neither autobiography nor reportage: She later described the aim of the novel as "to evoke existence at the moment of its upsurge" [*évoquer l'existence dans son jaillissement*] (FC I 272 TA; FC Fr I 372), and she succeeds in vividly evoking the "taste" of her characters' lives. Beauvoir must, I think, be taken at her word here: *The Mandarins* is not a *roman à clé*. The fictitious characters do not align neatly with the actual dramatis personae of Beauvoir's circle and, although the novel treats the impact of actual political events, the chronology is not accurate, and the details of some of the events have been altered.[13] However, as an evocation, *The Mandarins* is also thoroughly grounded in her own experience, and its "fictions" are in large measure woven from the autobiographical. As such the book is also a phenomenology of political experience. Furthermore, like all good phenomenologies, as well as many good novels, its evocation of particular experiences speaks to audiences whose own lives are very different. Beauvoir says she put important elements of herself and of her own experiences particularly into two different characters: Anne Dubreuilh and Henri Perron. It is above all through the character of Henri that Beauvoir explores the kinds of experience that attend arriving at political judgments. "Most of the time they are my own emotions and thoughts

---

12. In chapter 1, I suggested that what enables Beauvoir's phenomenology, in *The Second Sex*, to communicate some women's lived experience to others whose lives are radically different is a certain affinity with literature. Like the good novelist, Beauvoir enables the reader's identification with others to take place through her vivid phenomenological descriptions. Literary and theoretical projects may converge from either direction.

13. Among these fictionalizations the most important concerns the disclosure of the presence of forced-labor camps in the Soviet Union. This disclosure forms a key moment in the novel (which I discuss below), but it did not in actuality occur until several year after the time period in which Beauvoir places it. The camps were first brought to wide public attention in France in 1950 by the right-wing *Le Figaro* and not, as in the novel, by a leftist newspaper in 1946. See FC I 199–202; FC I Fr. 276–79 for Beauvoir's autobiographical account of these actual events. For her comments on how she fictionalized them in *The Mandarins*, see FC I 202n.; FC I Fr 280n.

that inhabit him," she writes (FC I 269; FC Fr I 368), and (in an interview given when she won the Prix Goncourt), "it is through Henri that I tried to pose the real problems [of practical politics]" (1954, 359). However, she is clear that she does not use the novel to advocate specific "solutions" to these problems.[14]

Henri Perron is a successful young novelist, Resistance activist, and editor of a leftist daily newspaper, L'Espoir [Hope], which he had cofounded during the Resistance. He struggles throughout the novel to make sense of the shifting political currents and events of the postwar period and to address his diverse and conflicting desires. He wants to engage effectively and responsibly in a leftist politics that navigates between the two great power blocs of the emerging Cold War; to find the time to write a new novel; to disengage from a stifling affair with his long-standing mistress, Paula; to enjoy other liaisons; to maintain his close friendship with Robert Dubreuilh, the older and highly charismatic intellectual who, in 1935, had helped Henri to get his first novel published.

By following Henri as he addresses various dilemmas and as he moves toward making his decisions, we may draw from Beauvoir's novel a phenomenological description of the experience of arriving at political judgments. In the course of the novel, Henri has to make a series of crucial judgments, each of which is at once personal and political. Each involves rational deliberation, and yet none, we learn, can be arrived at by reason alone. These include (among others) whether to join the SRL, the new "third way" leftist political organization Robert Dubreuilh is founding[15]; whether (once having decided to join it) to make L'Espoir its official newspaper; whether to publish information that is emerging about forced labor camps in the Soviet Union; whether to perjure himself to protect his mistress, who had previously had

---

14. As she wrote later: "Thesis-novels impose a certain truth that eclipses all others and calls a halt to the perpetual dance of conflicting views; whereas [in The Mandarins] I described certain ways of living in the postwar world, without offering any solution to the problems that were troubling my main characters. . . . I showed some people at grips with doubts and hopes, groping their way in the dark; I cannot think I proved anything" (FC I 270–71 TA; FC Fr I 369–70).

15. The model for the SRL is the Rassemblement Démocratique et Révolutionaire (RDR), a movement with which Sartre and others in Beauvoir's circle were centrally involved. Founded early in 1948 with the goal of being an internally democratic, nonaligned, and socialist movement, the RDR collapsed by the end of 1949, with its leadership divided about its nonaligned status. Sartre left the RDR when Rousset and Altman, its other leading figures, began to espouse a pro-American position and agreed to take money from American trade unions to support the movement. See Cohen-Solal (1987, 298–309); see also Beauvoir (FC I, 146–49; FC Fr I 205–209).

an affair with a German officer during the Occupation; and whether (at the very end of the novel) to withdraw to Italy to write fiction or to stay in Paris and remain politically engaged.

I focus here on only two of these decisions: whether to turn *L'Espoir* into the official organ of the SRL and whether to publish information that Henri receives about the use of forced labor camps in the Soviet Union. For, in these examples, Beauvoir demonstrates how the convergence of a multiplicity of factors shapes the project of arriving at a political judgment. She tells us that political judgments emerge as complex amalgams of diverse elements of self and situation, of freedom and facticity, and that it is profoundly misguided to expect them to be made with the head alone.

The Mandarins: L'Espoir and the SRL

The Mandarins begins with an account of a joyous Christmas party held in December 1944 in recently liberated Paris. Henri has devoted himself for four years to Resistance politics, above all to publishing *L'Espoir*, and is now aching to live life more fully again. He hungrily anticipates the end of the deprivations and drudgery of the Occupation years. He yearns to travel (he has an invitation that he will accept to give a number of lectures in Portugal) and, above all, he desires to write fiction again. "With no time for himself he had lost his taste for life and with it his taste for writing. He had become a machine . . . now he was above all determined to become a man again" (M 16 TA; M Fr 14). However, even during this joyous celebration Robert Dubreuilh approaches Henri and urges him to become involved in the political struggles looming in the new postwar era by participating in the SRL. In the Resistance life had been straightforward, as had been running the paper, and political judgments were fairly clear-cut. Henri knows that now "politics," in the sense of endless committees, conferences, meetings, maneuverings, and compromises, will consume his time and energy and both exasperate and bore him. However, when Dubreuilh approaches him, he does not feel he has "the right to look for an out," and so he agrees to lend his name to the SRL and to put in "a few appearances" (M 18; M Fr 15).

Already, the "impasse" is revealed. The trap is sprung. Henri wants to go back to being and doing what he was and did before the war. But, as he discovers, he is no longer the "same" Henri. For not only is he older and wearied by the experiences of the war and the weight of human suffering in the world, but he must also now act in a new national and international configuration not of his choosing. *Pace* Arendt, this will significantly shape "who he is" and what his possibilities are and will suffuse his judgments. A leftist armchair intellectual until 1939, Henri now feels obligated to be more politically active if he is to break away from the privileges of his class, if he is not to deserve the hatred of millions of oppressed people (M 17; M Fr 15). However, if he gets sucked into politics, he will not have time to write. Another character, the intensely anti-Soviet Russian émigré and writer Scriassine, puts this dilemma into a wider context:

> French intellectuals are facing an impasse . . . their art, their thought [*leur pen-sée*] will continue to have meaning only if a certain kind of civilization manages to endure. And if they want to save that civilization, they'll have nothing left over to give to art or thought. . . . What weight will the message of French writers have when world-wide hegemony belongs either to the Soviet Union or the United States? No one will understand them any more; nobody will even speak their language any more. (M 43–45 TA; M Fr 34–35)[16]

The SRL stands for a "third way," for a democratic socialist France. This must be built by creating a space between the imperialism of U.S.-dominated world capitalism and the deformed, expansionist socialism of the Soviet Union. Without an autonomous France there will no longer be a place for meaningful cultural expression by French intellectuals. However, even keeping such a possibility alive in the emerging Cold War context will be an all-consuming struggle.[17] For Henri and others in his circle, there is yet a further impasse within the "impasse." For their assessment is that, for all its deformations, the Soviet Union still remains the greatest force for progress and, as such, must be given support. Moreover, the French Communist Party (PCF), which takes its line from Moscow, is still the party that enjoys mass working-class support in France; thus, it de facto represents socialist potential in France. It follows that the SRL must not alienate the PCF but instead must give it "critical support" while still keeping its distance.[18] But if the SRL criticizes the Soviet Union and keeps its distance from the PCF, how then will it win over the mass of people to

16. In the novel, Anne Dubreuilh contests Scriassine's interpretation of the situation, but it becomes evident that there is more than a grain of truth to it.

17. With hindsight, it is apparent that a major theme of Beauvoir's novel is the crisis of French national identity, precipitated by France's loss of status as a world power and intellectual center. Gaullism (to which Beauvoir was profoundly hostile) was, of course, also a response to this crisis.

18. This "impasse" closely follows that generated by the policy of "critical support" that *Les Temps modernes* for a period offered the PCF and the Soviet Union.

its more democratic socialist agenda? It is within the context of these multiple dilemmas that Henri struggles, first, over the decision whether to
make *L'Espoir* the official organ of the SRL and, later, over the issue of
whether to publish an exposé of the use of forced labor camps in the Soviet
Union. How does one arrive at closure, and how does one make a definitive
judgment that will result in action in such equivocal situations as these?

With regard to the first dilemma, over time and as various elements come
to bear on him, Henri shifts from insisting that *L'Espoir* must remain independent to deciding to make it the official publication of the SRL. Afterward, when Henri finally agrees that *L'Espoir* is formally to become the SRL's
newspaper, he has a conversation with Robert Dubreuilh's wife, Anne. Henri
is resentful about the pressure Dubreuilh has put on him to give *L'Espoir* to
the SRL. "After all . . . you finally did agree," says Anne. Yes, Henri replies, he
did agree. However, he adds, it is hard not to feel resentful when you are
pushed into doing something "against your will [*à contre-coeur*]" (M 254–55;
M Fr 188–89). But how does one arrive at a "decision" that goes against
one's will? One does not do so, Beauvoir's account suggests, only or even
primarily through a process of dispassionate judgment, in which cool reason
is pitted against and triumphs over emotion. One is carried toward one's
final judgment by the confluence of many aspects of one's situation that are
not the object of one's rational deliberations. Furthermore, these are rarely
commensurable and so cannot be weighed objectively against each other.

This is not to say that Henri does not spend many hours trying to
decide what would be the most rational course of action to pursue, considering what appear to be the objective pros and cons of the matter
given his aim of forwarding a progressive politics in France and elsewhere. Indeed, he engages mightily in reflective judgment and even in
what Steinberger calls "intelligent performance"—but the results remain
inconclusive. On the side of keeping *L'Espoir* independent of the SRL he
can, most importantly, point to the need to maintain full editorial independence if he is to keep trust with his readers and maintain his own
commitments: Today was the time "to educate readers instead of cram-
ming things down their throats. Not dictating opinions to them, but
rather teaching them to judge for themselves" (M 28 TA; M Fr 23). He
can also point to the financial risk of losing readers who would be dis-
pleased if *L'Espoir* ceased to be independent, thus possibly leading to the
death of the paper. But he hears conflicting arguments from different
sides: The SRL will end up in bed with the Communists, and so will *L'Espoir*,
warns one. To the contrary, if the SRL has a newspaper of its own it will
become too strong a force for the PCF to accept, and it will be destroyed,
warns another. On the side of giving the paper to the SRL, the strongest

argument is that Henri is already a prominent member of the SRL: If he supports this movement, then surely he should help it to grow by providing it with a daily paper. Moreover, in the new postwar situation the paper itself now needs a clear program. Its "independence" threatens to become vacuous, a way of pleasing everyone by committing to nothing. The memory of the Resistance, the moment of the paper's founding, no longer provides an adequate political program. Indeed, the Resistance is fast becoming a nostalgic myth, not an orientation to action.

Still, as he considers all of these arguments Henri becomes aware of several things: One is that the "concrete evidence" one has at one's disposal will never provide a sufficient basis on which to arrive at an unambiguous judgment (an issue that becomes even more pressing later with regard to evaluating the Soviet labor camps). In politics we can never know enough to be sure that our decisions will have the desired outcome. Will the readership grow or shrink if the paper becomes the organ of the SRL? Will the SRL grow or shrink as a result? On so many political matters, Henri reflects, you have to act without knowing. "First, you've got to speak, because it's urgent; afterwards events prove you right or wrong. 'And that's precisely what's known as bluffing,' he said unhappily to himself. 'Yes, even I bluff my readers'" (M 175; M Fr 131). However, if he is bluffing, if he fails to give his readers what he has promised them, then why defend the independence of the paper? Similarly, he tells the younger journalist, Lambert, one cannot defend the paper's independence on the grounds that one must be free to follow one's own conscience, for this too is to act from ignorance: "'It's just a question of speaking as our consciences dictate!' Lambert said. 'Think what that means!' said Henri. 'Every morning I tell a hundred thousand people how they ought to think. And what do I guide myself by? The voice of my conscience! . . . It's a gigantic swindle'" (M 177 TA; M Fr 132).

Although he considers the arguments on each side very seriously, from the beginning Henri has what we might call a gut resistance to the idea of handing over *L'Espoir*. "No, he wouldn't give him [Dubreuilh] *L'Espoir*. That was so clear that it needed no justifying. Nevertheless, he wished he could find a few good reasons for his stand" (M 153; M Fr 114–15). But why this gut response? It is far from a "dumb emotion." For Henri has created the paper and has edited it for several years and, in doing so, he has made it vital to the very meaning of his own existence. The paper is his "world." It is not only his political project but also *his place*, a place where he is profoundly at home. Beauvoir describes Henri entering the offices alone, late at night: "He liked the smell of stale dust and fresh ink. The offices were still empty, the basement silent. But soon a whole world would rise from this silence, a world that was his creation. 'No one will ever lay hands on *L'Espoir*,' he repeated to himself. He sat down at his desk and stretched out" (M 166 TA; M Fr 124).

In addition, Henri's initial gut resistance to Dubreuilh's proposal is linked to his passionate desire to become again the "old" Henri, the creative and successful writer, the man with a zest for life. For putting *L'Espoir* into the hands of the SRL will entail his being sucked further into the desiccating world of politics. He is already "dry," and he will become more so. Then writing will be impossible. There is also the matter of personal relationships, above all with Dubreuilh. Henri feels obligated to him, and he desires to continue his friendship with the older man, who has been his mentor. At the same time he is also resentful that Dubreuilh is making him feel guilty and that he is using their friendship against him. Then, there is also Samazelle, a powerful player in the SRL. Henri actively dislikes this man and distrusts his politics, which are intensely anti-Soviet. He knows he will have to deal with him day after day if *L'Espoir* becomes the organ of the SRL.

Why then does Henri end by deciding to give *L'Espoir* to the SRL? It is not just that he chooses the rationally justifiable or morally superior course of action across the grain of his emotional preferences. Choosing against one's will here is not a matter of choosing reason over un-reason or emotion, or choosing selflessness over self-interest. Rather, it has to do with a profound shift in Henri's own *experience* of himself. It has to do with his realization that, for reasons both of his own making and many beyond his control, his very existence has changed. " 'It's funny,' " he remarks to himself, " 'but whenever you do the decent thing, instead of giving you certain rights it only creates obligations.' He had founded *L'Espoir*, and now that was driving him to throw himself body and soul into the tumult of politics" (M 190 TA; M Fr 142).

However, the problem is not only one of being "forced" into politics. For what Henri begins to realize—and to experience as a profound crisis—is that there is no going back to the prewar Henri. With regard to his desire to write, he begins to discover that the problem is not only one of lack of time—for actually he has nothing left to say! When he does sit down to work at his novel, he is blocked. For what should he now say? And to whom? Who now will be his audience? His whole life lacks meaning, lacks flavor. He is "living like an engineer in a mechanical world"; he has become "drier than a stone" (M 191 TA; M Fr 142). But that being the case, to refuse to get further involved in politics on the grounds that he needs time to write is a sham. Similarly, he comes to feel that his insistence on keeping control of *L'Espoir* is a sham, for he now realizes that the paper cannot make much of a difference. In fact, he suddenly feels, he has been "playing" at being an editor. He has considered *L'Espoir* his toy, "a complete set of equipment for the little junior editor—life size. A magnificent plaything!" (M 190; M Fr 142). He does not really believe in what he is doing any more: If Dubreuilh and Samazelle still have hope that they can change the world, then they should have the paper.

In the end, Henri is overwhelmed with a sense of the futility of his own life and life in general. For massive structural changes in world power relations, apparently distant forces that are now being brought to bear on him locally, conjoin with other, more particularistic elements of his own situation. They strongly predispose Henri toward his final decision to give up *L'Espoir* to the SRL—and so also to privilege politics over writing his novel. Here the tension between literature (and art more generally) and politics, an important subtheme of the novel, reaches a climax as Henri wonders whether, in a world of such misery and violence, writing a novel is not an act of sheer self-indulgence. The issue, he realizes, is not simply one about where to put one's time and energy, for it is also about the meaning of writing. The "impasse" also bears on why and for whom one writes.[19]

On the night that Henri finally arrives at his decision he has an abrupt and terrible epiphany. He suddenly recognizes, now not as a mere piece of intellectual information, for of course he "knew" this before, but as a profound shattering of his own world, that geopolitics changes the meaning of our actions.[20] It is this devastating realization that precipitates his final decision. Two things take place that night. One directly involves Henri, and the other seems more distant, and yet he realizes it is not. Early in the evening, Henri has been to see Tournelle, a man whom he had known as a comrade in the Resistance and who is now a government minister. At the

---

19. For the young Henri (like Beauvoir), writing had been a passion, an intense and even a profoundly sensuous experience. But now the brutal realities of the war and the postwar situation have destroyed his vitality. However, writing cannot be no more than a personal passion, for what one writes must also communicate to others, and it will do so only if one is intensely involved in life. Throughout *The Mandarins* Henri struggles to try to recapture the "old" Henri, the novelist who could engage his audience by writing so passionately about his own life, but he repeatedly fails. At the very end of the book he (apparently) abandons the fantasy he has had of isolating himself in a small village somewhere in Italy in order to write, and he somewhat diffidently commits himself again to the political struggle (M 755; M Fr 573). So perhaps one might read Beauvoir as telling her audience that the times call for a new type of novel, for the politically committed novel (such as she herself and Sartre had written)? Or not? For the end of the novel still remains open and inconclusive, and one cannot take from it, as an unambiguous message, that literature should be put in the service of politics.

20. This is, of course, what, much earlier in the book, Scriassine had diagnosed as the "impasse" of French intellectuals.

behest of the beleaguered old leftists he had met during his visit to Portugal early in 1945, Henri asks Tournelle for French government support of the Portuguese Left against Salazar's Fascist dictatorship. He already knows that, because of American influence on the French government, the answer will be "no," but he still feels morally obligated to try. " 'You know the situation as well as I,' " says Tournelle. " 'How can you expect France to do anything for Portugal, or for anyone else for that matter, when she can't do anything for herself!' " (M 204; M Fr 151). Tournelle is trapped, bitter. Now he is not even sure that the Resistance had been worth all the bloodshed . . . and suddenly the realization hits Henri: In this new world France is no longer a world power, and what its citizens say, write, or do now simply makes no difference. "Suddenly he realized he was living in the moribund capital of a very small country . . . Henri was nothing but an insignificant citizen of a fifth-rate power, and *L'Espoir* was a local sheet in the genre of the village weekly" [*dans le genre du* Petit Limousin] (M 205; M Fr 152). So what did it matter who controlled *L'Espoir*? He may as well give it to the SRL!

But Henri still hesitates. It is only later that night that he finally arrives at the definitive moment of decision as his dreadful realization is reinforced from yet another direction. For this is also the night the triumphant Soviet army is entering Berlin. Nazism is definitively defeated—but there is no cause for celebration. *L'Espoir* is irrelevant in the new configuration, in which France, Europe, and indeed the whole world are now the playthings of two great powers—and equally irrelevant is the project of being a writer:

> The Russians were sacking Berlin, the war was ending, or another one was beginning—how could one find pleasure in telling stories that never actually happened? . . . He was nowhere, he had nothing, he was nothing; there was nothing he could speak about. "Then I just have to shut up," he thought. "If I really commit myself, I'll stop tearing myself to pieces. Maybe I'll bear drudgeries I'm forced to do with a better will." . . . He had believed that he lived in a very special part of the world from which every word echoed across the entire planet. But now he knew that all his words died at his feet. (M 212–13 TA; M Fr 157–58)

And so Henri goes into a bar, gets drunk with an acquaintance, and "decides" he will give *L'Espoir* to the SRL. Moreover, drunk and maudlin, he declares to himself that he will abnegate his entire life to politics and simply follow orders: "[E]veryone had died in the war," including him. But "it's not upsetting being dead, if you give up pretending to be alive." So now, "act, act as a team, without worrying about yourself; sow, sow again, and never reap. Act, unite, serve, obey Dubreuilh, smile at Samazelle. He'd telephone them: " 'the paper is yours' " (M 215 TA; M Fr 159).

From the perspective of Beauvoir's earlier moral period essays Henri is acting in profoundly bad faith. He tells himself that because the world has changed
he is no longer free to take responsibility for himself. Because the world has
changed, he can no longer act meaningfully, and so instead he will commit
himself to blind obedience. He will abstain from questioning or judging, he will
just mindlessly follow orders in the SRL. Furthermore, he arrives at this
moment of final decision drunk! He flees his anguish by diminishing his capacity to think and see clearly. In the event, Henri does not abnegate himself in
this way for long and, as we will see, he later chooses expulsion from the SRL
rather than consent to remain silent about the use of forced labor camps in the
Soviet Union. Even so, we must ask about the significance of this moment, for
it seems to fly in the face both of Beauvoir's own earlier notions of freedom and
of those theories that conceive of judgment as a strictly inferential process.

Interestingly, Beauvoir does not invite her readers to criticize Henri. We
are not asked to assess him in a dispassionate mode, or to evaluate his decision by applying a set of criteria that a judgment "proper" should meet and
against which we will find his decision wanting. Rather, she invites us
to enter Henri's world and to discover that—from the perspective of lived
experience—reason, judgment, and responsibility have become much more
relative matters than she had once thought (or than rationalist theories of
judgment presume). These, she now realizes, must be qualified by the fact
that we so often act in an in-between zone, an ambiguous place of neither
freedom nor of determination *tout court*: a zone where individual and collective histories merge, where reason and emotion, far from being antithetical,
are mutually implicated, and where one must both deliberate *and* wager.

The Mandarins: The "Camps"

Henri's later decision to publish an article in *L'Espoir* exposing the Soviet
labor camps involves a more explicitly deliberative process of judgment. It
is also one in which he seeks (as Arendt says we must) to persuade a public
of his position (here, a public of diverse leftist interlocutors) even as he
deliberates with "himself." The judgment he arrives at will abruptly end the
relationship between *L'Espoir* and the SRL and lead to Henri's expulsion
from the latter. It will also result in a bitter break with Dubreuilh, who
opposes publishing the exposé.[21] But this decision too is driven by its wider

21. In actuality *Les Temps modernes* did publish an essay by Merleau-Ponty about
the Soviet labor camps, and Beauvoir and Sartre supported this decision. In *The*

political context, by contingent events and the actions of others, as well as by Henri's personal history, his dispositions and emotions, indeed, one might say, by "who he is."

For purposes of clarification we may distinguish three different components of the conscious, deliberative aspect of Henri's process of judgment, although they tend to merge experientially as well as blending with its various nonconceptual aspects. These three components involve adjudicating the truth of allegedly factual information; making judgments about both its historico-political and its moral significance; and deciding what action should be taken in light of these considerations. I begin, as does Henri, with the issue of the veracity of allegedly factual information.

Theoretical treatments of political judgment most often presume that the facts on which we must reflect are simply "there" before us. However, in Henri's case—and it is a ubiquitous problem for political judgment—the question of how to evaluate the veracity of information is itself a dilemma that is already politically shaped and requires the exercise of judgment. Did forced labor camps really exist? If so, how many people were kept in them? For how long and under what conditions? What proportion of them died? How can one know the truth about such questions? Which of the sources who provide "evidence" should one judge trustworthy? How might one evaluate their claims?[22]

Mandarins, Henri's article, like Merleau-Ponty's, endeavors both to indicate the serious negative implications of the camps and yet to affirm critical support for the Soviet Union as still offering greater promise to humanity than Western capitalism. Merleau-Ponty had written in his essay:

> The decadence of Russian communism does not make the class struggle a myth, "free enterprise" possible or desirable, or the Marxist criticism in general null and void. . . . The only sound criticism is thus the one which bears on exploitation and oppression, inside and outside the U.S.S.R.; and every political position which is *defined* in opposition to Russia and localizes criticism within it is an absolution given to the capitalist world. ([1950] 1964b, 269)

See FC I 198–202 and FC I Fr 275–81 for Beauvoir's autobiographical account of the camps issue.

22. Again, Arendt is more attuned than most to Beauvoir's concerns here. She also insists that thinking from the "perspective" of truth (by which she means the perspective of allegedly transcendental truth) is inimical to political judgment because it forecloses discussion and opinion. She is also well aware that the status of "facts" may be an integral—and tricky— aspect of judging:

> Factual truth is no more self-evident than opinion, and this may be among the reasons that opinion-holders find it relatively easy to discredit factual truths as

The initial evidence is brought by Scriassine, known by Henri to be strongly hostile to communism and whom he does not trust. Scriassine brings him a report on the camps provided, he asserts, by an "escaped" Soviet functionary now based in West Germany. Henri's first reaction is one of skepticism (M 387; M Fr 290). Yet he also finds himself discomforted, so he asks Lambert to read the material: "I've got these fragments in my hands, but I have no way of evaluating them," he says (M 393 TA; M Fr 295). The issue becomes one of how to evaluate information when the "facts" are themselves politically laden and the claim that they are true rests on the purported trustworthiness of their source. Pressure starts to mount on Henri. On the one side Samazelle says that it would be a great coup for *L'Espoir* to publish a full exposé now, though of course even before the war people knew the camps existed since the policy of "administrative internment" had been promulgated quite publicly in the Soviet Union. On the other side, although he acknowledges that there has long been a policy of internment in the Soviet Union, Dubreuilh argues that an escaped Soviet functionary is hardly a reliable source on which to base a detailed exposure (M 394; M Fr 295).

Scriassine brings his source, one George Peltov, to meet with the group. Peltov provides detailed information on the number and locations of camps and on conditions—a truly horrendous account of forced (essentially slave) labor, lack of food, disease, death. While Dubreuilh continues to doubt Peltov and to say they would be criminal to publish without more reliable information (M 397; M Fr 298), for Henri a profound existential crisis develops. Just as he had suddenly been struck by the realization, on the evening when he "decided" to give *L'Espoir* to the SRL, of the irrelevance of France and of people such as himself in the new geopolitical order, so now old certainties suddenly began to collapse: "Everything he had read absentmindedly a few hours earlier suddenly took on a terrifying meaning. There they were, translated into English, official documents admitting the existence of the camps. And one could not, except in bad faith, challenge the total of these accounts. . . . It was impossible to deny: in Russia, too, men were exploiting other men to the point of death" (M 396 TA; M Fr 297). Henri's world was dissolving: "Unless the whole thing was nothing but a

---

just another opinion . . . In the event of a dispute, only other witnesses but no third or higher instance can be invoked, and settlement is usually arrived at by way of a majority; that is, in the same way as the settlement of opinion disputes— a wholly unsatisfactory procedure since there is nothing to prevent a majority of witnesses from being false witnesses . . . to the extent that factual truth is exposed to the hostility of opinion-holders, it is at least as vulnerable as rational philosophical truth. (1977, 247)

pack of lies, it would be impossible henceforth to think of the Soviet Union as he used to think of it. Everything had to be reconsidered" (M 399; M Fr 299). Nonetheless, Henri still does not want to believe what he has heard. It is too devastating to the very meaning of his life and his world.

Peltov offers to provide further proof if somebody will accompany him to Germany. Lambert says he will go, but he demands that Henri publish an exposé if further proof is provided. Henri instantly says "yes" (M 400; M 300). But having assented, he wonders why he has done so. "He had said yes to Lambert without hesitation; it was almost a natural reflex. But as a matter of fact, he knew neither what he should believe nor what he should do; he knew nothing at all" (M 400 TA; M Fr 300). Of course, Henri had "known" abstractly that there were abuses in the Soviet Union. But, distant matters, he had excused them as minor, or as perhaps necessary in order to defeat Nazism. "He knew of the defects, of the abuses, of the Soviet Union; nevertheless, one day socialism, true socialism, where justice and freedom would be reconciled, would end by triumphing in the Soviet Union, and through the Soviet Union. If this evening that certainty had left him, then the whole future would sink into shadows; nowhere else in the world could one see even a glimmer of hope" (M 400–401 TA; M Fr 300–301). Henri's fear that these terrible claims are true makes him want to continue to doubt them and to demand further proof. However, for Scraissine and Samazelle, already strongly anti-Soviet, they simply confirm the evils of the Soviet regime and require no further authentication. Their preexisting political sensibilities profoundly color each one's reading of the "same" information.

At the end of the summer Lambert returns from Germany: He has not only seen the documents found in Nazi archives to which Peltov had referred but also read depositions from liberated former Polish internees. There are also translated documents Henri has now read that make it clear that, since the mid-1930s, the use of forced camp labor had been an explicit and important element in Soviet economic planning. One could doubt particular pieces of evidence, but not the sum total. "What was certain," Henri concludes, is that even if the actual number of "slave laborers" was uncertain, still "the camps existed, on a large scale, and in an institutionalised manner" (M 473; M Fr 357). But then the questions become ones of interpretation: What does this mean for one's assessment of the Soviet Union as a force for progress? And what, consequently, are the political implications for the French Left and, more specifically, for the SRL and *l'Espoir*?

Here Henri is still plagued by ignorance, for one would need to know much more—but how much more is a question—about the Soviet regime

to place the significance of the camps in an adequate political and historical context. But "ignorance is no alibi . . . When in doubt, and since he had
promised to tell his readers the truth, he had to tell them what he knew"
(M 474; M Fr 357)—and yet he still hesitates. To publish will mean being
attacked by the PCF, something he would strongly like to avoid. Even more
strongly, he admits, "he would have liked to hide from himself the fact that
in Russia, too, something was rotten" (M 493; M Fr 372). Yet not to publish would be "cowardice." Perhaps, he tells himself, those in the PCF who
are concerned about the camps but are not free to speak out because of
Party discipline would be grateful to him. Perhaps his exposé would even
help to build pressure on the Soviet Union from Western Communist Parties to reform its policies. Surely, he also tells himself, to keep silent would
be to write off the possibility of reform in Russia: "It would be irrevocably
to condemn the Soviet Union under the guise of not judging her" (M 493
TA; M Fr 372).

Yet Henri is still indecisive. To buy a little more time, he says he will take
the matter to the editorial committee, although he is sure they will agree
with him. But will they? Others predict that Dubreuilh will still remain
opposed to publication. Furthermore, Samazelle tells Henri that he has evidence that Dubreuilh has secretly become a member of the PCF. Henri
insists this cannot be true (and, indeed, later it is revealed to be a total
fabrication), but even so seeds of doubt and anger are sown that will complicate Henri's judgment and help to precipitate his break with his old
friend and mentor.

Henri goes to see Dubreuilh alone. Dubreuilh now agrees that the evidence that the camps exist is compelling: The basic facts, at least, are no
longer at issue. Nonetheless, he does not think the camps are an essential
component of the whole regime, and he insists that, in the present political
context, the Soviet Union should still be wholly supported. He emphatically asserts they would be wrong to publish. Given the belief both men still
firmly hold, that U.S. imperialism is the greater evil and that for all its warts
the Soviet Union is still the best hope for humankind, the reasons Dubreuilh
gives for his opposite judgment are cogent ones. He points out that the
information about the camps will become widely available anyway since the
right-wing press will willingly publish it. Thus the issue is only whether
there is a good reason for L'Espoir to publish first. If it does so, he argues,
this will inevitably be read as a full indictment of the Soviet Union and not,
as they intend, as only a limited critique. For there is not now a political space
in which their criticism will not, de facto, serve anti-Communism. "Even
though we took all imaginable precautions, what people would inevitably
see in our articles would be an indictment of the Soviet regime" (M 495 TA;

M Fr 373).[23] Furthermore, elections are imminent in France, and to publish the information now could contribute to the defeat of the Left. Thus, de facto, to publish would be an act of anti-Communism, and people would be right to see them as changing sides.

Henri replies that, even if the chances are slim, they must try to bring about change in Russia. Furthermore, the whole aim of the SRL has been to exert sympathetic but critical pressure on the PCF, and here is exactly the moment to do so: One should either speak out and tell the truth, or else one may as well join the PCF. It is important that they publish before the Right does since "our words would carry much more weight if we were the first to denounce the camps. Then no one could believe we were following a line" (M 497; M Fr 375). No, we'd just be seen as anti-Communists, counters Dubreuilh: "I don't want to start an anti-Soviet campaign, especially not now. I would find it criminal." To which Henri replies: "And me, I would find it criminal not to do everything in my power against the camps" (M 499; M Fr 376).

Two emphatically opposed judgments, and each is surely reasonable. Indeed, each could meet Steinberger's criterion of rational, *post festum* reconstruction and could qualify as a judgment "proper." Both men share a commitment to the regulative ideal of humanistic socialism, and they both agree (wrongly, as we know with hindsight) that the Soviet Union, for all its flaws, still offers the greatest hope for achieving it. Yet they interpret the same information and the same range of possible actions in ways that are incommensurable. Furthermore, neither judgment can be based on certitude about its outcomes, whether these be immediate or long term, local or international. Dubreuilh privileges the more immediate and local issues of French politics; Henri privileges contesting the camps, which are deforming the Soviet project—each choice is a reasonable "wager," and each has political risks attached to it.

If we ask how Henri finally comes to arrive at his judgment, there are many elements at play that would not be included in an account of judgment as uniquely an "intelligent performance," or even as Arendtian "reflective judgment." Significant among these are his prior relationship with Dubreuilh and the false information he has been given that Dubreuilh has secretly joined the PCF. When Henri asks him, Dubreuilh emphatically denies the latter charge. But Henri is distrustful because of past pressure and even deception, which he has experienced at the hands of his imperious

---

23. This is, indeed what happens. Attacked by the PCF, Henri is then pressured by the pro-American members of the editorial committee to take a fully anti-Soviet line (M 507–11; M Fr 383–86). He refuses to do so, and he later loses control of the paper to them and ceases to be its editor.

older mentor. In a sudden flash, he "sees" that Dubreuilh has indeed joined the PCF and that his secret task is in fact to prevent *L'Espoir* from publishing material embarrassing to the Party. This time, for once, Henri has decided he will stand up to Dubreuilh's authority and assert himself!

Perhaps, then, Henri's distrust, resentment, and anger are what have finally tipped the scales? Yet, we cannot definitively say so. Indeed, Henri himself does not know. Later, when Scriassine confesses that he had made up the story that Dubreuilh was a secret member of the PCF, Henri wonders how much of a difference the lie has made. He wonders whether things would have turned out the same way without it. Perhaps not, but "he hated to think that he had been playing with marked cards; it gave him a consuming desire to replay the hand" (M 515; M Fr 389). Marked cards; wanting to replay the hand: are we then in the realm of mere wager? Certainly, we are in the realm of contingency, of a judgment colored by the happenstance of false information. But we are not in the realm of *mere* chance. For although Henri could have responded differently to that information, elements of his personal history with Dubreuilh, his affective dispositions, his values, his sense of self—in Arendt's words, "who" he was—strongly predisposed him to come to the judgment he did.

Perhaps an important element in Henri's decision is a certain defiant machismo on his part. He repeatedly tells himself that it would be cowardice not to publish. Although his general disposition is to be accommodating and to avoid conflict, he now feels he must heroically take a stand and hold his ground, come what may, against the PCF and (as it turns out) also against antagonists within the SRL. Dubreuilh also alleges that Henri is concerned above all with how others see him: "All he's thought of in this whole business is what people would say about him . . . Henri doesn't want people to accuse him of letting himself be intimidated by the Communists; he prefers actually to go over to the anti-Communist camp," he says (M 532; M Fr 402). Dubreuilh is wrong with regard to Henri's political intentions but perhaps not wrong about Henri's concern with appearing, in his own eyes and those of others, as a man of strength and integrity.

Are the reasons Henri gives for his decision then merely bad faith excuses? Is he offering no more than specious, post hoc justifications for what is, at base, no more than a knot of intensely felt emotional responses to a complex political and individual situation? From the perspective of a theory of determinate judgment, Henri's deep personal feelings about the Soviet Union, his troubled relationship with Dubreuilh, his machismo, his concern about how he appears to others, and so forth must be deemed aberrant, indeed "dumb" emotional intrusions into what should have been an "intelligent performance." Likewise, for Arendt, such "idiosyncratic" and "private" aspects of Henri's life should have been left behind in the process of reflective judgment. However, matters such as these are in actuality integral to making judgments, including—and this is my key point—what may still remain *reasonable* judgments.

Henri judges as "who" he is, but (unlike for Arendt) this "who" is an embodied and affective self that cannot shed its "idiosyncrasies" or delimit its "private" from its "public" practices. The facticities of Henri's life, his personal history, his emotions, beliefs, and values are integral to how he deliberates and to how he arrives at what still remains a reasonable interpretation of the political situation he faces. That these personal elements play a role does not mean, however, that reason is absent, for Henri carefully considers the information at his disposal, trying to evaluate its veracity and its significance, as well as considering possible outcomes of his chosen course of action. This is not—and cannot be—a practice of "determinate judgment," but it does share some affinities with Arendt's account of "reflective judgment." We could even say that Henri engages in "representative thinking": He endeavors to think from the place of others, from "where he is not," as he holds interior dialogues with various interlocutors, both hypothetical and actual, assessing their different claims and interpretations of the situation. However, Arendt's notion of "enlarged mentality" remains far too rationalistic to encapsulate all that is at play here.

Reason, Non-reason, and Judgment

There is another strand of recent scholarship that also challenges rationalist accounts of judgment. Beauvoir's insistent rejection of mind-body dualism and her argument that subjectivity is always embodied might, at first sight, seem to anticipate recent studies that draw on neuroscience in order to account for judgment primarily in nonconscious terms. However, much of this literature tends toward a reductionism that is not Beauvoir's goal. For it argues that judgments are but manifestations of circuits of synaptic brain activity (for example, Churchland 1995; McDermott 2004; Thiele 2006). Here, veering to the opposite extreme from theories of determinate judgment, rational deliberation is denied any significant role. For what might appear to be deliberation is said to be no more than post hoc rationalization of preconscious neural processes. The "self" is conceived here as but a particular composite of neural pathways, wherein prior experiences have become encoded in "brain maps" that, in turn, structure our future preconscious responses. Thus, for example, in *The Heart of Judgment*, Leslie Paul Thiele presents experimental evidence that shows how forms of preconscious emotional "priming" shape judgments for which we afterward offer what are merely post hoc reasons. He goes on to say: "Affective biases often induce *post hoc* rationalizations. Here, reason truly displays its slavish relation to passion . . . moral judgments often signal an attempt to support affective predispositions with arguments. One might say, to recall Nietzsche, that reason supplies the *post hoc* paperwork" (171–72). Thiele similarly describes the conscious mind as merely the "secretary" that records the outcome of unconscious processes (149).

Political judgment does surely require the presence of a stock of tacitly accumulated experience, as well as forms of unconscious or preconscious cognition, emotions, and affects, as Thiele argues. Indeed, our ability to engage in rational deliberation simply would not be possible absent the to-and-fro between thinking, affect, and other preconceptual activity. However, this hardly justifies the claim that deliberation simply provides the "*post hoc* paperwork." It is true that the border between the kind of "thinking" that is (negatively) called post-hoc rationalization and that which is (approvingly) called reason is fluid and ambiguous. However, this does not mean that the latter is reducible to the former. Nor does it mean that the self is but a collection of "brain maps" laid down in synaptic pathways, as Thiele and others suggest.[24] To return to Beauvoir's example in *The Mandarins*, the disagreements between Dubreuilh and Henri are in no way *reducible* to their differing "brain maps." Rather, we have to say, with Beauvoir, that the entire *existence* of each—each an embodied subject, each ambiguously free and constrained—is present in their respective judgments.

A political judgment must be understood as an existential choice. It is not determined by brain circuitry, nor does it result from a process of abstract reason detached from the particularities of self and situation. We should not expect that, if given the same set of options, all reasonable actors would arrive at an identical judgment. Our affects and emotions, our dispositions and habits, our histories and personal experiences will enter into how we judge, and yet we cannot say that these will *cause* us to make a

---

24. Thiele writes (summarizing the neuroscience literature), "Brain mapping . . . occurs when specific neural connections assert their dominance with repeated use. . . . The synaptic circuits formed by this process produce a neural inventory of life. The worldly experiences that constitute an individual's existence, coupled with the internal reactions of the individuals to these experiences, are laid down as tracks in the mind." He then proceeds to make the more reductive and problematic claim that "this interactive scheme of brain maps—built upon genetically acquired neural foundations—produces a sense of self" (2006, 204).

certain judgment. Herein lies that moment of ambiguous freedom within constraint toward which Beauvoir rightly points us. Furthermore, even if we were able to be the abstract reasoners beloved of theorists of determinate judgment, we could still come to different, yet equally reasonable, conclusions. For, of necessity, we act from incomplete knowledge, in uncertainty about outcomes, and in fields of incommensurables where the ends we value most often conflict. It is here that we must recall Beauvoir's claim that a judgment is not only a "decision" but also a "wager." A political judgment is, even at its best, but an informed and reasonable guess, one made by a particular, "idiosyncratic" self in a particular situation—and like all human action it is subject to failure. As in her strictures on abstract humanism, Beauvoir urges us to avoid the hubris that attends too great a faith in reason even as we continue—as we must—to make reasonable judgments. "Politics is made with the head, but it is certainly not made with the head alone," Weber had said—and Beauvoir helps us to see why.

5

"An Eye for an Eye": The Question of Revenge

The kinds of political violence that we call "atrocities"—shocking, evil, and irreparable harms committed on a mass scale—have moved back onto the agenda of political theory and philosophy with pressing urgency since September 11, 2001.[1] It is not, of course, that atrocities such as mass murder, mutilation, torture, rape, or, indeed, terrorism were actually absent from politics before that. Far from it. But in the United States (as well as most other places that deem themselves stable, liberal, and democratic) in the late twentieth century, such violence seemed to be an issue

---

1. I draw here on Claudia Card's *The Atrocity Paradigm* for an approximate meaning of the term *atrocity*, although, wisely, she does not give a formal definition. An atrocity, she says, is an "evil" that not only involves "culpable wrong" by its perpetrators but also inflicts extreme levels of harm on its victims, and that occurs on a large scale and with a viciousness that is shocking. She writes,: "Many evils lack the scale of an atrocity. Not every murder is an atrocity, although murder is also a paradigm of evil. Atrocities shock, at least when we first learn of them. They seem monstrous. We recoil from visual images and details" (2002, 9). More recently she has added the notion of being "inexcusable" to her definition: Atrocities are "evils that are *inexcusable*, not just culpable" (Card 2010, 4). Scholars in international law now tend to link the term *atrocity* to "crimes against humanity," as designated in the Rome Statute of 1998, which established the International Criminal Court: "At the very core of the extraordinariness of atrocity crimes," writes Mark Drumbl, "is conduct—planned, systematized, and organized—that targets large numbers of individuals based on their actual or perceived membership in a particular group that has become selected as a target on discriminatory grounds" (2007, 4). See also Hughes, Schabas, and Thakar (2007).

that generally affected only "other," distant parts of the world. It did not impinge on the daily life and consciousness of most people with any immediacy. Nor did it impinge significantly on theorizing about the politics of liberal societies. Discussions about liberalism and communitarianism, about the just society, about the value of civil society, deliberative democracy, multiculturalism, and so forth—not to mention political judgment—have proceeded pervasively (if problematically) from the tacit assumption that politics is a domain where groups and individuals may negotiate their divergent interests and values through agreed procedures and in reasonable and civil ways.

But no longer. Thus, suggestively, William Connolly begins his book *Pluralism* (2005) by portraying the events of September 11, 2001, as a profoundly traumatic, personal encounter with the kind of violence we may call an atrocity.[2] And it is one that, with many others, he calls "the experience of evil." However, Connolly was not in New York on that day, and he does not say that anybody he personally knew died. It is not as somebody directly connected to the victims of the attack that he writes. His account thus raises intriguing questions about how we respond to such evils when they are wreaked on others: questions concerning our sense of interconnectedness with others whom we did not even know, and questions also about the deep rootedness of certain of our social and political identities. For Connolly also responds very much as an "American" in an "America" that has been atrociously attacked. He describes how the initial news, followed by the endlessly replayed TV images of the collapsing twin towers, hit him in what he calls "the visceral register of being" (11).[3] Terrorism, he observes, "issues in the *lived experience of evil*" and "when you experience evil *the bottom falls out of your stomach* because it has fallen out of the world"

---

2. The book develops an argument for the greater cultivation of and respect for a plurality of differences as a counter to the troublingly chauvinist and aggressive popular and political responses to September 11 in the United States.

3. Most people in the United States, irrespective of social differences, experienced a similar "gut" reaction to the sight on their TVs of other human beings leaping to their deaths from the windows of the collapsing buildings. National identity seems to have trumped many divisions, including race. Significantly (although some African Americans soon began pointing out both that "atrocity" was hardly new to the African American experience and that the "war on terrorism" was going to be used to legitimize yet heavier policing of African Americans), the immediate reactions of most African Americans were much like those of the white population (Malveaux and Green 2002). A poll conducted on September 20, 2001, found that 94 percent of African Americans supported Bush's initial declaration of the "War on Terror" (Stanford 2002, 96).

(13; my emphasis). The desire for revenge, the desire to return injury for injury is, he continues, our most immediate response to such evil: "Evil . . . generates imperious demands to identify and take revenge on the guilty parties" (13). Nearly a decade later, responses to the killing of Osama Bin Laden in early May 2011 seem to bear out Connolly's point. For irrespective of what policy ends his killing may have been intended to serve, many (though certainly not all) in the United States savored it above all as revenge. "Payback" was among the words most frequently used in response to the killing and, indeed, "revenge" itself. "Justice is a politician's word; it's all about revenge for me," as the brother of a September 11 victim told a New York Times reporter.[4]

Connolly's account of his feelings on September 11 draws our attention to the immediate and embodied quality of our experience of atrocity: It took place at a "visceral level of being" as "the bottom falling out of your stomach." For the phenomenological experience is—and Connolly well captures it—both immediate and situational: It involves a *total* response of the self, at once physical, affective, cognitive, and moral. Although, post hoc, neuroscientists or other outside observers may pull apart and analyze these elements as discrete, our lived experience is otherwise. For (to return to Beauvoir's conceptual register) it is as embodied and situated subjectivities that we experience such events. The bottom "falls out of your world" when your tacit, taken-for-granted, habitual ways of "being-in-the-world" are suddenly and violently shattered by the overwhelming disruptive force of an atrocity. For in normal daily life we do not put into question the integrity of our own and others' bodies, the constancies of space and place through which we orient ourselves, or the routine flow of time in our lives.

Nor do most of us (even if sometimes perhaps we should) question the stability of those institutions, cultural practices, and norms that structure our field of action and enable us to give it meaning. These norms include tacit assumptions of reciprocity through which—unless a radical disruption occurs—we may spontaneously engage with each other in what we (sometimes correctly, sometimes erroneously) take to be one and the same

---

4. Cited in New York Times, May 3, 2011, F1. While *The Village Voice* emblazoned the headline "Payback" across its front page (56 [18], May 4–10, 2011) and *Newsweek*'s editorial announced: "When President Obama announced the tragedy of 9/11 had at last been avenged, the news reached into the heart and soul of every American and created a global anthem of response that justice had at last been done" (May 16, 2011, 4). Other motives for the jubilation were also conjoined, including patriotic pride and a (doubtless misguided) sense of relief that the world would now be safer for Americans.

world.[5] Atrocity violently shatters such norms. Indeed, we often experience atrocities committed against others as bodily harm to ourselves. We become traumatically decentered, and suddenly we are no longer the source of our own actions in the world, no longer the locus of our own meanings and values. Abruptly revealed as wholly vulnerable, our bodies become subject to uncontrollable and painful sensations that we experience as "ours" and yet "not ours"—hence the profoundly disturbing quality of the "visceral" register of our response. As Connolly writes, the experience of evil "generates imperious demands to identify and take revenge on the guilty parties. . . . The accumulation of such events becomes layered into the soft tissues of life, finding expression in both modes of explicit recollection and embodied dispositions to judgment subsisting below the threshold of recollection" (13).

Commonly, the vocabulary in which the desire for revenge is described—from popular journalism to works of philosophy—casts it as a fundamental biological drive, as an instinct, as self-evidently "natural." Revenge is "primitive," "animalistic." It is an "appetite" and is often described using metaphors of eating. As the journalist Ellis Cose puts it, "Lurking in virtually all of us is a bit of a monster, a fiend who cackles—wickedly, uncontrollably—as he savors revenge. There is something exhilarating, deliciously primal about payback . . . The instinct as we will call it, is older than the Bible" (2004, 65). Quite similarly, the philosopher Charles Griswold writes that "Revenge impulsively surges in response to wrong and becomes perversely delicious to those possessed by it" (2007, xiii), while the political theorist Judith Shklar calls it "an insatiable urge of the human heart" (1990, 93), and (perhaps surprisingly) Hannah Arendt also calls revenge "the natural, automatic reaction to transgression" (1958, 241). "Instinct," "appetite," "impulse"—and "insatiable"—the desire for revenge has also been compared to the desire for sex in its intensity and as "hard-wired" into us.[6] Commenting on the outburst of spontaneous jubilation in New York and elsewhere that followed the news of Bin Laden's killing, "expert" psychologists were quoted in the

---

5. As discussed in chapter 3, the unquestioned assumptions made by members of privileged groups that others experience the world just as they do are highly problematic. But my point is that, irrespective of whether or not such assumptions are illusory, the shattering of the felt-unity of one's world may be traumatic.

6. "The taboo attached to revenge in our culture today is not unlike the illegitimate aura associated with sex in the Victorian world," writes Susan Jacoby, who warns that misguided attempts to deny outlets to what she calls this "ineradicable impulse" are, like sexual repression, harmful to society (Jacoby 1983, 5, 12–13). French (2001, 81, 98–99) cites J. L. Mackie, who describes the desire for revenge as genetically "hard-wired" into us.

New York Times as saying that revenge is "natural" and that "people everywhere have a strong belief in 'just deserts' punishment."[7]

While, as Connolly rightly indicates, the desire for revenge lies in embodied dispositions that often "subsist below the threshold of recollection," this does not mean it is an instinctive or "natural" desire; it is not one that is biologically or genetically programmed. To the contrary, revenge appears to be a distinctly human desire, and it is rare or perhaps absent among even the higher primates.[8] However, the desire for revenge does not operate uniquely or even primarily at the level of conscious cognition, and it cannot be grasped adequately through philosophical analysis concerning matters such as its moral justification or its rationality. Whether or not revenge is ever morally justifiable, its relation (or lack of thereof) to justice, what might be the proper ethical bases for the punishment of those who commit atrocities, and so forth certainly are important questions for reflection. However, their investigation is not alone sufficient, for we also need to attend phenomenologically to the immediate, embodied, often predeliberative affects and emotions, the often inchoate desire to return injury for injury that politically motivated and world-destroying irreparable harms so often incite. In her essay "An Eye for an Eye," Beauvoir provides a significant contribution to such a phenomenology.[9]

The Context of the "Purges"

Beauvoir published "An Eye for an Eye" [*Œil pour œil*] in February 1946, in a France still riven by the brutalities and bitter animosities of the German Occupation and the Vichy regime.[10] Her title refers, of course, to the Old

---

7. *New York Times*, May 6, 2011, A17.

8. Although intraspecies aggression is frequent among chimpanzees, for example, the primatologist de Frans de Waal notes that acts to which we might ascribe the term *revenge* are rare. When they do occur, they appear to be intentional and not instinctive actions (Waal 1990, especially 240–41 and 270–71). But revenge is, of course, but one particular motive for aggression among other possible ones, such as defense of territory or competition for females. As such, it has to be imputed to chimpanzees by human observers, and the risk of anthropocentrism is high here.

9. Because my focus is on responses to mass political atrocities, my discussion does not address those lesser cases where some sort of material restitution for a wrong may be satisfactory. Likewise, although some of Beauvoir's insights also apply to responses to irremediable personal wrongs, these are not my main concern here.

10. The essay was originally published in *Les Temps modernes*, no. 5, February 1946, 813–30, and was republished as chapter 4 of *L'Existentialisme et la sagesse des nations* (Paris: Nagel, 1948, 125–64). The English translation (in Beauvoir 2004) is based on the latter.

Testament injunction to avenge injury with injury.[11] It also refers, in the context of France in 1946, to the "purges" of those who had collaborated with the Nazis during the Occupation. Many of these became targets of the extralegal, spontaneous "justice" meted out to collaborators by former members of the Resistance and others. Others were formally tried by the newly created French government and, in some cases, executed for various crimes of collaboration with the enemy.[12]

The specific focus of Beauvoir's essay was the high-profile trial and execution a year earlier of Robert Brasillach, but the continuing trials of collaborators and accused Nazi criminals throughout 1946 formed its backdrop.[13] Brasillach was a young, right-wing intellectual. Graduating from the prestigious École Normale in the same cohort as Sartre, he had enjoyed a considerable reputation on the Paris intellectual scene as a poet and novelist, in addition to his political presence. During the Occupation he had been editor in chief for more than two years of the fascist weekly newspaper *Je suis partout* [*I Am Everywhere*]. Among other unsavory practices, the paper would list the names and whereabouts of Jews and members of the Resistance, who could then face Nazi deportation, torture, or execution. A variety of his explicitly pro-German and anti-Semitic writings were cited at the trial. However, Brasillach was not tried on charges related to any specific deportation or death or for his anti-Semitism but for "complicity" with an enemy power [*d'intelligence avec l'ennemi*].[14] Reflecting a year after the trial on its significance, on her own emotions, and on her refusal to sign a petition that had been circulated among French intellectuals asking for

---

11. It refers to the Talionic Law. See Exodus 21.

12. For a general account of the purges see Lottman (1986), and for the purges of intellectuals in particular see Assouline (1985).

13. Brasillach's trial lasted only one day, taking place on January 19, 1945, and his execution was carried out soon thereafter, on February 6.

14. *Je suis partout* had a significant circulation: about 250,000 in 1942 (Kaplan 2000, 50). Brasillach also wrote for other pro-Nazi journals and attended meetings with intellectuals in Germany. He was tried under article 75 of the French legal code and found guilty of intentionally assisting Germany, or other enemy powers, or their agents. Jacques Isorni, his defense lawyer, afterward published a transcript of the trial, in which he lists the precise questions the jury was asked to consider in establishing Brasillach's guilt (1946, 209–10). It is worth noting that, although it had some precursors after World War I, the concept of "crimes against humanity" first took on substance only in the context of the Nuremberg trials. These began some months after Brasillach was executed but were ongoing at the time Beauvoir wrote her essay. Perhaps surprisingly, "crimes against humanity" became incorporated into French law only in 1964 (Kaplan 2000, xi).

clemency for Brasillach, Beauvoir offers a nuanced phenomenology of the desire for revenge. She also insists, as we will see, on its almost invariably self-defeating qualities.

Beauvoir begins, like Connolly, from her own experience, and her essay has an impassioned and sometimes confessional tone. As an anti-establishment leftist, Beauvoir had been firmly opposed to the death penalty before the war, and she had believed herself to be above such "base" sentiments as hatred and revenge (EE 245–46; OO 125–26). She saw criminals as victims of an unjust system of bourgeois law from which she herself benefited, and she did not presume to pass judgment on them. But with the Occupation her feelings changed in dramatic and disturbing ways. "Under the Nazi oppression, faced with traitors who became their accomplices, we saw poisonous sentiments [des sentiments vénéneux] bloom in our hearts, of whose flavor we had never previously had a presentiment" (EE 245 TA; OO 125). She continues: "Since June 1940 we have learned rage and hate. We have wished humiliation and death on our enemies" (EE 246; OO 126).

However, Beauvoir was never a direct victim of Nazi violence herself. In occupied Paris, she suffered from the sense of menace, from the myriad humiliating restrictions on life, and from shortages of food and fuel. She also recalls in her autobiography her tremendous shock the first time she saw a German wall-poster announcing that a French citizen had been shot for an act of resistance (PL 376; FA II 542). People she knew personally and cared about were arrested, disappeared, or were killed. She recalls the for-lorn hope, as the camps were opened at the end of the war, that some of the missing would return. But, as with Connolly, she was not an immediate victim of the atrocities that she called "absolute evil" [le mal absolu].[15]

---

15. Far from being a victim, Beauvoir has been accused by some of having had rather too pleasant an Occupation. Tarred with the same brush as Sartre (whom the Communists rumored might be a secret provocateur), she has even been ac-cused of "collaboration" with the regime (see Bair 1990, 258–60). The latter rumor is, as Galster writes, obviously "absurd" (1996, 288), although given Sartre's hos-tile relationship at the time with the Communists (who were the backbone of the organized Resistance), its origin is comprehensible. Both Beauvoir and Sartre were profoundly hostile to Nazism. They engaged in minor acts of resistance, includ-ing, at some personal risk, illegally traveling into the Vichy zone in 1941 to try to make contact with Resistance groups there and to distribute leaflets. However, the question of complicity (as opposed to active collaboration) is more complicated. As Beauvoir later realized with regard to Algeria, unless one is prepared to risk one's life in resistance, one bears a certain degree of responsibility for the atrocities com-mitted by a regime under which one lives. Beauvoir certainly made some question-able accommodations, such as signing the required "Vichy" oath, affirming that

Beauvoir's hatred of the Nazis was outstripped only by her loathing for their French collaborators, notably those public figures who broadcast Nazi propaganda on the radio or published pro-Nazi journals like *Je suis partout*.[16] "We said to ourselves in a fit of rage, 'they will pay.' And our anger seemed to promise a joy so heavy that we could scarcely believe ourselves able to bear it" (EE 246 TA; OO 128). But Beauvoir is also deeply shocked by her reactions: her rage and hatred, her desire for revenge and for the humiliation and death of those who had committed "absolute evil." How, as a good humanist, could she feel such things? Thus she set about trying to understand the existential meanings of this desire for revenge.

Because Beauvoir's project is to understand the desire for revenge phenomenologically, to disclose its existential meanings and implications, she does not try to delve "beneath" it to seek for causes. She does not consider revenge as instinctive; it is not, as is so widely assumed, simply a "natural" response to injury or atrocity. Nor does she attempt to explain it psychoanalytically, as the displacement of subconscious drives, desires, or fears.

---

she was neither a Jew nor a Communist, in order to be able to teach, and working on a music program for a German-controlled radio station. She also published her first novel, *L'Invitée*, in 1943 under conditions of Nazi censorship, when some other writers were simply refusing to publish. As Galster remarks, such actions may indirectly have helped to give the Occupation regime a veneer of normalcy (1996, 288), but they certainly do not justify the tendentious accusations of "collaboration," made notably by Gilbert (1991).

See also Susan Suleiman's troubled, yet sympathetic, reading of Beauvoir's wartime diaries and other writings. Discussing Beauvoir's business-as-usual and hedonistic lifestyle, especially during the early part of the war, she writes: "If one tries to imagine what it was actually like to live as a civilian in Paris during the winter of 1939–1940, *without knowing what was in store*, it becomes easier to understand Beauvoir's apparent insensitivity, her selfish pursuit of pleasure even as catastrophe is about to strike" (1996, 224). But Suleiman is also profoundly disturbed by Beauvoir's actions. Beauvoir had been a heroine for her in her youth, but she now describes experiencing a profound sense of "separation," observing that "had I been in her place, I would not have had the choice of signing the oath, or working for Radio-Paris. . . . My choices, as a Jewish woman, even if I had been a self-identified *French* Jewish woman, would have been very, very different" (220; Suleiman's emphasis).

16. Beauvoir's especially intense hatred of intellectual collaborators such as Brasillach may perhaps be explained by the fact that they were active in creating the world in which she found herself also to be complicit in evil. As Merleau-Ponty wrote of the Occupation in the first issue of *Les Temps modernes*, nobody who survived had clean hands ([1945] 1964c).

She also does not attribute it, like Nietzsche, to the displacement of a fundamental "will to power."[17]

Beauvoir expressly reserves the term *punishment* to refer to the purely retaliatory treatment that revenge demands (an eye for an eye), and she does not make a distinction between "revenge" and "retribution." She would disagree with those thinkers who try to distinguish them by designating "retribution" as a form of justice, as proportionate or just deserts, and castigating "revenge" as a wild excess.[18] However, she does distinguish punishment from what she calls "sanctions," by which she means those

---

17. Rather, Beauvoir argues that revenge must be distinguished from a "will to power," although it may superficially appear similar. Hate, she says, may sometimes become a "pretext" [*un prétexte*] for exercising a will to power, an excuse for the pleasure of domination over others—but then one is no longer engaging in revenge proper but in something else (EE 251; OO 143). Although, as we have seen, Beauvoir refers to the human desire "to seek the death of the other" as ubiquitous, she does so with reference to Hegel, and she does not align this desire with a Nietzschean notion of the "will to power." Indeed, I am not aware of other uses of the concept of "will to power" in Beauvoir's œuvre, and it sits rather strangely in this essay. Possibly she alludes to it here because other thinkers so often explicate revenge through Nietzschean lenses.

18. Judith Shklar, for example, insists that unlike "social retaliation, which has the more general aim of attacking public wrongs . . . revenge is uniquely subjective, not measurable, and probably an unquenchable urge of the provoked human heart. It is the very opposite of justice, in every respect, and inherently incompatible with it . . . [for] revenge is not detached, impersonal, proportionate, or rule-bound" (1990, 93). See also Minow: "A trial . . . transfers the individual's desire for revenge to the state or official bodies. The transfer cools vengeance into retribution, slows judgment with procedure, and interrupts . . . the vicious cycle of blame and feud" (1998, 26).

However, other thinkers still plausibly insist, with Beauvoir, that vengefulness *is* the core of "just deserts" or "retributive" theories of justice and that the difference is merely a matter of degree. Feinberg, for example, writes: "I think it is fair to say of our community, however, that punishment generally expresses more than judgments of disapproval; it is also a symbolic way of getting back at the criminal, of expressing a kind of vindictive resentment. . . . [The criminal's] punishment bears the aspect of legitimized vengefulness. Hence there is much truth in J. F. Stephen's celebrated remark [in 1863] that 'The criminal law stands to the passion of revenge in much the same relation as marriage to the sexual appetite'" (cited in Feinberg 1970, 100–101). See also French (2001) and Murphy (2003) for recent, explicit defenses of justice as legitimized vengefulness. In what follows, I also treat revenge and retribution as roughly equivalent.

One should note that, although the notion of *"justice rétributive"* exists in French legal discourse, the most common meaning of *"la rétribution"* is nearer to the English "remuneration," a payment or recompense, such as a salary.

penalties that have intended purposes other than revenge. Many contemporary discussions of punishment tend to conflate the two, as when it is claimed that the punishment of certain criminals is necessary to protect society from them, or that their punishment will have a needed deterrent effect on others, or reform the wrongdoer. Such arguments for sanctions (to use Beauvoir's distinction) may have utilitarian justifications, but they fall out of the purview of revenge and so of what Beauvoir calls punishment proper. "What distinguishes punishment," she writes, "is that it expressly aims [*il vise expressément*] at the individual who suffers it. It does not seek to prevent him from committing new crimes, for if one is able to punish him, this means he is already beyond the condition where he could do further wrong. Nor is it a matter of making an example. . . . Thus, vengeance is not justified by realistic considerations." To the contrary, she goes on, "a concern for efficacy often demands that one renounce punishment. . . . Vengeance appears to be a luxury. Nonetheless, it answers a need so deep that it can hold practical interests in check" (EE 247 TA; OO 131).[19]

From a utilitarian perspective, punishment that seeks revenge is dismissed as irrational. "If you hate much punish much" is, in Bentham's classic formulation, the byword of an unacceptably "capricious" view of punishment; one based on the whims of "sympathy and antipathy" and not on a rational calculus of pains.[20] Beauvoir concurs that the pursuit of revenge may be counterproductive with regard to other, rational objectives we may hold. But, more importantly, she argues that revenge as a response to atrocity is almost always a failure *on its own terms*. For it cannot actually restore the prior situation or cancel out the prior suffering. Nor can it provide full moral satisfaction by establishing actual reciprocity.[21]

---

19. In many instances the justifications for punishment are, of course, more mixed and are not purely vengeful. But it is often the case that by the time the perpetrators of mass atrocities are brought to trial the political situation has changed to such an extent that neither deterrence nor the protection of society remains a justification for the penalty inflicted. As Murphy also notes, "The goal of vengeance is simply to provide vindictive satisfaction to victims, and victims may require something other than what is necessary to control crime or what wrongdoers deserve" (2003, 17).

20. "But all punishment in itself is evil. Upon the principle of utility, if it ought at all to be admitted, it ought only to be admitted in as far as it promises to exclude some greater evil" (Bentham 1973, 170, para. II).

21. Thus, although some of those who lost family members on September 11 joyously celebrated the killing of Bin Laden as "payback," others cited in press reports said it provided no "closure" and in no way redeemed their loss.

Yet, however self-defeating it may be, the desire for revenge after atrocity should not be dismissed as mere caprice. For we are not—and should not be exhorted to be—merely rational actors. Thus Beauvoir situates the phenomenology of revenge within the ambiguities of embodiment and the necessary failures of human action. Hate, she points out, "is not a capricious passion" but rather an appropriate response to our encounter with those who commit absolute evil (EE 248; OO 133). Between reason and caprice there lies a range of complex, and often paradoxical, emotions and dispositions that more dualistic philosophies usually ignore.

Acts of evil may sometimes be committed quite unthinkingly or (as discussed in chapter 2) through indifference. But in the case of collaborators in France there had been a deliberate targeting of victims: Named communists and Resistance members were shot and tortured; known Jews denounced to the Gestapo. In 1945, few of the victims were there in person to demand their revenge. Thus, Beauvoir finds it necessary to distinguish between those cases where revenge is sought on one's own immediate behalf and those (more common cases) where revenge is sought on behalf of others who are no longer living. She begins with the former since it represents what she calls the "privileged" case. For here we see revenge in its most "spontaneous" form (EE 247; OO 132). With regard to the latter she also distinguishes between the immediate and extralegal vengeance that was wreaked on some collaborators as the war ended and punishment that was exacted through formal legal processes via the courts. This last, she argues, is more complex, for although it is vengeful it also aims beyond revenge. However, in all cases, she will show, revenge fails to accomplish much of what is desired. I follow Beauvoir's essay in discussing all three cases: the desire for revenge on one's own behalf; on behalf of others; and in the context of legal prosecution. In all three cases revenge is both meaningful and an existential failure.

Turning the Tables: The "Privileged" Case

In the "privileged case" [*le cas privilégié*], a (still living) victim of atrocity tries symmetrically to turn the tables on the perpetrator. Beauvoir argues that what the former victim demands is not only an equivalence of physical suffering ("an eye for an eye") but also, and more significantly, a reciprocal recognition of her or his subjectivity from the one who had previously sought to deny it. For absolute evil lies not only in killing or maiming but also in the integral refusal to recognize its victim as a *subject*.[22] In some (it seems rare) instances, when the Nazi concentration camps were liberated, the inmates turned on their jailers. Then, says Beauvoir, "revenge existed for them in the most concrete and obvious way possible. The victims and their torturers had really exchanged situations" (EE 250–51; OO 141).[23] For revenge, in its privileged form, seeks a direct reversal. It seeks an equivalence through which the perpetrator must now be made not only to

---

22. To recall, in discussing Sade, Beauvoir had pointed out that his project was not fully to deny the subjectivity of his victims since what he sought from them was an acknowledgment of his sovereignty. However, this "normal" sadist project is not necessarily the aim in all torture or atrocity. Although most often the project is to degrade victims in ways that still maintain their consciousness, so that they are aware of their degradation and of the sovereignty of the torturer, on other occasions such extreme physical destruction is wrought that the victim is reduced to no more than a bundle of agonized sensation for whom no reflexive relation to self, other, or world is now possible.

In *Being and Nothingness*, Sartre argues that full objectification is never possible since the victim can always turn the tables on the perpetrator through the "look." He cites the passage from Faulkner's *Light in August* in which the castrated and dying negro, Christmas, "looks" at his murders as evidence of the indestructibility of subjectivity. Sartre writes: "The sadist discovers that it was *that freedom* which he wished to enslave, and at the same time he realizes the futility of his effort" ([1943] 1966, 497). Similarly, in his play *Morts sans sépulture* (first performed in 1946), consciousness is never obliterated by torture. The central characters are a group of captured Resistance activists who are being tortured to try to make them disclose where their leader is hidden. They not only clear-headedly refuse to talk but are also able to engage in a reasoned debate with each other until the very end about what is at stake in a plan to provide false information to their captors (Sartre 1947).

However, in "An Eye for an Eye" Beauvoir's view is strikingly different from Sartre's. She argues that it is possible fully to destroy subjectivity by reducing another to mere "panting flesh" (as I discuss below). Later on, in the case of Djamila Boupacha, we learn that she entirely lost consciousness during her torture, so that she was never sure whether she had "merely" been raped with a bottle or also in a more "conventional" manner (Beauvoir and Halimi 1962a, 31; 1962b, 24). It seems not to be uncommon that victims are tortured to the point of unconsciousness or extreme disorientation, if not death. However, the fact that (as we now have learned) torture victims are often hooded may suggest that their "look" is indeed felt to be threatening to their torturers, as Sartre claims.

23. This reversal seems to have taken place but not often. Or, at least, it has not been well documented in Holocaust research. For a recent discussion of what is known and why cases of direct revenge may have been ignored in "post-Holocaust" studies, see Berel Lang (2005); see also John Sack (1995) for an account of such a brutal turning of the tables.

acknowledge (through pain or knowledge of his impending death) his own vulnerable embodiment but also to acknowledge the subjectivity of his victim, which he had previously sought to deny. "The torturer believes himself to be sovereign consciousness and pure freedom in the face of the miserable thing he tortures. When he in turn becomes a tortured thing, he feels the tragic ambiguity of his condition as a man. What he must understand [ce qu'il droit comprendre] though, is that the victim, whose abjection he shares, also shares with him the privileges that he believed he could arrogate to himself. And he must not understand this by the thought alone, in a speculative manner, but must realize this reversal of situation concretely" (EE 248–49 TA; OO 135). Such an "understanding" [compréhension], Beauvoir says, is not merely "an abstract intellection" but is rather an "understanding" in a Heideggerian sense. That is, it is "a process [une opération] by means of which our entire being realizes a situation" (EE 248; OO 134–35; my emphasis).

But even in this "privileged case" a full reversal is rarely possible. The victim now demands from the former torturer a reciprocal recognition of her or his subjectivity. However, this runs up against a fundamental difficulty. For "It aims for nothing less than to 'compel' [contraindre] a 'freedom' [and] these terms are contradictory" (EE 249; OO 136). The impossible intent of revenge is, through inflicting suffering, to incite feelings of remorse and to obtain a recognition from the perpetrator that, in actuality, may be offered only voluntarily. One may reduce the former torturer himself to mere materiality, but then he will not be capable of the desired sentiments. For "if the suffering inflicted is excessive, the consciousness of the criminal is swallowed up in it [s'engloutit]. Entirely taken up in suffering, he is nothing more than panting flesh [une chair panteleante]—torture misses its aim" (EE 249 TA; OO 138). However, if his consciousness is not so engulfed, then he still remains free to respond to his punishment as he wishes. He may, for example, "undergo it with a sense of irony, with resistance, with arrogance, or with a resignation lacking in remorse. Here again punishment ends up in a defeat" (EE 250 TA; OO 138). Thus, Beauvoir argues, the desire for vengeance can virtually never be satisfied: It vainly seeks "to reestablish an impossible reciprocity" (EE 251; OO 144).

And what of inflicting death? In a certain way killing the perpetrator satisfies the desire for revenge better than other punishments. For, as Beauvoir observes, even if one could momentarily succeed in effecting the desired reversal, still vengeance "cannot keep a consciousness in subjection for its entire life." Death, by contrast, produces a certain moment of closure: It freezes the flux of time through which the project of revenge would otherwise have become dissipated. The act of execution extinguishes the life of the evil doer "with the hope that the abjection of those last instants will be eternalized by death" (EE 250; OO 140–41). Thus "the moment when Mussolini cries 'No, no' in front of the firing squad satisfies hate far more than the moment when he collapses beneath the bullets" (EE 250; OO 140).[24] But there is defeat here also, for any possibility of reciprocal recognition has now been definitively foreclosed: "[T]he concrete restitution of a relation of reciprocity between perpetrator and victim would require the living presence of the perpetrator turned victim in his turn" (EE 250 TA; OO 141).

Revenge on Behalf of Others

Much of the literature on revenge focuses on the privileged case; that is, on revenge as the desire to reverse the roles of victim and perpetrator. However, a further question, one that is not as often addressed, is, Why do we so often desire revenge when we are not the directly injured party, when, like Beauvoir or Connolly, we are bystanders? To address this second question it is necessary to explore the inherent sociality of individuated existence. Given Beauvoir's critique of the conception of the self as a sovereign, rational actor, it follows that to be a "bystander" is not, in actuality, to occupy the position of a detached observer; it is not primarily through dispassionate or rational judgment that we call for revenge. Because we are embodied and profoundly social beings, there are sentient and affective ways in which our lives are deeply implicated in those of others. Thus, we may "assume" the suffering of victims of atrocity as "our own." We may do so via several different routes, but three are especially salient: our embodied responses to suffering; our experiences of shared worlds; and our intense personal bonds with others.

Embodied Responses

Witnessing the physical suffering of others, their torture, injury, or violent death, may arouse pain in our own bodies. This is not, of course, to say that we literally feel the same pain as the victims of an atrocity. Far from it. But we may have a visceral or "gut" response to the suffering of others that is

---

24. More recently, the baiting of Saddam Hussein on the gallows has also exemplified this desire for the abjection of the perpetrator.

itself painful.[25] For example, we may feel nauseous and shaky at the sight of another's bloody wounds or mutilations, or at the sight of the dead or dying. However, such responses are never physiological alone. For if we desire the suffering of others we will receive pleasure, and not pain, from viewing their pain. We can also sometimes block our embodied responses. For example, those who provide humanitarian assistance in situations of extreme suffering often find they must learn to do this in order to remain functional. Furthermore, such embodied responses do not only arise when we directly witness an atrocity (as did those in New York who actually saw people leaping to their deaths). We may also experience them when an event is mediated by film or TV, or when we hear or read about it. However, these mediated responses involve a greater degree of imaginative empathy on our part. Thus there must be further, social aspects to how we come to experience injury to others as injurious to ourselves.

Experiences of Shared Worlds

Felt commonality of place or world is often one such vital aspect. Thus, on September 11, the trauma Connolly and many others felt was not merely that some three thousand deaths took place—such numbers of people frequently die in any number of atrocities, wars, and disasters. Rather, for the onlookers, these deaths threatened the destruction of their entire world. Mass rape and murder in Srebrenica or Rwanda (or, indeed, atrocities in Iraq or Afghanistan) may stir a liberal American professor to moral outrage, but it is not likely to provoke the same overwhelming gut reactions as the deaths on September 11. For these more distant atrocities do not as profoundly disrupt our own world. They do not put our very being-in-the-world, the meaning and solidity of our lives, into question. By contrast, the violation of "our own" place, whether it be the national territory that we take as a given, or the specific built spaces that are part of the "there-ness" of our world (for Beauvoir, the specific streets of Paris through which she routinely passes and the cafés now full of Germans; for Connolly, New York and its iconic World Trade Towers), is experienced as a profound violation of a self that inhabits and is inhabited by that world.[26]

---

25. I discuss this phenomenon more fully in Kruks (2001).

26. Connolly is highly critical of intense patriotism, and he is well attuned to its dangers. Thus, it is significant that when he recalls other events that have produced a similar visceral reaction on his part, they are moments of specifically American trauma: the Cuban missile crisis and the deaths of John F. Kennedy, Martin Luther King Jr., and Robert Kennedy (2005, 11).

For not only must we say that "I am my body" but also that "I am my situation," and it follows that its spatial and social aspects are constitutive of "myself."

Likewise we must also say that "I am other people" since, even while I am not literally them, their presence and my affective relations with them (whether caring or conflictual) are also strongly constitutive of who I am. Thus, Beauvoir writes of how she experienced a oneness with others in occupied Paris. They were "a multitude who were faceless yet whose presence inhabited me [*dont la présence m'investissait*]; they were everywhere, outside me and within me; it was they who, through the beating of my own heart, were stirred up, who hated" (PL 398 TA; FA II 575). For our world is suffused, our existence shaped, by our participation (often unchosen) in various anonymous social collectivities. I am also my (sometimes very diverse) social and cultural identities, and these shape my affective sense of belonging (or not belonging) to various groups. Such affective identities may often involve a language shared with others and a citizenship-based identity. Being "French" for Beauvoir in occupied Paris or "American" for Connolly after September 11 are among the untheorized background conditions for the experience of evil that each recounts. Such background conditions suffuse what we normally take for granted as our field of action, and they often affectively color our relations with others within that field. Thus, our tacit assumptions about those who live within our political system, speak our language, share our spaces, and so forth, even if we do not know them personally (and whether rightly or, perhaps, mistakenly), are that they are sufficiently "like" us that violence against them is experienced as an injury to ourselves.

We may, of course, extend this sense that we are integrally bound up with them to groups with whom we have no physical proximity or daily contact. This is why we may well feel outrage about atrocities in Srebrenica or Rwanda. But in these cases our bonds are less intense. Distances of various kinds stretch our affective bonds thinner. Thus, although we may feel profoundly angry and demand that retribution be exacted from those who have engaged in such genocidal acts, our own world does not disintegrate around us. We are unlikely to say that "the bottom falls out of our world" as we hear of such atrocities or even when we see their suffering victims on our TVs or computers. Moreover, we are free to turn off the screen, to protect ourselves from the pain of experiencing the suffering of others. But such options are nonexistent or very minimal when atrocity penetrates our own immediate world.

Personal Bonds with Others

When we have known victims of an atrocity in person, and especially when they have been a significant part of our own immediate affective universe, then the bottom does indeed fall out of our world. Thus Beauvoir writes in *The Prime of Life* of the murder by the Germans of "Bourla"—Jewish, nineteen years old, a former student of Sartre's, a lover of "Lise," one of Beauvoir's women students (with whom she also had an affair), and a member of the "little family" she and Sartre had created around them—as tearing her world apart. She tells that Bourla and his father were seized by the Gestapo and taken off to Drancy (the predeportation holding center for Jews on the edge of Paris) in a dawn raid. For a while a young German intermediary promised that (for a fee) he would protect them, but then he admitted that they had already been deported and killed. Beauvoir tries to imagine Bourla's last moments:

> Death . . . had he stood for an instant and seen it face to face? And who had been killed first, his father or him? If he was conscious, I felt certain, he must have cried *No!*, aloud or silently, and this last atrocious convulsion remained for ever and vainly frozen in eternity. He had cried *No!*, and then there had been nothing. I found the very thought unbearable; but I had to bear it. . . . The last four years had been a balancing act between fear and hope, between patience and anger, between desolation and moments of returning joy. Now, abruptly, all accommodation [*toute conciliation*] appeared impossible, and I was torn asunder. . . . Never before had I encountered with such obviousness the random horror of our mortal state [*jamis je n'avais touché avec une telle évidence la capricieuse horreur de notre condition mortelle*]. . . . Because of his death and all that it meant, my moments of outrage and despair reached an intensity I had never hitherto known: truly hellish. (PL 457–58 TA; FA II 662–63)[27]

---

27. As Susan Suleiman has pointed out, Beauvoir's memories of this episode are erroneous. Beauvoir describes going out to Drancy with Lise and discovering one day in the spring of 1943 that the camp had been emptied, except for two figures they saw waving high up in the building. They believed these figures to be Bourla and his father until, when asked for proof that they were still alive, the German intermediary angrily said they had already been killed. However, Drancy continued to be occupied until August 1944, more than a year after the events that Beauvoir "describes," and so her account is inaccurate. Suleiman attributes this inaccuracy to what she calls Beauvoir's "ambivalent memory" about Jews during the Occupation: her admixture of shame and guilt even as she continued to live her life with her customary zest (Suleiman 2010). But whatever explanation one might offer for Beauvoir's inaccurate recalling of these events, one cannot doubt the profound despair and rage they aroused in her.

Beauvoir ends this volume of her autobiography with a meditation on the significance death has held in her life, and she returns again to Bourla's death as the one that has haunted her the most. She had also earlier presented this death in fictional form in *The Mandarins* in the account of Anne's reaction to the death of her daughter's lover, Diego.[28] No closure was possible for Bourla's death. The was no body, no funeral—only an absence that could not be grasped:

> Bourla; when I walked through the Paris streets I tried to say, he is not there. But in any case he would not have been in the precise spot where I was. From where, then, *was* he absent? From nowhere and everywhere: his loss overran [*infestait*] the entire world. And yet this world was full; *no place remains there for one who no longer occupies his place. What separation! What betrayal!* Each of our heart-beats disavows his life *and* his death. (PL 478 TA; FA II 693; my emphases)

How then could she not hate? How could she not desire revenge against those who not only were complicit in such a death but were also making her complicit in his absence, who were causing *her* to betray him?[29] Above all, the French collaborators, and especially those Parisian intellectuals such as Brasillach, who had in significant ways shared her world and so had destroyed it from within, were the object of her hatred:

---

28. Here, the account is very similar to that in *The Prime of Life*, but Beauvoir locates the event as taking place in May 1944, again before Drancy was emptied (Suleiman 2010). However, as noted in chapter 4, Beauvoir's "fictions" in *The Mandarins* frequently included changing the chronology of actual events. Anne, to recall, is the second character in the novel into which Beauvoir says she put a great deal of herself. Anne is haunted by the death of Diego. Her profound sense of guilt and her impossible attempt to grasp his definitive, yet ungraspable, absence resonate with Beauvoir's account of her own struggles. Anne says: "Everything that's been given to me, I stole from them. 'They were killed.' Which one first? His father or him? Death didn't enter into his plans. Did he know he was going to die? Did he resist or was he resigned? How to know? And now that he's dead, what difference does it make? No date of death, no tombstone. That's why I still grope around for him through this life that he loved with such passion" (M 35 TA; M Fr 28).

29. In *Force of Circumstance* Beauvoir describes learning about the horrors of the camps as they were opened: "In '45, we received these revelations in all their immediacy, they concerned our friends, our comrades, our own life," and she names those she had known who did not come back. "Once more, I was ashamed to live" (FC I 32; FC Fr I 53–54). Again, in *The Mandarins*, Anne experiences this shame as the surviving deportees return to Paris: "Before these returning ghosts I was ashamed, ashamed of not having suffered enough, of being there unscathed, of being ready to give them advice from the heights of my good health" (M 217 TA; M Fr 160).

I had never really known what hatred was before, I realized; my rages had been more or less abstract. But now I knew its flavor and aimed it with particular violence against those of our enemies whom I knew the best. Pétain's speeches hit me more intensely than Hitler's. I condemned all collaborators, but I felt a deep, specific and quite excruciating loathing with regard to those of my own kind—intellectuals, journalists, writers. When men of letters, when artists, went to Germany to assure the conquerors of our spiritual loyalty, I felt I had been personally betrayed. (PL 398 TA; FA II 575)

As previously mentioned, when Brasillach was found guilty and condemned to death, Beauvoir refused to sign the petition asking for clemency for him. In "An Eye for an Eye" she offers an explanation for her refusal, couched in terms of his freedom and responsibility, that I find dubious. Brasillach fully accepted responsibility for what he had done, and he expressed no remorse. Thus, she argues, "in claiming his freedom he also claimed his punishment" (EE 257 TA; OO 161), and she ends the essay by asserting that the justification for the punishment is that it recognizes the freedom with which evil has been undertaken (EE 259; OO 165). However, that Brasillach acted freely (which he no doubt did) is not in itself an argument for imposing or carrying out the death penalty, and Beauvoir's later, autobiographical remarks better explain (even if they do not, in my view, justify) her refusal to sign the petition. She was not, in fact, just a bystander. She was not a dispassionate observer, and her refusal was far more visceral than her "reasoned" justification suggests.

In *Force of Circumstance* Beauvoir names those friends who had died or suffered at the hands of the Nazis and their collaborators: "It was with these friends, dead or dying, that I felt solidarity," she writes. "if I had lifted a finger to help Brasillach, I would have deserved to have them spit in my face. There was not even a moment's hesitation on my part, the question did not even arise" (FC I 21 TA; FC Fr I 37).[30] The desire for revenge—the

---

30. Albert Camus, by contrast, had a change of heart and did sign the petition. A few weeks earlier he had responded to a similar request (with regard to some other death sentences) that it was not up to him to request a pardon; only the victim's surviving family members might legitimately ask for one, he said. Although the death sentence horrified him, Camus still insisted, like Beauvoir, that he could not "betray" those who had died (2006, 233). However, shortly afterward, in the case of Brasillach, he did sign the clemency petition. Later that year he explained: "I could no longer accept any truth that might place me under an obligation, direct or indirect, to condemn a man to death," and he now condemned the use of the death penalty against collaborators, calling it no more than "legitimate murder" (2006, 260–61).

demand for recognition that the dead can no longer make—now becomes the immediate, unreflective project of the living. For the dead live on within us, the "other within."[31] Their absence is a presence that still inhabits our world, as Beauvoir had said of Bourla. To refuse to avenge their deaths would not only be to destroy our solidarity with them, to be complicit in their infinite absence; it would also be to betray ourselves.

However, here again, Beauvoir realizes that revenge must also *fail*—and this is why she surely could have chosen otherwise and signed the clemency petition on behalf of Brasillach. For although we carry their deaths within us, still we are not those who have actually ceased to exist, and nothing can restore them or fully heal the loss. "In truth, one can no more avenge the dead than one can resurrect them," she writes (EE 252; OO 144). Human existence is simultaneously intersubjective and yet also individuated. Thus, even though the bottom falls out of our world when atrocities are committed against others, still we are not them. The restoration of reciprocity that the victim seeks (or would have sought) directly from the perpetrator is absolutely impossible here—and, Beauvoir warns, the failure of the project of revenge on behalf of others may be more dangerous.

"Official Justice": Legal Sanctions and Revenge

As France was liberated at the end of the war, many immediate and extra-legal acts of revenge were committed. Beauvoir was hardly unique in her hatred and desire for revenge, but many others acted on this desire, whereas she did not. Scores were viciously settled as members of the Resistance beat up or murdered known (or alleged) collaborators; women who had "slept with the enemy" had their heads shaved and were publicly humiliated. Although she says she understands the passion for vengeance "with her entire being," Beauvoir did not condone such counterviolence: To *experience* the desire for revenge and to *act* on that desire are very different matters. For, beyond the real risk that violence may be done to innocent parties, other dangers attended this "private vengeance."

Beauvoir was particularly concerned about the actions of those she called "vigilantes": groups that went around attacking collaborators (and alleged collaborators) who had not injured them personally and against whom they held only a generalized hatred. "I do not think anyone was

---

31. Beauvoir later uses this phrase in *The Coming of Age* to describe the way that age inhabits us.

revolted by the way the concentration camp inmates massacred their torturers," she writes, but it is otherwise with the vigilante. Since he is not the
directly injured party himself, the vigilante in effect claims the right to
judge from on high: He claims that he is entitled to inflict vengeful punishment on others in the name of universal rights. However, Beauvoir argues,
since he is neither the directly injured party nor the institutional embodiment of the general values of society, the vigilante "is not qualified to
defend the universal rights of man." What he is doing is tyrannically to set
himself up as a "sovereign consciousness," and "this is why private vengeance always has a disquieting character" (EE 251; OO 142).[32] Thus, even
though Beauvoir helps us to make sense of the prevalence of such extralegal revenge, she does not condone it. Instead she turns, in the last part of
her essay, to consider state prosecutions and legal penalties as a preferable,
although still flawed, alternative. Beauvoir attended Brasillach's trial as an
observer, and although she felt deep personal satisfaction at his sentencing
and execution, she was also profoundly disturbed. The trial, she said, left
"the taste of ashes" in her mouth (EE 246; OO 129).

In the "privileged" case, we saw, the pursuit of revenge involves an
immediate, concrete relationship of former victim and perpetrator. Revenge
serves no utilitarian social function, and it looks only backward in time, in
the victim's attempt to gain from the perpetrator the recognition that was
previously denied. However, with the turn to legal process, to what Beauvoir calls "official" or "social" justice [la justice sociale] the aim can no longer
be to reestablish this "impossible reciprocity" (EE 251; OO 144). Instead,
says Beauvoir, "the notion of vengeance is replaced by that of sanction,
which is elevated to the level of an institution and cut off from its base in
the passions." Rather, it is asserted, "one must punish without hate, in the
name of universal principles" (EE 251; OO 143). But this ideal of objectivity

---

32. In *The Mandarins* Beauvoir gives a very negative portrait of such vengeful
killers in the character Vincent. Vincent is a sullen and angry youth who has killed
a dozen Nazis and collaborators during the war while he was in the Resistance.
Now the war is over, but he wants to continue killing. He and a gang of his friends
are going around executing alleged collaborators. Beauvoir puts some of her objections into the mouth of Henri: "I've heard talk about gangs who enjoy playing
at being judges. Now if it's a question of settling a personal account, I can understand. But these guys who think they're saving France by killing a few collaborators here and there, they are either sick men or stupid bastards" (M 164–65 TA;
M Fr 123). And later in the novel: "Bringing down collaborators in 1943, that was
all right. But now there's no point to it. There's practically no risk involved, it's not
action, it's not work, it's not even a sport. It's just an unhealthy little game. There
are certainly better things to do" (M 202 TA; M Fr 150).

is, of course, untenable. For (as we have already seen in the discussion of political judgment and elsewhere) passions such as hatred cannot be fully expunged. With regard to the vigilantes, Beauvoir had said that the claim to set oneself up as a judge in the name of universal principles is but a specious mask for hatred and revenge, but this may also be the case with legal punishment, especially in times of such intense national feeling.[33] Futhermore, even setting this difficulty aside, the project of reaffirming a society's principles through legal penalties has a certain self-defeating quality.

Beauvoir begins "An Eye for an Eye" by saying that the sentences passed on the collaborators expressed her own sentiments. For, in the face of such evil, she discovered that she did share common values with her society at large and that these were expressed in the verdicts: "We participated in [the collaborator's] condemnation. . . . It is our values, our reasons for living, that are affirmed by their punishment" (EE 246; OO 127). Although, as a leftist social critic, she still considered the legal system generally to be the upholder of a unjust socioeconomic system, such "absolute evil" was another matter. It trumped class divisions. She writes: "To the extent that it refuses tyrannies, that it strives to reestablish the dignity of man, this society is our own. We feel a solidarity with it; we are complicit in its decisions" (EE 246 TA; OO 127–28).

In the case of the collaborators, punishment cannot be justified by classic utilitarian ends such as deterrence or the protection of society, for the accused already belongs to the definitively defeated party. But there is a social value to the penalty, and this is its *expressive* quality. Brasillach is not condemned to death only on the basis of "an eye for an eye" but also as an expression of the values that his crimes have violated. He is to suffer as an expression of society's extreme revulsion at this violation.

---

33. The collaborators' trials (as well as those of Nazi leaders at Nuremberg and elsewhere) have sometimes been described as handing out a vengeful "victor's justice." Brasillach was tried and executed in early 1945, before the war was definitively over in other places. Thus, matters of national pride and patriotism were also at play in his sentencing, and it is striking that the death penalty was not generally imposed on those who were brought to trial somewhat later. Kaplan argues that the early purge trials were an important plank in de Gaulle's postwar project to reassert the values and dignity of "France," and in doing so to consolidate his own power: "With Brasillach's punishment, the government committed an irrevocable act, an execution that consolidated de Gaulle's power and proved the might of his new Court of Justice only four months into its operations. Brasillach's death had a legitimating function" (2000, 229). However, if Beauvoir was aware of these political currents surrounding the trial, she did not say so, either in "An Eye for an Eye" or in her autobiography.

So why then, Beauvoir asks, did the trial also leave the "taste of ashes" in her mouth? Paradoxically, the problem lay in the very goal of objectivity, in the formal, abstract nature of legal procedure: "The official courts claim to take refuge behind this objectivity that is the worst part of the Kantian heritage. They want only to express an impersonal right and to deliver verdicts that are nothing more than the subsumption of a particular case under a universal law. But the accused exists in his singularity, and his concrete presence does not so easily take on the guise of an abstract symbol" (EE 258 TA; OO 162–63).[34]

Thus, although the trial was expressive of the values society places on human life and functioned to reaffirm rights and human dignity, it also had the paradoxical effect of dehumanizing life. For the legal process profoundly objectified Brasillach, reducing him to that *abstract* entity, "the criminal." It reduced him to a mere *symbol* of the evil that society rejects, so that ultimately "the condemned is never far from appearing as an expiatory victim" (EE 252; OO 146). Beauvoir experienced a profound sense of dissociation. For, she realized, "in the end it is a man who is going to experience in his consciousness and in his flesh the penalty aimed at this *abstract* social reality, the condemned criminal" (EE 252; OO 146; my emphasis).[35]

This dissociation arises, Beauvoir notes, not only through the shift from revenge for the actual deeds committed to still-vengeful punishment for the violation of societal values but also from the temporal dissociation of deeds from punishment that the legal process necessitates. In the privileged case revenge aims, however unsuccessfully, to establish an immediate reciprocity between victim and perpetrator. But now, removed in time and place, perhaps months or even years later, and in the courtroom, "someone else" was being punished. Thus the still-vengeful and the expressive functions of the trial enter into conflict. Beauvoir writes of the lonely and dignified figure in

---

34. Beauvoir made a similar point (as mentioned in chapter 2) in discussing Sade's refusal to condemn those brought before him as traitors, when he served as a Grand Juror after the Revolution. For, "when murder becomes constitutional it is nothing more than an obnoxious expression of abstract principles: it becomes inhuman" (MWBS 19 TA; FBS 27).

35. More recently Mark Drumbl has also noted, with regard to international criminal tribunals, what he calls the "disconnect between aspirations of punishment and realities of sentence" (2007, 15 ff). In cases of atrocious "crimes against humanity" he also considers "expressive" goals to be a better justification for punishment than retribution or deterrence. But, analogously to Beauvoir, he warns that "the expressive goals of punishment are fragile. Their attainment is jeopardized by the selectivity and formalism of the legal proceedings" (2007, 17).

the accused's box: "We desired the death of the editor of *Je suis partout*, not of this man completely occupied in dying well" (EE 253; OO 149). Indeed, she reflects, "the dignity with which he carried himself in this extreme situation demanded our respect in the moment we most desired to despise him" (EE 253; OO 149).[36]

In addition to this temporal disjuncture, the grandiose symbolism of the court building, the ritualistic procedures of the trial, the inscrutability of the jury also transformed "justice" into a disturbingly formal and abstract performance—but one out of which she knew real blood would flow:[37]

> Death is a real concrete event, not the fulfillment [*l'accomplissement*] of a rite. The more the trial takes on the aspect of a ceremony, the more outrageous it seems [*plus il semble scandaleux*] that it might end in a real spilling of blood. . . . The questioning, the defence, unrolled with all the pomp of a comic drama. Only the accused belonged to that world of flesh where bullets can kill. Between these two universes no passage seemed conceivable. In renouncing vengeance, society renounces tying the crime to punishment with a concrete bond, and so punishment appears to be but an arbitrarily imposed penalty; for the guilty party it is nothing but an atrocious accident. . . . For all their concern for purity, legal sanctions fail to achieve the concrete goal they have set themselves. (EE 254 TA; OO 151–52)

Thus, "official justice," legal punishment, insofar as it also aims "beyond" revenge, has in significant measure a self-defeating character. For in trying to meet its expressive aims the legal process turns the guilty party into a symbolic object so divorced from his actual deeds that his fate seems arbitrary; his death seems to become yet another atrocity and not an act of justice. Moreover, as in the privileged case, there is no way that the vengeful aspect of legal punishment can ensure that the guilty party will feel remorse, or that he will acknowledge the evil he has perpetrated against society.[38] His

---

36. She also writes of the court appearance of Pierre Laval. Having held top government positions in the Vichy regime and now charged with (and to be executed for) collaboration with the enemy, Laval had aged so much that he seemed barely recognizable. "The vanquished foe was no more than a pitiful old man. It became difficult to wish for his death" (EE 253; OO 148).

37. Arendt also comments on the striking theatricality of the Eichmann trial in 1960 (Arendt 1963, 4). For an insightful comparative discussion of Arendt on the trial of Eichmann and Beauvoir on that of Brasillach, see Marso (2012).

38. As already mentioned, Brasillach did not express remorse. He was still defending his anti-Semitism while in prison before the trial and was writing heroic poetry while awaiting execution (Kaplan 2000, 48–91, 189–90).

execution will neither adequately satisfy the desire for revenge nor adequately reaffirm the values he has violated. Even so, Beauvoir defended both the trial and the penalty, arguing that they were preferable to vigilante "justice." For after atrocity, there are no good solutions. Legal justice is preferable, but there is no adequate way to provide recompense for the "absolute event" of such evil.

"Restorative Justice"?

Today, in a world where the mass atrocities for which we now have the name of "crimes against humanity"—genocides, civilian slaughters, mass rapes, and mutilations, perpetrated in both civil and international wars, and in the violence of states against their own populations—are all too common, the call is often made to *avoid* revenge in their aftermath. An increasingly frequent response to mass atrocities is to set up "truth and reconciliation" commissions and to urge surviving victims and other affected individuals to be "healed" through "reconciliation" or even "forgiveness." Such practices, with their strongly therapeutic orientation, were not part of legal practice, jurisprudence, or political discourse in 1945. They have emerged more recently in the context of wider practices of "restorative justice" that aim to enable societies to cohere and function after profoundly divisive internal conflicts.[39] Thus, we might ask whether or not they now offer a viable alternative to the vengeful forms of justice that Beauvoir discusses.

In the last two decades, "truth and reconciliation commissions" (hereafter TRCs) were established after mass atrocities in many countries, from Peru to South Africa to East Timor. Their advocates argue that these may express a society's abhorrence of atrocities as effectively as trials and punitive legal justice and that, furthermore, they do so in ways that better overcome the profound social antagonisms that atrocities leave in their wake. Advocates also argue that TRCs provide individual victims with the meaningful recognition they seek and aid them to "heal" better than more vengeful forms of justice do.

---

39. As well as truth and reconciliation commissions, reparations may be another important form of "restorative justice," as may government apologies. Schiff describes "victim orientation, perpetrator rehabilitation," and the "full exposure of history" as the central foci of the new restorative justice (2008, 33). He dates practices of restorative justice as having emerged since the 1980s.

The best known (although not the first) of these TRCs is the South African Commission, and it has inspired many others. Archbishop Desmond Tutu, its chairperson, described the TRC as engaging in something new: "a restorative justice which is concerned not so much with punishment as with correcting imbalances, restoring broken relationships—with healing, harmony and reconciliation" (1998, 9). The TRC asked surviving victims of apartheid-era atrocities, and others affected, to forgo not only direct revenge but also punitive forms of legal justice; they were also urged to be reconciled with, or to forgive, perpetrators. Indeed, this urging sometimes bordered on heavy pressure, for forgiveness was often presented as a duty and its refusal as a moral and political failing, or else as a psychological pathology on the part of the victims (Brudholm 2008, 26–41).[40] In exchange for forgoing retribution, victims were provided with a space where they could speak about what they had undergone and where, under the protection of amnesty, perpetrators could also publicly confess to the atrocities they had committed. Amnesty was seen as the most effective way of obtaining a full record of the past, uncovering the truth on the basis of which both national and individual healing could begin. It was generally acknowledged that amnesty was also a politically necessary compromise with the old apartheid regime in order to enable a peaceful transition.[41] "Revealing is healing," claimed banners at the TRC headquarters (Hamber 2003, 160). While Archbishop Tutu wrote: "The past refuses to lie down quietly. It has an uncanny habit of returning to haunt one. . . . However painful the experience, the wounds of the past must not be allowed to fester. They must be opened. They must be cleansed. And balm must be poured on them so they can heal" (1998, 7).

Many have celebrated the TRC as a bold new step that helped to prevent a cycle of revenge in South Africa; others are more doubtful or critical. Some question how far establishing the truth *does* help reconciliation rather than merely keeping old wounds open. Others question whether an agreed-upon account of the truth of apartheid's atrocities can even be

---

40. "Reconciliation" and "forgiveness" are not, of course, identical. However, they were not clearly distinguished in TRC discourse (Gready 2011; esp. chap. 5) and, accordingly, I use them interchangeably.

41. As Tutu himself wrote: "There is no doubt that members of the security establishment would have scuppered the negotiated settlement had they thought they were going to run the gauntlet of trials for their involvement in past violations" (1998, 5). Although most of the cases involved murder and torture perpetrated by agents of the apartheid regime, some cases involving atrocity by members of the resistance movements were also brought before the TRC.

established.[42] There seems to be a consensus that the TRC did contribute toward much-needed national unity by providing South Africans with what has been described as "a semiofficial narrative of a common past" (Forsberg 2003, 73). At the level of public discourse, it also helped to promote the values of human rights and due process, which had been sorely absent under apartheid. Indeed, an editorial in one of the main English-language newspapers described the final TRC report (rather than the constitution) as "the founding document" of the new South Africa: "The Constitution is a theoretical exercise, in large part a product of intellectual effort in the ivory towers of academia. The final report, in a very real and immediate way, defines us" (cited in Verwoerd 2003, 269–70).

However, in exchange for confession, those granted amnesty escaped legal penalties and also kept their jobs. Thus, many have talked critically of a "culture of impunity" or of the TRC as "perpetrator friendly" (Hamber 2009, 133–34). For even policemen who had confessed to the routine use of the most horrendous torture and to murder continued to keep their jobs. In addressing critics of amnesty, Archbishop Tutu insisted that amnesty was not impunity: Not all applications for amnesty were accepted; when they were, the applicants had to admit responsibility for their actions "in the full glare of publicity," and the personal costs to them were high. They underwent "public shaming." Often their exposure before family and friends, who may have had no previous knowledge of their actions, was traumatic (1998, 9). However, for many survivors these must have seemed rather trivial penalties, given the kinds of tortures to which they had been subjected. Even so, most evaluations of the TRC conclude that, for all its flaws, it played a significant role in articulating a *societal* revulsion at former atrocities. It succeeded in its symbolic or "expressive" role, and it did so without recourse to the punitive element that Beauvoir had thought necessary in the context of post-Occupation France, or the "victors' justice" meted out at the Nuremberg trials. However, it is less clear that such expressions of revulsion offered *individual* victims the recognition they desired.

The TRC was legislated into being in late 1995.[43] Victims of atrocity were urged by the TRC to come forward and provide depositions and in some

---

42. Andre Brink, the white South African author, has described the TRC as the process of establishing a narrative "in which not history but imaginings of history are invented" (cited in Forsberg 2003, 83n21). More prosaically, it has been pointed out that the TRC had little actual investigative capacity, for example, to find the bodies of those who had "disappeared" (Hamber 2009, 147–50).

43. It submitted its five-volume report in 1998. However, its Amnesty Commission continued to work longer and submitted a further two volumes in 2003.

cases also to give testimony at its public hearings. This was hardly the direct recognition from their torturers that Beauvoir argues is desired in the "privileged case," but it could offer victims a certain recognition. Their personal stories were heard by the Commission members; their subjectivity and suffering were acknowledged. Some have described experiencing a dramatic catharsis. For example, one man who had been shot in the face and blinded told the Commission: "I feel that what has been making me sick all the time is the fact that I couldn't tell my story. But now it feels like I got my sight back by coming here and telling you my story" (cited in Hamber 2003, 159).

However, for many other (and perhaps most) victims, their brief moment of testimony before the commission could do little to repair their wounds; and for some, the process of testifying was itself very stressful and could even induce "re-traumatization" (Picker 2005).[44] Some, but not most, were able directly to confront their torturers or the murderers of their loved ones.[45] In certain instances perpetrators not only gave full accounts of their deeds but also expressed deep remorse, and on a number of occasions personal reconciliation between remorseful perpetrators and their victims did take place. But more often perpetrators denied much of what they had done, or expressed only the most pro-forma regret, or none at all. Expressions of remorse were not required for amnesty—and, as Beauvoir pointed out, remorse cannot be coerced but must be freely given. For some victims there was a further devastating experience when no acknowledgment or remorse was forthcoming. One former victim of torture and rape later described her shattered expectations to the journalist Ellis Cose. Before she met him, this woman had imagined a confession

---

44. It could also have (or be feared to have) negative practical consequences, such as harassment by neighbors or loss of a job (Picker 2005).

45. Depositions were taken from about twenty-two thousand victims, of which only about 8 percent were taken on to the Human Rights Violations Committee for a fuller hearing (Picker 2005). It was the TRC that decided which cases should go forward, and it has been argued that this process was too "top down" to satisfy many victims since cases were often chosen so as to be "show" events (Van Der Merwe 2003). Cases where perpetrators asked for amnesty went to the separate Amnesty Committee and totaled 7,116, of which 1,312 were granted (Brudholm 2008, 24). High-profile cases (e.g., of infamous torturers) were extensively broadcast and discussed in the media. Thus, the political impact was greater than the number of cases alone suggests. "The brutal horrors of apartheid found their way, via the media, into the living rooms of most South Africans" (Hamber 2009, 142).

coming from her torturer, remorse, an apology—and then she herself for-
giving him. But it did not work out that way. She said, "That was my
chance to tell him, 'Everything that you and your friends did to me, I forgive you.' But I couldn't say that because he was saying 'I don't know you.
I haven't seen you [before].' And I said, 'You are the one who suggested
that black policeman should put a sack over my head. *You* are the one.' He
said, 'No, I don't remember.' . . . I felt like I was empty" (cited in Cose
2004, 15).

But although the TRC gave some of the victims a space in which reconciliation might take place, many wanted a more punitive outcome and they
were resistant to the suggestions from the Commission that they reconcile
or forgive. That torturers and murders should not only be walking free but
still have well-paying jobs, especially when the victims' own lives continued
to be so hard, was seen as profoundly unjust. The same woman continued:
"If I say 'I reconciled with my perpetrator' and my perpetrator is now a station commander and is earning fifty thousand rands a month and I am
living in a shack, can you call that reconciliation?"[46] (cited in Cose 2004,
16). Hamber's interview-based studies of TRC participants lead him to
conclude that "the granting of amnesty is also at odds with the feelings of
most survivors of violence. Ideally these survivors want truth from the
perpetrators, but they also want them to be prosecuted. Justice through
the courts is the preferred way of dealing with perpetrators among victims" (Hamber 2003, 165–66; see also Backer 2007 for a study of victims'
attitudes). Indeed, many of them wanted, through the courts or otherwise,
the kind of retributive punishment that Beauvoir calls revenge. Hamber
cites a torture victim, an elderly woman frustrated with the response she
had received to her testimony, as saying to the Commission: "I am not satisfied. Even Samson got his eyes gouged out. These people's eyes must be
gouged out" (Hamber 2009, 118).

---

46. One of the TRC committees was concerned with material reparations. However, it was the least active part of the Commission, and few victims actually received monetary recompense. A follow-up study of victims who had participated
in hearings of the Human Rights Violations Committee found that many had expected reparations after testifying, and the TRC's failure to provide these often
undermined trust and possible healing: "The issue of monetary reparations takes
on paramount importance for impoverished survivors of violence—the majority
of the South African victims. . . . To see the perpetrators gaining immediate benefits from the TRC in the form of amnesty while they have to wait a very long time
for reparations [and many waited in vain] fuels their perception of the process as
biased and unjust" (Picker 2005).

Ambiguity and the Irreparable

In the context of post-Occupation France, Beauvoir had defended the desire for revenge as an appropriate response to atrocity. Although this desire may so rarely be satisfied, this does not mean that it is necessarily an "unhealthy" psychological condition from which sufferers need to be "healed." For it is neither blind nor capricious, but is rather a meaningful demand for recognition and restitution. Nor do the failures that also attend "official" justice and punishment imply that they are worthless. Thus, we may ask whether or not Beauvoir would have given a sympathetic hearing to the arguments for "truth and reconciliation" in South Africa as an alternative to revenge, had she still been alive.

Here we must return to Beauvoir's arguments (discussed in chapter 1) against the use of a priori, or abstract, principle as the justification for a course of action in politics. To recall, she had criticized French pacifists who, in the 1930s, refused to contemplate the possibility of declaring war on Hitler, claiming that in all circumstances war would be wrong (MIPR 185; IMRP 85). While, in *The Ethics of Ambiguity* she had written: "[W]e challenge every a priori condemnation as well as every such justification of violence practiced with a view to a valued end. They must be legitimized concretely" (EA 148; PMA 206–207). Likewise, she surely would not have accepted any a priori claim for the superiority of either revenge or forgiveness as *the* correct response to atrocity. The "purist" who insists either that retribution or that forgiveness is the only correct path to pursue, irrespective of concrete circumstances and possible consequences, is in bad faith hiding behind "ready-made values."

Thus, Beauvoir would surely have examined the South African TRC process with considerable sympathy, exploring what the pros and cons of "truth and reconciliation" might have been in this particular context. She would have acknowledged that it was necessary for society to expose the atrocities of the apartheid period and would, I think, have agreed that there was a practical necessity for amnesty in order to encourage perpetrators to confess. However, she would also have seen the vengeful desires of certain individual victims as quite appropriate, and she surely would have questioned the triumphant banner outside the TRC headquarters, which definitively asserted that "revealing is healing." She would have been profoundly troubled by a certain moral purism in the speeches of Archbishop Tutu and more generally in the rhetoric of the Commission. For forgiveness was unambiguously presented as a virtue, and the desire for revenge as a moral fault or as a sickness to be healed. Both the desire for revenge and the willingness to forgive may have their place as appropriate responses—whether political, moral, or therapeutic—to atrocity. However, both responses will necessarily be subject to failure, she would also have insisted. This is not only because "what is good for different men differs" but also because it is in the very nature of atrocity that repair is impossible. As Hannah Arendt wrote of the Holocaust, "there are crimes which men can neither punish nor forgive" ([1951] 2004, 591)—but for Beauvoir this is not to say that either punishment or forgiveness is misguided.

The legal scholar Martha Minow has rightly described forms of restorative justice such as TRCs as "the attempt to repair the irreparable" (1998, 23). Atrocities cannot be reversed, and neither revenge *nor* forgiveness can restore the dead, or make the physically or psychologically maimed whole again. Yet to say a situation is irreparable is not to justify silence or to reject its contestation as meaningless. Rather, it is to demand that one abandon a purism of expectations and instead embrace the inherent ambiguity of action. For, as Beauvoir insisted at the end of "An Eye for an Eye," failure haunts all human action, love as much as vengeance (EE 258–59; OO 164). In the case of the TRC, to embrace ambiguity is to accept that not only "healing" but also significant harm to victims sometimes results from "revealing"; that the desire for revenge is not always reprehensible or pathological; and that forgiveness is not a universal virtue. Since the evils of atrocity cannot be allowed to sink silently, unacknowledged, into historical oblivion, we must continue to seek repair whether it be through revenge or forgiveness. But as we do so we must recognize, with Beauvoir, the element of wager that is present in all action and that "failure is a condition of life itself."

Beauvoir's insistence on failure may seem too somber a note on which to end my study of her political thinking, but I do not think it is. For Beauvoir's message is not one of pessimism or despair. Rather, she demands that we continue to struggle for greater freedom in the world, even though we know our efforts will be fraught with risks and frustrations. For, to accept that struggles conducted in the name of humanism may also dehumanize; that resistance to oppression may also necessitate oppression; that the enjoyment of privilege is not simply a matter of free personal choice; that judgments are also wagers; or that revenge and forgiveness may each have their limits is to accept that ambiguity is the very stuff of human existence.

BIBLIOGRAPHY

Abu-Lughod, Lila. 1993. *Writing Women's Worlds: Bedouin Stories.* Berkeley: University of California Press.

Aïvazova, Svetlana. 2002. "*Le deuxième sexe* en russe: les aléas et les problèmes de la transmission." *Cinquantenaire du "Deuxième sexe,"* edited by Christine Delphy and Sylvie Chaperon with Kate Fullbrook and Edward Fullbrook, 482–87. Paris: Éditions Syllepse.

Alcoff, Linda. 1998. "What Should White People Do?" *Hypatia: A Journal of Feminist Philosophy* 13(3): 6–26.

———. 2006. *Visible Identities: Race, Gender, and the Self.* New York: Oxford University Press.

Alfonso, D. Rita. 2005. "Transatlantic Perspectives on Race: Simone de Beauvoir's Phenomenology of Race in *America Day by Day.*" *Philosophy Today* 49(5): 89–99.

Althusser, Louis. 1969. *For Marx.* Translated by Ben Brewster. New York: Pantheon.

Altman, Meryl. 2007. "Beauvoir, Hegel, War." *Hypatia: A Journal of Feminist Philosophy* 22(3): 66–91.

Anzaldúa, Gloria. 1987. *Borderlands = La Frontera: The New Mestiza.* San Francisco: aunt lute.

Arendt, Hannah. 1946a. "French Existentialism." *Nation* (February 23): 226–28.

———. 1946b. "What Is Existenz Philosophy?" *Partisan Review* 13(1): 34–56.

———. 1958. *The Human Condition.* Chicago: University of Chicago Press.

———. 1963. *Eichmann in Jerusalem: A Report on the Banality of Evil.* New York: Viking.

———. 1977. *Between Past and Future: Eight Exercises in Political Thought.* New York: Penguin.

———. [1951] 2004. *The Origins of Totalitarianism.* Introduction by Samantha Power. New York: Schocken.

Arendt, Hannah, and Karl Jaspers. 1992. *Hannah Arendt/Karl Jaspers Correspondence: 1926–1969.* Edited by Lotte Kohler and Hans Saner. Translated by Robert Kimber and Rita Kimber. New York: Harcourt Brace Jovanovich.

Aronson, Ronald. 2004. *Camus & Sartre: The Story of a Friendship and the Quarrel That Ended It.* Chicago: University of Chicago Press.

Arp, Kristana. 2001. *The Bonds of Freedom: Simone de Beauvoir's Existentialist Ethics.* Chicago: Open Court.

Assouline, Pierre. 1985. *L'Épuration des intellectuels.* Brussels: Éditions Complexe.

Astell, Mary. 1694. *A Serious Proposal to the Ladies for the Advancement of their True and Greatest Interest by a Lover of her Sex.* London: Wilkin.

Backer, David. 2007. "Victims' Responses to Truth Commissions: Evidence from South Africa." In *Security, Reconstruction, and Reconciliation: When the Wars End*, edited by Muna Ndulo, 165–96. London: University College London Press.

Bailey, Alison. 1998. "Locating Traitorous Identities: Toward a View of Privilege-Cognizant White Character." *Hypatia: A Journal of Feminist Philosophy* 13(3): 27–42.

———. 2004. "Privilege: Expanding on Marilyn Frye's 'Oppression.' " In *Oppression, Privilege, and Resistance: Theoretical Perspectives on Racism, Sexism, and Heterosexism*, edited by Lisa Heldke and Peg O'Connor, 301–16. Boston: McGraw-Hill.

Bair, Deirdre. 1990. *Simone de Beauvoir: A Biography*. New York: Summit.

Bartky, Sandra. 2002. *"Sympathy and Solidarity" and Other Essays*. Lanham, MD: Rowman and Littlefield.

Bauer, Nancy. 2001. *Simone de Beauvoir, Philosophy, and Feminism*. New York: Columbia University Press.

Bauman, Zygmunt. 2003. "The Project of Humanity." In *Becoming Human: New Perspectives on the Inhuman Condition*, edited by Paul Sheehan, 127–47. Westport, CT: Praeger.

Beauvoir, Simone de. 1948. *The Blood of Others*. Translated by Roger Senhouse and Yvonne Moyse. New York: Knopf.

———. 1954. "Interview de Simone de Beauvoir par J.-F. Rolland." *L'Humanité Dimanche* (December 19). Reprinted in Claude Francis and Fernande Gontier, eds., *Les écrits de Simone de Beauvoir*, 358–62. Paris: Gallimard, 1979.

———. 1955. *Privilèges*. Paris: Gallimard.

———. 1965. "Que peut la littérature?" In *Que peut la littérature?* Edited by Yves Buin, 73–92. Paris: Coll. "L'Inédit," 10/18, Union Générale d'Éditions.

———. 1966. Preface to *Treblinka*, by Jean-François Steiner. Paris: Fayard.

———. 1998. *A Transatlantic Love Affair: Letters to Nelson Algren*. Compiled and annotated by Sylvie Le Bon de Beauvoir. New York: New Press.

———. [1945] 2000. *Le sang des autres*. Paris: Coll. Folio, Gallimard.

———. 2004. *Simone de Beauvoir: Philosophical Writings*. Edited by Margaret A. Simons et al. Foreword by Sylvie Le Bon de Beauvoir. Urbana: University of Illinois Press.

———. 2006. *Diary of a Philosophy Student: 1926–27*. Edited by Barbara Klaw, Sylvie Le Bon de Beauvoir, and Margaret A. Simons. Translated by Barbara Klaw. Urbana: University of Illinois Press.

———. 2008. *Cahiers de jeunesse, 1926–1930*. Edited by Sylvie Le Bon de Beauvoir. Paris: Gallimard.

Beauvoir, Simone de, and Gisèle Halimi. 1962a. *Djamila Boupacha: The Story of the Torture of a Young Algerian Girl Which Shocked Liberal French Opinion*. Translated by Peter Green. New York: Macmillan.

———. 1962b. *Djamila Boupacha*. Paris: Gallimard.

Beiner, Ronald. 1983. *Political Judgment*. Chicago: University of Chicago Press.

Bentham, Jeremy. 1973. *An Introduction to the Principles of Morals and Legislation*. New York: Hafner.

Bergoffen, Debra B. 1997. *The Philosophy of Simone de Beauvoir: Gendered Phenomenologies, Erotic Generosities*. Albany: State University of New York Press.

Bilge, Sirma. 2010. "Recent Feminist Outlooks on Intersectionality." *Diogenes* 57(1): 58–72.

Blanchard, Marc Eli. 2004. "On the Style of the Coming Philosophy: 'Le style, c'est la femme' (Buffon)." *Modern Language Notes* 119(4): 696–717.

Brightman, Carol. 1992. *Writing Dangerously: Mary McCarthy and Her World*. New York: Harcourt Brace.

Brudholm, Thomas. 2008. *Resentment's Virtue: Jean Améry and the Refusal to Forgive*. Philadelphia: Temple University Press.

Burnier, Michel-Antoine. 1968. *Choice of Action: The French Existentialists on the Political Front Line*. Translated by Bernard Murchland. New York: Random House.

Butler, Judith. 2004. *Precarious Life: The Powers of Mourning and Violence*. London: Verso.

———. 2009. *Frames of War: When Is Life Grievable?* London: Verso.

Camus, Albert. 2006. *Camus at Combat: Writing 1944–1947*. Edited and annotated by Jacqueline Lévi-Valensi. Translated by Arthur Goldhammer. Princeton, NJ: Princeton University Press.

Caputi, Mary. 2006. "Beauvoir and the Case of Djamila Boupacha." In *Simone de Beauvoir's Political Thinking*, edited by Lori Jo Marso and Patricia Moynagh, 109–26. Urbana: University of Illinois Press.

Card, Claudia. 2002. *The Atrocity Paradigm: A Theory of Evil*. New York: Oxford University Press.

———. ed. 2003. *The Cambridge Companion to Simone de Beauvoir*. Cambridge: Cambridge University Press.

———. 2010. *Confronting Evils: Terrorism, Torture, Genocide*. New York: Cambridge University Press.

Chafiq, Chahla. 2008. "Simone de Beauvoir et l'islamisme: L'expérience iranienne." Special issue, *Les Temps modernes*, "La transmission Beauvoir," 63 année, numéros 647–48 (January–March): 265–85.

Cheah, Pheng. 2006. *Inhuman Conditions: On Cosmopolitanism and Human Rights*. Cambridge, MA: Harvard University Press.

Churchland, Paul M. 1995. *The Engine of Reason, the Seat of the Soul: A Philosophical Journey into the Brain*. Cambridge, MA: MIT Press.

Code, Lorraine. 1991. *What Can She Know? Feminist Theory and the Construction of Knowledge*. Ithaca, NY: Cornell University Press.

Cohen-Solal, Annie. 1987. *Sartre: A Life*. Edited by Norman MacAfee. Translated by Anna Cancogni. New York: Pantheon.

Connolly, William E. 2005. *Pluralism*. Durham, NC: Duke University Press.

Cose, Ellis. 2004. *Bone to Pick: Of Forgiveness, Reconciliation, Reparation, and Revenge*. New York: Atria.

Cudd, Ann. 2006. *Analyzing Oppression*. New York: Oxford University Press.

Davies, Howard. 1987. *Sartre and "Les Temps Modernes."* Cambridge: Cambridge University Press.

Davies, Tony. 1997. *Humanism*. London: Routledge.

Deutscher, Penelope. 2008. *The Philosophy of Simone de Beauvoir: Ambiguity, Conversion, Resistance*. New York: Cambridge University Press.

Digby, Tom, ed. 1998. *Men Doing Feminism*. New York: Routledge.

Douzinas, Costas. 2007. *Human Rights and Empire: The Political Philosophy of Cosmopolitanism*. London: Routledge-Cavendish.

Drake, David. 2005. *Sartre*. London: Haus.

Drumbl, Mark A. 2007. *Atrocity, Punishment, and International Law*. New York: Cambridge University Press.

Duchen, Claire. 1994. *Women's Rights and Women's Lives in France, 1944–1968*. London: Routledge.

Ellison, Ralph. 1990. *Invisible Man*. New York: Vintage.

Elshtain, Jean Bethke. 1981. *Public Man, Private Woman: Women in Social and Political Thought*. Princeton, NJ: Princeton University Press.

Evans, Martin. 1997. *The Memory of Resistance: French Opposition to the Algerian War (1954–1962).* Oxford: Berg.

Evans, Mary. 1985. *Simone de Beauvoir: A Feminist Mandarin.* London: Tavistock.

Fallaize, Elizabeth, ed. 1998. *Simone de Beauvoir: A Critical Reader.* London: Routledge.

Fanon, Frantz. [1961] 1963. *The Wretched of the Earth.* Translated by Constance Farrington. Preface by Jean-Paul Sartre. New York: Grove.

———. [1952] 1967. *Black Skin, White Masks.* Translated by Charles Lam Markmann. New York: Grove.

———. [1964] 1988. *Toward the African Revolution: Political Essays.* Translated by Haakon Chevalier. New York: Grove.

———. [1959] 1989. *Studies in a Dying Colonialism.* Translated by Haakon Chevalier. New York: Grove.

Feinberg, Joel. 1970. *Doing and Deserving: Essays in the Theory of Responsibility.* Princeton, NJ: Princeton University Press.

Ferguson, Ann. 1998. "Resisting the Veil of Privilege: Building Bridge Identities as an Ethico-Politics of Global Feminisms." *Hypatia: A Journal of Feminist Philosophy* 13(3): 95–113.

Ferrara, Alessandro. 1999. *Justice and Judgment: The Rise and the Prospect of the Judgment Model in Contemporary Political Philosophy.* London: Sage.

Folbre, Nancy. 1994. *Who Pays for the Kids? Gender and the Structure of Constraint.* London: Routledge.

Forsberg, Thomas. 2003. "The Philosophy and Practice of Dealing with the Past: Some Conceptual and Normative Issues." In *Burying the Past: Making Peace and Doing Justice after Civil Conflict,* edited by Nigel Biggar, 65–84. Washington, DC: Georgetown University Press.

Foucault, Michel. 1977. *Discipline and Punish: The Birth of the Prison.* Translated from the French by Alan Sheridan. London: Penguin.

———. 1978. *The History of Sexuality: An Introduction.* Translated from the French by Robert Hurley. New York: Pantheon.

———. 1984. "What Is Enlightenment?" In *The Foucault Reader,* edited by Paul Rabinow, 32–50. New York: Pantheon.

Frankenberg, Ruth. 1993. *White Women, Race Matters: The Social Construction of Whiteness.* Minneapolis: University of Minnesota Press.

Fraser, Nancy. 2009. *Scales of Justice: Reimagining Political Space in a Globalizing World.* New York: Columbia University Press.

Frazer, Elizabeth, and Kimberly Hutchings. 2007. "Argument and Rhetoric in the Justification of Political Violence." *European Journal of Political Theory* 6(2): 180–99.

French, Peter A. 2001. *The Virtues of Vengeance.* Lawrence: University Press of Kansas.

Frye, Marilyn. 1983. "Oppression." In *The Politics of Reality: Essays in Feminist Theory,* 1–16. Trumansburg, NY: Crossing Press.

———. 1992. "White Woman Feminist, 1983–1992." In *Willful Virgin: Essays in Feminism, 1976–1992,* 147–69. Freedom, CA: Crossing Press.

Fullbrook, Edward, and Kate Fullbrook. 1994. *Simone de Beauvoir and Jean-Paul Sartre: The Remaking of a Twentieth-Century Legend.* New York: Basic Books.

Galster, Ingrid. 1996. "Simone de Beauvoir face à l'occupation allemande: Essai provisoire d'un réexamen à partir des écrits posthumes." *Contemporary French Civilization* 20(2): 278–93.

———. 2004. *Le deuxième sexe de Simone de Beauvoir.* Paris: Presses de l'Université Paris-Sorbonne.

Geuss, Raymond. 2008. *Philosophy and Real Politics*. Princeton, NJ: Princeton University Press.

Gilbert, Joseph. 1991. *Une si douce occupation: Simone de Beauvoir, Jean-Paul Sartre, 1940–1944*. Paris: Éditions Albin Michel.

Gordon, Lewis R. 1995. *Bad Faith and Antiblack Racism*. Atlantic Highlands, NJ: Humanities Press.

Gready, Paul. 2011. *The Era of Transitional Justice: The Aftermath of the Truth and Reconciliation Commission in South Africa and Beyond*. New York: Routledge.

Green, Karen, and Nicholas Roffey. 2010. "Women, Hegel, and Recognition in *The Second Sex*." *Hypatia: A Journal of Feminist Philosophy* 25(2): 376–93.

Griswold, Charles L. 2007. *Forgiveness: A Philosophical Exploration*. New York: Cambridge University Press.

Grosholz, Emily, ed. 2006. *The Legacy of Simone de Beauvoir*. Oxford: Oxford University Press.

Habermas, Jürgen. 1984. *Reason and the Rationalization of Society*. Vol. 1 of *The Theory of Communicative Action*. Translated by Thomas McCarthy. Boston: Beacon.

Halimi, Gisèle. 1960. "D'Henri Aleg à Djamila Boupacha." *Les Temps modernes*, 15 année, numéro 171 (June): 1822–27.

———. 1988. *Le lait de l'oranger*. Paris: Gallimard.

———. 2002. "Simone de Beauvoir, une femme engagée: De la guerre d'Algérie au procès de Bobigny." In *Cinquantenaire du "Deuxième sexe,"* edited by Christine Delphy and Sylvie Chaperon with Kate Fullbrook and Edward Fullbrook, 293–99. Paris: Éditions Syllepse.

Hamber, Brandon. 2003. "Does the Truth Heal? A Psychological Perspective on Political Strategies for Dealing with the Legacy of Political Violence." In *Burying the Past: Making Peace and Doing Justice after Civil Conflict*, edited by Nigel Biggar, 155–74. Washington, DC: Georgetown University Press.

———. 2009. *Transforming Societies after Political Violence: Truth, Reconciliation, and Mental Health*. New York: Springer.

Hamon, Hervé, and Patrick Rotman. 1982. *Les porteurs de valises*. Paris: Éditions Albin Michel.

Haraway, Donna. 1999. "The Biopolitics of Postmodern Bodies." In *Feminist Theory and the Body: A Reader*, edited by Janet Price and Margrit Shildrick, 203–14. Edinburgh: Edinburgh University Press.

Harding, Sandra. 1991. *Whose Science? Whose Knowledge?* Ithaca, NY: Cornell University Press.

Hawkesworth, Mary. 2010. "From Constitutive Outside to the Politics of Extinction: Critical Race Theory, Feminist Theory, and Political Theory." *Political Research Quarterly* 63(3): 686–96.

Heinämaa, Sara. 2003. *Toward a Phenomenology of Sexual Difference: Husserl, Merleau-Ponty, Beauvoir*. Lanham, MD: Rowman and Littlefield.

Holveck, Eleanore. 2002. *Simone de Beauvoir's Philosophy of Lived Experience: Literature and Metaphysics*. Lanham, MD: Rowman and Littlefield.

Honneth, Axel. 2008. *Reification: A New Look at an Old Idea*. Edited by Martin Jay. With commentaries by Judith Butler, Raymond Geuss, and Jonathan Lear. Oxford: Oxford University Press.

Hughes, Edel, William A. Schabas, and Ramesh Thakar, eds. 2007. *Atrocities and International Accountability: Beyond Transitional Justice*. New York: United Nations University Press.

Hutchings, Kimberly. 2003. *Hegel and Feminist Philosophy*. Cambridge: Polity.

Imbert, Claude. 2006. "Simone de Beauvoir: A Woman Philosopher in the Context of Her Generation." Translated by Emily R. Grosholz. In *The Legacy of Simone de Beauvoir*, edited by Emily R. Grosholz, 3–21. Oxford: Oxford University Press.

Inoué, Takako. 2002. "La réception au Japon et ses deux traductions." *Cinquantenaire du "Deuxième sexe,"* edited by Christine Delphy and Sylvie Chaperon with Kate Fullbrook and Edward Fullbrook, 463–67. Paris: Éditions Syllepse.

Isorni, Jacques. 1946. *Le procès de Robert Brasillach*. Paris: Flammarion.

Jacoby, Susan. 1983. *Wild Justice: The Evolution of Revenge*. New York: Harper Colophon.

Judt, Tony. 1992. *Past Imperfect: French Intellectuals, 1944–1956*. Berkeley: University of California Press.

Kail, Michel. 2006. *Simone de Beauvoir, philosophe*. Paris: Presses universitaires de France.

Kandell, Lilliane. 2008. "Le sexisme et quelques autres ennemis principaux." Special issue, *Les Temps modernes*, "La Transmission Beauvoir," 63 année, numéros 647–48 (January–March): 117–21.

Kaplan, Alice. 2000. *The Collaborator: The Trial and Execution of Robert Brasillach*. Chicago: University of Chicago Press.

Kristeva, Julia. 1981. "Women's Time." Translated by Alice Jardine and Harry Blake. *Signs: Journal of Women in Culture and Society* 7(1): 13–35.

———. 1982. *Powers of Horror: An Essay on Abjection*. Translated by Leon S. Roudiez. New York: Columbia University Press.

———. 2009. "Beauvoir and the Risks of Freedom." Translated by Catherine Porter. Introduction by S. K. Keltner. *PMLA: Publications of the Modern Language Association of America* 124(1): 224–30.

———, Pascale Fautrier, Pierre-Louis Fort, and Anne Strasser, eds. 2008. *(Re)découvrir l'œuvre de Simone de Beauvoir: Du Deuxième Sexe à La Cérémonie des adieux*. Paris: Éditions Le Bord de l'eau.

Kruks, Sonia. 1991. "Simone de Beauvoir: Teaching Sartre about Freedom." In *Sartre Alive*, edited by Ronald Aronson and Adrien VanDenhoven, 285–300. Detroit: Wayne State University Press. Reprinted in *Feminist Interpretations of Simone de Beauvoir*, edited by Margaret A. Simons, 79–95. University Park: Pennsylvania State University Press, 1995.

———. 2001. *Retrieving Experience: Subjectivity and Recognition in Feminist Politics*. Ithaca, NY: Cornell University Press.

———. 2005. "Beauvoir's Time/Our Time: The Renaissance in Simone de Beauvoir Studies." *Feminist Studies* 31(2): 286–309.

———. 2009. "Ambiguity and Certitude in Simone de Beauvoir's Politics." *PMLA: Publications of the Modern Language Association of America* 124(1): 214–20.

———. 2010. "Simone de Beauvoir: Engaging Discrepant Materialisms." In *New Materialisms: Ontology, Agency, and Politics*, edited by Diana Coole and Samantha Frost, 258–80. Durham, NC: Duke University Press.

Lang, Berel. 2005. *Post-Holocaust: Interpretation, Misinterpretation, and the Claims of History*. Bloomington: Indiana University Press.

Lazreg, Marnia. 1994. *The Eloquence of Silence: Algerian Women in Question*. New York: Routledge.

Le Bon de Beauvoir, Sylvie. 2004. Foreword to *Simone de Beauvoir: Philosophical Writings*, edited by Margaret A. Simons, x–xi. Urbana: University of Illinois Press.

Le Doeuff, Michèle. 1991. *Hipparchia's Choice: An Essay Concerning Women, Philosophy, etc.* Translated by Trista Selous. Oxford: Blackwell.

———. 2006. "Toward a Friendly Transatlantic Critique of *The Second Sex*." Translated by Emily R. Grosholz. In *The Legacy of Simone de Beauvoir*, edited by Emily R. Grosholz, 22–36. Oxford: Oxford University Press.

Lloyd, Genevieve. 1984. *The Man of Reason: "Male" and "Female" in Western Philosophy*. Minneapolis: University of Minnesota Press.

Locke, John. [1690] 1988. "The Second Treatise of Government." In *The Two Treatises of Government*, edited by Peter Laslett. Cambridge: Cambridge University Press.

Lottman, Herbert R. 1986. *The People's Anger: Justice and Revenge in Post-Liberation France*. London: Hutchinson.

Lugones, María. 1990. "Playfulness, 'World'-Travelling, and Loving Perception." In *Making Face, Making Soul/Haciendo Caras: Creative and Critical Perspectives by Feminists of Color*, edited by Gloria Anzaldúa, 390–402. San Francisco: aunt lute.

———. 2003. *Pilgrimages/Peregrinajes: Theorizing Coalition against Multiple Oppressions*. Lanham, MD: Rowman and Littlefield.

Lundgren-Gothlin, Eva. 1996. *Sex and Existence: Simone de Beauvoir's "The Second Sex."* Translated by Linda Schenck. London: Athlone.

Mackenzie, Catriona, and Natalie Stoljar, eds. 2000. *Relational Autonomy: Feminist Perspectives on Autonomy, Agency, and the Social Self*. New York: Oxford University Press.

Mairs, Nancy. 1996. *Waist-High in the World: A Life among the Nondisabled*. Boston: Beacon.

Malveaux, Julianne, and Reginna A. Green, eds. 2002. *The Paradox of Loyalty: An African American Response to the War on Terrorism*. Chicago: Third World Press.

Marcuse, Herbert. 1964. *One Dimensional Man: Studies in the Ideology of Advanced Industrial Society*. Boston: Beacon.

Markowitz, Sally. 2009. "Occidental Dreams: Orientalism and History in *The Second Sex*." *Signs: Journal of Women in Culture and Society* 34(2): 271–94.

Marso, Lori Jo. 2012. "Simone de Beauvoir and Hannah Arendt: Judgments in Dark Times." *Political Theory* 40 (April): 165–93.

Martinez, Roy, ed. 2010. *On Race and Racism in America: Confessions in Philosophy*. University Park: Pennsylvania State University Press.

Marx, Karl. 1964. *Karl Marx: Early Writings*. Edited and translated by T. B. Bottomore. New York: McGraw-Hill.

———. 1978. "The German Ideology." In *The Marx-Engels Reader*, 2nd ed., edited by Robert C. Tucker, 146–200. New York: Norton.

May, Larry. 1992. *Sharing Responsibility*. Chicago: University of Chicago Press.

———. 1998. *Masculinity and Morality*. Ithaca, NY: Cornell University Press.

McBride, William L. 1991. *Sartre's Political Theory*. Bloomington: Indiana University Press.

———. 2005. "The Conflict of Ideologies in *The Mandarins*: Communism and Democracy, Then and Now." In *The Contradictions of Freedom: Philosophical Essays on Simone de Beauvoir's "The Mandarins,"* edited by Sally J. Scholz and Shannon M. Mussett, 33–45. Albany: State University of New York Press.

McDermott, Rose. 2004. "The Feeling of Rationality: The Meaning of Neuroscientific Advances for Political Science." *Perspectives on Politics* 2(4): 691–706.

McIntosh, Peggy. [1988] 2011. "White Privilege: Unpacking the Invisible Knapsack." In *Gender through the Prism of Difference*, 4th ed., edited by Maxine Baca Zinn, Pierrete Hondagneu-Sotelo, and Michael A. Messner, 235–38. New York: Oxford University Press.

McNay, Lois. 2008. *Against Recognition*. Cambridge: Polity.

Memmi, Albert. [1957] 1991. *The Colonizer and the Colonized*. Translated by Howard Greenfield. Introduction by Jean-Paul Sartre. Afterword by Susan Gilson Miller. Boston: Beacon.

Merleau-Ponty, Maurice. [1945] 1962. *Phenomenology of Perception*. Translated by Colin Smith. London: Routledge and Kegan Paul.

———. [1945] 1964a. "Faith and Good Faith." In *Sense and Non-Sense*. Translated by Hubert L. Dreyfus and Patricia Allen Dreyfus, 172–81. Evanston, IL: Northwestern University Press.

———. [1950] 1964b. "The USSR and the Camps." In *Signs*, translated by Richard C. McCleary, 263–73. Evanston, IL: Northwestern University Press.

———. [1945] 1964c. "The War Has Taken Place." In *Sense and Non-Sense*. Translated by Hubert L. Dreyfus and Patricia Allen Dreyfus, 139–52. Evanston, IL: Northwestern University Press.

Miao, Xin. 2008. "Simone de Beauvoir et *Le deuxième sexe* en Chine." In *(Re)découvrir l'œuvre de Simone de Beauvoir: Du Deuxième Sexe à La Cérémonie des adieux*, edited by Julia Kristeva, Pascale Fautrier, Pierre-Louis Fort, and Anne Strasser, 432–33. Paris: Éditions Le Bord de l'eau.

Miller, William Ian. 1993. *Humiliation: And Other Essays on Honor, Social Discomfort, and Violence*. Ithaca, NY: Cornell University Press.

Mills, Charles W. 1997. *The Racial Contract*. Ithaca, NY: Cornell University Press.

———. 2004. "'Ideal Theory' as Ideology." In *Moral Philosophy: Feminist Ethics and Social Theory*, edited by Peggy DesAutels and Margaret Urban Walker, 163–82. Lanham, MD: Rowman and Littlefield.

Minow, Martha. 1998. *Between Vengeance and Forgiveness: Facing History after Genocide and Mass Violence*. Boston: Beacon.

Moi, Toril. 1994. *Simone de Beauvoir: The Making of an Intellectual Woman*. Oxford: Blackwell.

———. 1999. *What Is a Woman? and Other Essays*. Oxford: Oxford University Press.

———. 2002. "While We Wait: The English Translation of *The Second Sex*." *Signs: Journal of Women in Culture and Society* 27(4): 1005–35.

———. 2009. "What Can Literature Do? Simone de Beauvoir as a Literary Theorist." *PMLA: Publications of the Modern Language Association of America* 124(1): 189–98.

Moorehead, Caroline. 1974. "A Talk with Simone de Beauvoir." *New York Times Magazine*, June 2, E 16ff.

Morgan, Anne. 2009. "Simone de Beauvoir's Ethics, the Master/Slave Dialectic, and Eichmann as a Sub-Man." *Hypatia: A Journal of Feminist Philosophy* 24(2): 39–53.

Morris, Phyllis Sutton. 1996. "Self-Creating Selves: Sartre and Foucault." *American Catholic Philosophical Quarterly* 69(4): 537–49.

Moser, Susanne. 2008. *Freedom and Recognition in the Work of Simone de Beauvoir*. Frankfurt am Main: Lang.

Murphy, Jeffrie G. 2003. *Getting Even: Forgiveness and Its Limits*. New York: Oxford University Press.

Murphy, Julien. 1995. "Beauvoir and the Algerian War: Toward a Postcolonial Ethics." In *Feminist Interpretations of Simone de Beauvoir*, edited by Margaret A. Simons, 263–97. University Park: Pennsylvania State University Press.

Mussett, Shannon M. 2006. "Conditions of Servitude: Woman's Peculiar Role in the Master-Slave Dialectic in Beauvoir's *The Second Sex*." In *The Philosophy of Simone de Beauvoir: Critical Essays*, edited by Margaret A. Simons, 276–94. Bloomington: Indiana University Press.

Muthu, Sankar. 2003. *Enlightenment against Empire*. Princeton, NJ: Princeton University Press.

Myrdal, Gunnar. 1944. *An American Dilemma: The Negro Problem and Modern Democracy*. With the assistance of Richard Sterner and Arnold Rose. New York: Harper.

Nedelsky, Jennifer. 2005. *Law, Autonomy, and the Relational Self: A Feminist Revisioning of the Foundations of Law*. New York: Oxford University Press.

Nielfa, Gloria. 2002. "La diffusion en Espagne." *Cinquantenaire du "Deuxième sexe,"* edited by Christine Delphy and Sylvie Chaperon with Kate Fullbrook and Edward Fullbrook, 453–59. Paris: Éditions Syllepse.

O'Brien, Mary. 1981. *The Politics of Reproduction*. Boston: Routledge and Kegan Paul.

Okely, Judith. 1986. *Simone de Beauvoir*. New York: Pantheon.

Oshana, Marina. 2006. *Personal Autonomy in Society*. Aldershot, UK: Ashgate.

Parshley, H. M. [1952] 1989. "Translator's Note." In *The Second Sex*, by Simone de Beauvoir, xxxvii–xlii. Edited and translated by H. M. Parshley. Foreword by Deidre Bair. New York: Vintage.

Picker, Ruth. 2005. *Victims' Perspectives about the Human Rights Violations Hearings*. Centre for the Study of Violence and Reconciliation, Johannesburg, South Africa. Accessed March 21, 2012. http://www.csvr.org.za/docs/humanrights/victim-sperspectivshearings.pdf.

Pilardi, Jo-Ann. 1999. *Simone de Beauvoir Writing the Self: Philosophy Becomes Autobiography*. Westport, CT: Greenwood.

Plummer, Kenneth. 2001. *Documents of Life 2: An Invitation to a Critical Humanism*. London: Sage.

Pratt, Minnie Bruce. 1984. "Identity: Skin Blood Heart." In *Yours in Struggle: Three Feminist Perspectives on Anti-Semitism and Racism*, edited by Elly Bulkin, Minnie Bruce Pratt, and Barbara Smith, 11–63. Ithaca, NY: Firebrand.

Pucheu, Jacques. 1957. "Un an dans les Aurès." *Les Temps modernes*, 12 année, numéro 139 (September): 433–47.

Purvis, Jennifer. 2003. "Hegelian dimensions of *The Second Sex*: A Feminist Consideration." *Bulletin de la société Américaine de philosophie de langue française* 13(1): 128–56.

Rawls, John. 1971. *A Theory of Justice*. Oxford: Oxford University Press.

———. 1993. *Political Liberalism*. New York: Columbia University Press.

Rothenberg, Paula. 2000. *Invisible Privilege: A Memoir about Race, Class, and Gender*. Lawrence: University of Kansas Press.

Rowley, Hazel. 2005. *Tête-à-tête: Simone de Beauvoir and Jean-Paul Sartre*. New York: HarperCollins.

Sack, John. 1995. *An Eye for an Eye*. New York: Basic Books.

Said, Edward W. 1978. *Orientalism*. New York: Pantheon.

———. 2004. *Humanism and Democratic Criticism*. New York: Columbia University Press.

Salaita, Steven. 2008. *The Uncultured Wars: Arabs, Muslims, and the Poverty of Liberal Thought: New Essays*. London: Zed.

Sandoval, Chela. 1991. "U.S. Third-World Feminism: The Theory and Practice of Oppositional Consciousness in the Postmodern World." *Genders* 10 (Spring): 1–24.

Sartre, Jean-Paul. 1947. "Morts sans sépulture." In *La p . . . respectueuse: Pièce en un acte et deux tableaux; suivi de "Morts sans sepulture": Pièce en deux actes et quatre tableaux*. Paris: Gallimard.

———. 1957. "Vous êtes formidable." *Les Temps modernes*, 12 année, numéro 135 (May): 1642–47.

———. [1946] 1965. *Anti-Semite and Jew*. Translated by George J. Becker. New York: Schocken.

———. [1943] 1966. *Being and Nothingness*. Translated by Hazel E. Barnes. New York: Washington Square.

———. [1960] 1976. *Critique of Dialectical Reason: Theory of Practical Ensembles*, Vol. 1, Edited by Jonathan Rée. Translated by Alan Sheridan-Smith. London: New Left Books.

———. [1969] 1983. "Itinerary of a Thought." In *Between Existentialism and Marxism: Sartre on Philosophy, Politics, Psychology, and the Arts*, translated by John Matthews, 33–64. London: New Left Books.

Scarry, Elaine. 1985. *The Body in Pain: The Making and Unmaking of the World*. New York: Oxford University Press.

Scarth, Fredrika. 2004. *The Other Within: Ethics, Politics, and the Body in Simone de Beauvoir*. Lanham, MD: Rowman and Littlefield.

Schiff, Benjamin N. 2008. *Building the International Criminal Court*. New York: Cambridge University Press.

Schott, Robin May. 2003. "Beauvoir on the Ambiguity of Evil." In *The Cambridge Companion to Simone de Beauvoir*, edited by Claudia Card, 228–47. Cambridge: Cambridge University Press.

Scott, Joan Wallach. 1988. *Gender and the Politics of History*. New York: Columbia University Press.

Shklar, Judith N. 1990. *The Faces of Injustice*. New Haven, CT: Yale University Press.

Simons, Margaret A., ed. 1995. *Feminist Interpretations of Simone de Beauvoir*. University Park: Pennsylvania State University Press.

———. 1999. *Beauvoir and "The Second Sex": Feminism, Race, and the Origins of Existentialism*. Lanham, MD: Rowman and Littlefield.

———, ed. 2006. *The Philosophy of Simone de Beauvoir: Critical Essays*. Bloomington: Indiana University Press.

———. 2010. "Confronting an Impasse: Reflection on the Past and Future of Beauvoir Scholarship." *Hypatia: A Journal of Feminist Philosophy* 25(4): 909–26.

Soper, Kate. 1986. *Humanism and Anti-Humanism*. London: Hutchinson.

Spelman, Elizabeth V. 1988. *Inessential Woman: Problems of Exclusion in Feminist Thought*. Boston: Beacon.

———. 1989. "Anger and Insubordination." In *Women, Knowledge, and Reality: Explorations in Feminist Philosophy*, edited by Ann Garry and Marilyn Pearsall, 263–73. Boston: Unwin Hyman.

———. 1997. *Fruits of Sorrow: Framing Our Attention to Suffering*. Boston: Beacon.

Spivak, Gayatri. 1988. "Can the Subaltern Speak?" In *Marxism and the Interpretation of Culture*, edited by Cary Nelson and Lawrence Grossberg, 271–313. Urbana: University of Illinois Press.

Stanford, Karin L. 2002. "The War Within: African American Opinion on the War against Terrorism." In *The Paradox of Loyalty: An African American Response to the War on Terrorism*, edited by Julianne Malveaux and Reginna A. Green, 95–116. Chicago: Third World Press.

Steinberger, Peter J. 1993. *The Concept of Political Judgment*. Chicago: University of Chicago Press.

Strasser, Anne. 2005–2006. "La Vieillesse comme mutilation: Essai et Autobiographie." *Simone de Beauvoir Studies* 22: 38–52.

Suleiman, Susan Rubin. 1996. "Life-Story, History, Fiction: Reflections on Simone de Beauvoir's Wartime Writings." In *Debating Gender, Debating Sexuality*, edited by Nikki R. Keddie, 217–37. New York: New York University Press.

———. 2010. "Memory Troubles: Remembering the Occupation in Simone de Beauvoir's *Les Mandarins*." *French Politics, Culture, and Society* 28(2): 4–17.

Sullivan, Shannon. 2006. *Revealing Whiteness: The Unconscious Habits of Racial Privilege.* Bloomington,: Indiana University Press.

——, and Nancy Tuana, eds. 2006. "Introduction: Feminist Epistemologies of Ignorance." *Hypatia: A Journal of Feminist Philosophy* 21(3): vii–ix.

——. 2007. *Race and Epistemologies of Ignorance.* Albany: State University of New York Press.

Tahon, Jean-Luc. 1958. "En 'pacifiant' l'Algérie." *Les Temps modernes*, 13 année, numéros 147–48 (May–June): 2094–112.

Tamzali, Wassyla. 2008. "Simone de Beauvoir l'Algérienne." Special issue, *Les Temps modernes*, "La Transmission Beauvoir," 63 année, numéros 647–48 (January–March): 286–90.

Tessman, Lisa, ed. 2009. *Feminist Ethics and Social and Political Theory: Theorizing the Non-Ideal.* New York: Springer.

——. 2010. "Idealizing Morality." *Hypatia: A Journal of Feminist Philosophy* 25(6): 797–824.

Thiele, Leslie Paul. 2006. *The Heart of Judgment: Practical Wisdom, Neuroscience, and Narrative.* New York: Cambridge University Press.

Tidd, Ursula. 1999. *Simone de Beauvoir: Gender and Testimony.* Cambridge: Cambridge University Press.

Tuana, Nancy. 2006. "The Speculum of Ignorance: The Women's Health Movement and Epistemologies of Ignorance." *Hypatia: A Journal of Feminist Philosophy* 21(3): 1–19.

Tutu, Desmond. 1998. Chairperson's Foreword. In *Truth and Reconciliation Commission of South Africa Report.* Accessed March 21, 2012. http://www.justice.gov.za/trc/report/.

Van Der Merwe, Hugo. 2003. "National and Community Reconciliation: Competing Agendas in the South African Truth and Reconciliation Commission." In *Burying the Past: Making Peace and Doing Justice after Civil Conflict*, edited by Nigel Biggar, 101–24. Washington, DC: Georgetown University Press.

Verwoerd, Wilhelm. 2003. "Toward a Response to Criticisms of the South African Truth and Reconciliation Commission." In *Dilemmas of Reconciliation: Cases and Concepts*, edited by Carol A. L. Prager and Trudy Govier, 245–79. Waterloo, Ontario: Wilfrid Laurier University Press.

Vintges, Karen. 1996. *Philosophy as Passion: The Thinking of Simone de Beauvoir.* Bloomington: Indiana University Press.

——. 2001. "'Must We Burn Foucault?' Ethics as Art of Living: Simone de Beauvoir and Michel Foucault." *Continental Philosophy Review* 34(2): 165–81.

Waal, Frans B. M. de. 1990. *Peacemaking among Primates.* Cambridge, MA: Harvard University Press.

Walzer, Michael. 2002. "Albert Camus's Algerian War." In *The Company of Critics: Social Criticism and Political Commitment in the Twentieth Century*, 2nd ed., 136–53. New York: Basic Books.

Weber, Max. 1958. "Politics as a Vocation." In *From Max Weber: Essays in Sociology.* Edited and translated by H. H. Gerth and C. Wright Mills, 77–128. New York: Oxford University Press.

Wenzel, Hélène V. 1986. "Interview with Simone de Beauvoir." Special issue, *Yale French Studies*, "Simone de Beauvoir: Witness to a Century," 72: 5–32.

Wildman, Stephanie. 1996. *Privilege Revealed: How Invisible Preference Undermines America.* With contributions by Margalynne Armstrong, Adrienne D. Davis, and Trina Grillo. New York: New York University Press.

Young, Iris Marion. 1990. *Justice and the Politics of Difference*. Princeton, NJ: Princeton
    University Press.
————. 1994. "Gender as Seriality: Thinking about Women as a Social Collective." *Signs:
    Journal of Women in Culture and Society* 19(3): 713–38.
————. 2005. *On Female Body Experience: "Throwing like a Girl" and Other Essays*. New
    York: Oxford University Press.
Zerilli, Linda M. G. 2009. "Toward a Feminist Theory of Judgment." *Signs: Journal of
    Women in Culture and Society* 34(2): 295–317.

INDEX

abortion, 16, 67, 122
abstract humanism, 26, 28–30, 35–36,
    38–42
    as bourgeois ideology, 93
    determinate judgment and, 124
    masculinity and, 63, 71
Abu-Lughod, Lila, 31
African Americans, 106–107, 152n3. *See
    also* race
aged, the, 19–20, 61, 81–89, 90
Alcoff, Linda, 36n13, 102n13
Alfonso, D. Rita, 79n27, 90n48
Algerian war of independence: Beauvoir
    and, 18, 23, 92, 107–115, 117–120
    complicity and, 18, 107–108, 114
    French identity and, 118
    torture and, 18, 107–108, 113–115,
    119
    underground resistance and, 109, 112
Algren, Nelson, 16
All Said and Done (Beauvoir), 34n10, 35,
    82n33, 111n24, 112–113
alterity (*L'altérité*). *See* "The Other"
Althusser, Louis, 26, 30
ambiguity: Beauvoir's philosophy of,
    4–8, 33–38
    embodied subjectivity and, 7, 13,
    45–46, 163
    failure and, 18, 22, 23, 25, 39,
    105, 181
    flight from, 33, 69, 75, 87n43
    indeterminacy and, 6–7
    of political action, 25, 39, 40, 53n36,
    54–55, 123
    privilege and, 22–23, 92, 96, 116–117,
    123. *See also* ambiguous humanism

ambiguous humanism: 22, 32, 39, 46,
    53–55
America Day by Day (Beauvoir), 16, 22,
    64, 74–81, 88, 91
Antigone, 41
Arendt, Hannah: freedom and, 128–129
    The Holocaust and, 58, 181
    political judgment and, 23–24,
    128–130, 142n22, 147–148
    representative thinking and, 23–24,
    130, 132, 148
    revenge and, 154, 181
    Sartre and, 129n8
    sovereign self and, 128–129
Arp, Kristana, 13n14
Astell, Mary, 28
asymmetrical recognition, 56–57, 59–60,
    63–64, 74–75, 89–90
atrocity. *See* revenge; truth and
    reconciliation commissions
aversion, 22, 81–90

bad faith: abstract humanism as, 39, 93
    Beauvoir in, 109
    flight and, 33, 69, 87n43
    in *The Mandarins*, 141, 143, 147
    ready-made values as, 39, 41–42, 180
    Sartre on, 12n12
    the serious as, 41
    willful ignorance and, 94n2, 121.
    See also the serious
Bailey, Alison, 97
Bair, Deirdre, 5, 122, 157n15
Bartky, Sandra, 101, 107–108
Bauer, Nancy, 5n3, 59n6
Bauman, Zygmunt, 28